Best Practices in Online Program Development

Teaching and Learning in Higher Education

Elliot King
Neil Alperstein

Routledge
Taylor & Francis Group

NEW YORK AND LONDON

First published 2015
by Routledge
711 Third Avenue, New York, NY 10017

and by Routledge
2 Park Square, Milton Park, Abingdon, Oxon OX14 4RN

Routledge is an imprint of the Taylor & Francis Group, an informa business

Library of Congress Cataloging-in-Publication Data

King, Elliot, 1953–
    Best practices in online program development : teaching and learning in higher education / by Elliot King, Neil Alperstein.
        pages cm
    Includes bibliographical references and index.
    1. Education, Higher—Computer-assisted instruction.   2. Education, Higher—Effect of technological innovations on.   3. Internet in education.   I. Title.
    LB2395.7.K56 2015
    378.078′5—dc23
    2014018411

ISBN: 978-0-415-72443-2 (hbk)
ISBN: 978-0-415-72444-9 (pbk)
ISBN: 978-1-315-85717-6 (ebk)

Typeset in Minion
by Apex CoVantage, LLC

Printed and bound in the United States of America by Publishers Graphics, LLC on sustainably sourced paper.

Best Practices in Online Program Development

Best Practices in Online Program Development is a practical, hands-on guide that provides the concrete strategies that academic and administrative departments within institutions of higher learning need to develop in order to create and maintain coherent and effective online educational programs. Unlike individual courses, an online education program requires a comprehensive, inter-departmental effort to be integrated into the ongoing educational project of a college or university. This book focuses on the:

- Integration of online education into the institutional mission
- Complex faculty-related issues including recruiting, training, and teaching
- Multifaceted support required for student retention and success
- Need for multilayered assessment at the course, program, technical, and institutional levels
- Challenges posed to governance and by the need to garner resources across the institution
- Model to insure ongoing, comprehensive development of online educational programs.

Best Practices in Online Program Development covers the above topics and more, giving all the stakeholders in online educational programs the building blocks to foster successful programs while encouraging them to determine what role online education should play in their academic offerings.

Elliot King is a Professor and Chair of the Communication Department at Loyola University, Maryland, USA. He is the author or co-author of seven books and has written extensively about the application and impact of new computer and communication technology since the 1980s. He is a co-founder of Loyola's Master of Arts program in Emerging Media, an online program.

Neil Alperstein is a Professor in the Communication Department at Loyola University, Maryland, USA. He is the Founding Director of its Master of Arts program in Emerging Media, an online program, and a leader in the use of educational technology in the classroom. He is the author of the book *Advertising in Every-day Life*, numerous book chapters, and scores of scholarly articles.

Best Practices in Online Teaching and Learning

Series Editor Susan Ko

Best Practices for Teaching with Emerging Technologies by Michelle Pacansky-Brock

Best Practices in Online Program Development: Teaching and Learning in Higher Education by Elliot King, Neil Alperstein

From Elliot: To Anita, Aliza, Marcie, Jordan, Brad, and baby Lila. You are always first and foremost.

From Neil: To Gabriel and Spencer, who at some point in their lives will undoubtedly attend school online.

Contents

Preface

In the spring of 2011, we received the green light to develop what would become the first largely online master's degree program at Loyola University Maryland. We were excited, and perhaps naïve, about this opportunity, as we considered the institutional change this new program would bring to the university. Although we both had experience teaching online and made extensive use of educational technology in our classes, we quickly realized that we had no idea about the complexity of establishing an online program. Soon we found ourselves in meetings with people with whom we had never interacted before—the records office to work out course numbers, student administrative services to hammer out the mechanics of registration for students who would not be coming to campus, regulatory staff members to work on state authorizations, and so on. If only we had a guide to the process, we thought. But none existed, as far as we could tell.

So we decided to write this book. But we didn't want a book that merely reflected our experience, as Loyola is a relatively small largely liberal arts-oriented university, and probably not representative of universities across the United States. As we reflected on our own experience, we conducted interviews with more than a dozen individuals around the country representing various types of institutions to better understand their efforts in online education, and we surveyed the available literature. In doing so, we came to the following two general conclusions: First, while many online programs already exist, their development has been very idiosyncratic and they grew organically as a reflection of their particular institutional settings; and, second, many of the programs in traditional, non-profit universities are clustered in continuing and professional education sequences or college completion programs, and the programs have not yet been integrated into the mainstream educational offerings.

That is about to change. MOOCs (Massive Open Online Courses) have put online education front and center in the debates about higher education. As a result, online education is on the cusp of transitioning from being in the domain of early adopters to the domain of the early majority. Or put more simply, in the words of Malcolm Gladwell, online education seems to be about to hit the "tipping point," in which virtually every institution of higher education is going to have to determine what role online education will play. Some may decide that online education will not play any role at their institution, in the same way that some universities have remained primarily teaching institutions and did not adopt the research model for the university that emerged 100 years ago. But even those schools will have to develop strategies to confront the challenge posed by online education or be left floundering.

Many colleges and universities, however, will have to determine how they are going to incorporate online programs into their primary educational offerings and then create programs to achieve their educational goals. This book is designed to help those institutions in that process. The move to online education is not just about teaching and learning. Online education will shape the very character of the institution and how it operates. This book is geared to aid the various stakeholders in institutions of higher learning that are at various stages of considering, developing and offering online programs and who will ultimately make important contributions to the success of individual online educational programs.

This book addresses and presents practical guidance to virtually all the different constituencies inside and outside of the university from state legislatures and boards of trustees to administrators, faculty, and students. It will lay the foundation regarding all that it takes to create, develop, and implement an online program, and it will provide a common language for those constituencies to talk to one another. Along the way, the book will offer very concrete advice about how to develop and implement effective online educational programs. Finally, the book is designed to guide colleges and universities that have already entered into online education. It will provide them with tools to assess themselves on all the facets of an online educational program, including the issues that have an impact on faculty, students and the institution generally in a way that leads to continuous improvement of the overall educational experience.

Organization of the Book

This book serves as handbook for all aspects of developing an online education program. In doing so, it addresses the issues facing or posed by each of the major constituencies involved in higher education—the students, the faculty and the administration of both the academic and institutional leadership, and the stewards of higher education including boards of trustees, regulatory bodies and Federal and state governments. The book presents the challenges to developing high quality online educational programs, and it offers solutions to the problems that online program developers face. As would be expected, many of the issues raised by the development of online educational programs have an impact on many of the constituencies involved. Those issues will be explored in each chapter from the perspective of that constituency. This approach can help clarify the different perspectives within the organizational complexity of institutions of higher learning.

The book has seven chapters:

Chapter 1: The Online Revolution is Upon Us
Chapter 2: Moving Online Programs Forward

Chapter 1 describes the economic, social, political, and technological drivers behind the growth of online education and places the turbulence higher education is now experiencing within the history of reform in higher education. Colleges and universities have undergone radical reformation several times. Chapter 2 lays out an overview to creating online educational programs and the internal and external approval processes for online educational programs. The subsequent three chapters take an in-depth look at the issues online educational programs raise for faculty, program development, and students. Chapter 6 surveys the challenges to staff and other stakeholders posed by online program development and suggests a set of best practices for addressing those issues. The final chapter proposes a Generational Model of Online Program Development that can help institutions assess the state of online program development across many dimensions and guide them in implementing stable and effective practices. Overall, this book serves as a way to facilitate a campus-wide conversation about the role of online education and provides a basis for determining the appropriate approach to online education given the history and goals of the institution.

University 5.0. That is what we believe will emerge as online education and other applications of educational technology impact the student experience. University 5.0 refers to the next iteration of higher education, a phase in which place—literally geographic location—is becoming less of a central factor. With the advent of blended learning, flipped classrooms, and other collaborative approaches, among other alternatives to traditional learning, the university is extending beyond its physical borders. With online education, there literally are no borders.

We see higher education and online education as being at major turning points. But it is not the first turning point colleges and universities have faced. In the mid-19th Century, higher education embraced teaching practical arts along with the classical liberal arts. In the early 20th Century, colleges and universities were transformed into research centers charged with creating new knowledge and also became the gatekeepers to an array of professions, including medicine and law. And in the 1960s, colleges and universities opened their doors to women and other underserved populations. In each period, new colleges and universities were created and existing colleges and universities had to craft strategies to survive. In each case, some schools flourished and grew while others did not succeed. This book is geared to help colleges and universities navigate through these turbulent times and help them craft and implement strategies that will lead to their success for generations to come.

Acknowledgments

This book represents the culmination of ideas, practices, and experiences regarding the use of educational technology in teaching and learning over the past 25 years. The university where we both teach has been generous in letting us be early adopters of those new technologies and to use that experience to launch Loyola University Maryland's first online program. The Emerging Media graduate program has attracted students from across the United States. Setting it up hasn't been easy, but we have learned a lot in the process and would like to thank our first cohort of students in joining us on this journey. You know who you are.

We would also like to thank the following people at Loyola who have been instrumental in establishing our program: Dr. Timothy Law Snyder, who championed online education at Loyola from the beginning, Dr. Amanda Thomas, who guided the process in creating the program, Dr. Cindy Moore, who was our immediate point of contact, and Dr. Sharon Nell who was the right person at the right meeting and got it all started. In the Instructional Design team, we would like to thank Tracy McMahon, Suzanne Monthie, Ryan Servant, Simone Christian and Louise Finn, Loyola's CIO, for their assistance and support.

When we first started thinking about writing a book about online education, we became aware that there are a lot of people forging new ideas in this area. We are particularly grateful for the insights we received from the following people already deeply involved in developing online educational opportunities at their campuses and elsewhere: George Otte, City University of New York, Ronald Chambers, Hofstra University, Brian Salerno, Brandeis University, Kristin Palmer, University of Virginia, Dennis McElhoe, University of North Carolina at Charlotte and Holly Shiflett at Deltak. Neil found Cathy Davidson's MOOC, The Future (Mostly) of Higher Education helpful in giving the project a sense of history regarding higher education.

We thank Alex Masulis, our editor at Routledge (Taylor & Francis) for agreeing that online education program development is fertile ground and for his assistance in shaping the book, as well we thank Daniel Schwartz and the production team at Routledge. We thank Susan Ko for including us in the series of which she is the general editor.

Finally, Neil would like to make his most important acknowledgment: "I literally would not be here were it not for my wife Nancy. She is a great partner who I can bounce ideas off of, knowing I'll get sound feedback. She is, in a way, a shadow writer of this book. But most important, Nancy is my collaborator in life in all the things I do, and I thank her for all the support she has provided during the writing of this book." Elliot would like to give a shout out to his wife Anita as well: "Your faith and confidence in me helps me to tackle new projects. You are my life partner always."

The authors have collaborated with each other for more than 20 years. It has been a relationship of mutual support not often found in the academic world. We have built a successful department that is a leader in the use of educational technology and now the home for Loyola's first online program. We thank our colleagues in our department for creating such a great environment in which to work. We are all partners in this project.

Finally, to those who read this book, we hope it will inspire you to move your college or university forward in a way that makes online education programs not a stepchild of the university, but a central function that stands side by side with traditional residential education. We recognize that online program development starts with an idea, and we hope that this book will stimulate ideas for your institution. Whether the idea for an online program comes from the administration, faculty or staff, we all need to embrace the future, which will to a greater extent take place online.

1
The Online Revolution is Upon Us

If you are not worried about the impact of online education on the nature and structure of higher education, you should be. And if you are not excited about the impact of online education on the nature and shape of higher education, you should be. For many reasons, higher education has entered a turbulent period. Online education is a major element of that turbulence. Every college and university and every stakeholder in higher education including students, faculty, staff, administrators, top leadership, boards of trustees and governmental bodies have to react and respond to the disruption taking place. How you respond may help shape the character of your institution for the generation to come.

You may know that the largest graduate class offered on the campus of Stanford University in the fall of 2013 was CS229 (Kosner 2013). The course covered both statistical and biological approaches to machine learning and was taught by Andrew Ng, a professor of computer science with a specialization in artificial intelligence. It was no surprise that Ng's course would be popular. Ng had built the largest computer-based artificial brain in the world, with more than 11 billion neural connections running on 16 computer servers (Gillespie 2014). But the 760 students Ng attracted to his course in machine learning were practically the equivalent of an intimate class compared to the number of students that enrolled in a course taught by his colleague Daphne Koller in the fall of 2011. That semester, more than 100,000 students enrolled. The huge enrollment was spurred by the fact that the course was free and online. But the scale and scope of the course in 2011 helped to focus the higher education community as well as the general public on a potentially new alternative in higher education—the Massive Open Online Course or MOOC.

And then it was off to the races. The following spring, the *New York Times'* John Markoff reported that Ng had raised $16 million in venture capital and partnered with Stanford, the University of Pennsylvania, Princeton University and the University of Michigan to launch a new company called Coursera (Markoff 2012). Another professor of computer science at Stanford, Sebastian Thrun, had taught a course on artificial intelligence with

1

Peter Norvig, a colleague at Google, which had attracted 160,000 students. A course Thrun taught in the spring of 2012 about building a search engine had 90,000 people sign up (Lewin 2013). MOOCs were the new darlings of higher education. *New York Times* columnist and technology evangelist Thomas Friedman rhapsodized that MOOCs represented a revolution in college education and would provide students around the world with access to the very best education (Friedman 2012). He imagined a time when the United States might rent space in a remote village in Egypt, install a couple of dozen computers and a high speed Internet connection via satellite, and those students would have access to a world class education. He reported anecdotes in which students and professors opined that MOOCs were more intellectually exciting than their traditional classroom experiences. And he forecast a time when people would design their own college degrees selecting courses from the best professors from around the world and paying small sums for certificates of completion (Friedman 2013). In December, *Time* magazine called 2012 "The Year of the MOOC." The article noted that three dozen major universities including Duke and Princeton had signed deals with Ng's Coursera. Thrun had established a second company to develop and support MOOCs called Udacity. And Harvard and the Massachusetts Institute of Technology had partnered to establish yet a third MOOC initiative called edX. In 2012, more than one million students had enrolled in MOOCs (Webley 2012).

The allure was not hard to understand. World-class name brand universities were apparently willing to open some of their courses to anybody, anywhere, for free. The opportunity seemed to be amazing. After all, Harvard's freshman acceptance rate in 2012 was 5.9%. Stanford's acceptance rate was 6.6% and MIT's was 8.9%. If the availability of Internet technology forced other industries to begin to give away their best product for free, most notably newspapers, perhaps the same sort of process would take place in higher education. But as quickly as the hullabaloo about MOOCs swelled, it faded. First, many observers noted that although thousands of students enrolled in MOOCs, far fewer completed them. A study conducted jointly by Harvard and MIT examining 17 MOOCs offered by those institutions found that only 5% of the nearly 850,000 students who enrolled received a certificate of completion and 35% never viewed any course material. Of the 5% that did complete the course, almost 75% already held at least one college degree (Kolowich 2014). A study by researchers at the University of Pennsylvania Graduate School of Education, pointed out that of the 16 MOOCs that the university offered, the average completion rate was 4%, with a range of 2% on the low end and 14% at the top (Penn 2014). And perhaps most troubling, a study by a team at Princeton University, based on an assessment of 73 courses, found that not only did student participation plunge during the course of a MOOC, but also faculty participation fell (Brinton et al. 2014).

And that's not all. Shortly after the president of San Jose State announced the university's interest in experimenting with MOOCs, the faculty objected. In an open letter to Michael Sandal, a Harvard University professor who had created an online course about justice that was offered via edX, Harvard and MIT's joint MOOC platform, members of the philosophy department at San Jose State opined that the idea of offering the same course about justice across the country was "downright scary." The Philosophy faculty worried that the quality of education would be hurt if people untrained in an academic field would offer the course and rely solely on the material offered through the MOOC. And while administrators at San Jose State argued that no one was compelled to use Sandel's MOOC in their classroom, several professors said that they felt administrative pressure to do so (Lewin 2013). The growth of MOOCs raised several other thorny issues as well. And by 2013, Sebastian Thrun himself suggested that MOOCs did not offer a very good education product, describing them in one interview as "a lousy product" (Chafkin 2013).

But both the enthusiasm sparked by MOOCs and the objections to them are beside the point. What you have to recognize is that MOOCs drove the issue of online education from the margins of higher education to the mainstream. Once largely the domain of continuing and professional education or a way to serve non-traditional students such as older students, working students, or those whose college education had been interrupted by military service, MOOCs positioned online education as one of the most exciting innovations in higher education over the last generation and one of the most viable options to addressing the perceived flaws in higher education.

The rise of the Internet has disrupted many aspects of society and forced many institutions to adjust. The news media, the music industry, retailing and telecommunications have been completely reshaped over the past 20 years. In contrast, in many ways, mainstream higher education has been slow to react to the potential of the Internet. Educational policy to some degree is stuck in the late 19th and early 20th Centuries. But it has become increasingly clear that for many colleges and universities, the current models for higher education rooted in 19th Century thinking are no longer viable. A new paradigm, in which online education will inevitably play a significant role, must be created. As Mitchell Daniels, the president of Purdue University and former governor of Indiana, pointed out in an open letter to the Purdue community regarding the ten initiatives he felt would reshape Purdue for the future:

> When critics and skeptics contrive dramatic metaphors like "tsunami" and "avalanche" to forecast wrenching changes in higher education, they are thinking of two intersecting phenomena: first, the appearance of disruptive alternatives to site-based, "seat-time" residential education.

Why, he wondered, will students still find it wise to pay lots of money to go and live somewhere for four or more years, when a host of competitors are offering to bring them excellent teachers and instruction inexpensively in the comfort of their own homes?

Daniels was not alone in expressing his concern about the future. In 2010, Smith College, under the leadership of Carol T. Christ, laid out its vision for the future. With a storied history and an endowment of over $1 billion, Smith is a pillar of higher education. Nonetheless, the Smith task force that crafted the document anticipated that the nine-month residential experience will play an increasingly smaller role in higher education over time, with online education, education at other institutions and a variety of other learning experiences playing a larger role (The Futures Initiative 2010/2011). If the residential model for higher education is going to contract, every stakeholder in the institution is going to have to play a role in determining what will come next. Traditionally, the gathering of scholars and students in one place represented the very heart of higher education. But over the next decade, every institution will have to develop a strategy reflecting the technology-based world in which we live. And once that strategy is in place, every institution will have to learn how to develop and implement, along with other new and emerging technologies, online educational programs in response to the growing pressure from many quadrants within society, not the least of which are internal to institutions of higher learning.

Waves of Change

While the popular image of colleges and universities makes it seem as though they are cloistered institutions impervious to change, that is not true. Clark Kerr, the former president of the University of California, once observed that approximately 85 institutions have survived in a recognizable form for the past 500 years. Among them are the Catholic Church and the Parliament in Iceland as well as 70 universities (Tagg 2012). To be able to survive for 500 years, you have to be nimble. And it is critical to understand the dynamics of change in higher education among those 70 surviving institutions of higher learning to determine how online education can be incorporated effectively in modern colleges and universities.

Since the founding of what is generally seen as the first Western university in the 11th Century, the University of Bologna in Italy in 1088 (the first university to use the term at its founding and still in operation), higher education has experienced waves of radical innovations driven by changing economic, political and social conditions. The initial universities were corporations of students and teachers and this is the very concept that online education challenges, and if it is not implemented appropriately, the idea of the university as a gathering place of teachers and students could be diminished if not destroyed. Instruction at the University of Bologna focused on civil and canon law, and religious education was its primary mission. It often required six years to obtain a Bachelor of Arts degree and the instruction focused on what were called the liberal arts: arithmetic, geometry, astronomy, music theory, grammar, logic, and rhetoric, with a special emphasis on logic. Master's and doctorate degrees were offered in law, medicine, and theology. Course offerings were fixed and revolved around specific books. The liberal arts curriculum, geared toward the upper class, remained as the centerpiece in university education for several hundred years. For example, Harvard University was founded in the United States in 1636 primarily to train ministers and magistrates. Those who intended to enter other professions generally apprenticed with a master in that field. And access to universities was limited to a relatively select group. According to one estimate, by 1800 there were approximately 200 professors at the 19 institutions that offered Bachelor of Arts degrees in America. Fifty years earlier there were as few as ten professors (Carrell 1968).

In their first incarnation, colleges and universities were hardly democratic social institutions. However, that began to change in the 19th Century when the groundwork for universities in their current configuration began to be put in place. Starting in the 1820s, states began to establish universities whose scope stretched beyond classical education and training of clergy and to other members of the elite to include instruction in the practical arts associated with farming and industry. In 1855, the Agricultural College of the State of Michigan, the forerunner of Michigan State University, was chartered, which was followed shortly thereafter by the Farmers' High School of Pennsylvania that awarded its first degree as the College of Agricultural Sciences in 1861 and eventually served as the foundation for Penn State University.

The movement to broaden the purview of, and access to, higher education was accelerated by the passage of the Morrill Act of 1862 that directed Congress to give the states 30,000 acres for each member of their congressional delegation. The land was then to be sold and the proceeds used to establish public universities to "promote the liberal and practical education of the industrial classes in the several pursuits and professions in life" (1862). The universities established by the act were not expected to exclude teaching the liberal arts, sciences or military tactics but the core project was to teach subjects associated with agriculture and the mechanical arts. Over time, 69 universities were funded by these land grants, including Cornell University and the Massachusetts Institute of Technology.

The land-grant universities established a dichotomy in higher education between practical knowledge that can be usefully applied in industry and elsewhere and a liberal arts-oriented education geared toward developing mental discipline, habits of the mind and a general progressive attitude toward education. This split was further amplified as online educational programs became more common, as most are geared toward teaching applied skills; as well, there is some concern regarding whether online students can develop the critical thinking associated with liberal arts education.

As the land-grant institutions began to expand and flourish in the last part of the 19th Century, two additional strands in higher education began to emerge in the United States. The first was the idea that universities should be producers of knowledge as well as distributors of knowledge, that is, the concept of the research university. The second was that people entering various careers such as medicine, law, business, journalism, and other areas, previously assigned to apprenticeships and vocational education, should receive post-graduate education at the university level, that is, the concept of the professional school.

The research university, or the notion that one of the roles of university faculty is to discover new knowledge, has its roots in Germany in the early 1800s. In the 1820s, faculty at German universities began to conduct research in philology and linguistics. To do so, they needed access to primary texts and universities with larger libraries began to have an advantage. In 1826, a German chemist established the first laboratory devoted to both teaching and research. As German industrialization accelerated during the 19th Century, research at universities began to give them a competitive advantage. In the United States, although faculty at land-grant universities were expected to conduct research, particularly in fields of interest like agriculture, the idea of a research institution did not really gain traction until the 1870s, when U.S. industrialization boomed. While Harvard established the Jefferson Physical Laboratory in the early 1870s, new universities, often underwritten by wealthy benefactors, such as Johns Hopkins University and Stanford University, established the first laboratories at U.S. universities devoted to research and teaching. Johns Hopkins was established in 1876 as a research institution and over the next two decades awarded more PhD degrees than Harvard and Yale combined (Atkinson, & Blanpied).

The critical role that research played at universities expanded significantly after World War II. In 1945, Vannevar Bush, an esteemed scientist and the director of the U.S. Office of Scientific Research and Development, which had been established to coordinate scientific research and application in the war effort, wrote a report called "Science The Endless Frontier," in which he argued that a steady flow of new scientific knowledge was critical to making progress on everything from the fight against disease to industrial development to national defense, and he argued that new knowledge could only be discovered through basic research. In short, basic research was critical to the nation's health, prosperity and security. He proposed the creation of a permanent Federal agency geared to funding basic research in the colleges, universities, and research institutes in medicine, the natural sciences, and new military weapons (Bush 1945). In 1945, the National Institute of Health, an arm of the Public Health Service, began to fund external research projects. And in 1950, the National Science Foundation was established (National Science Foundation 1994). From that point on, the Federal government became a major funder of university-based research and universities with large research initiatives grew in prestige. This represented a significant shift in higher education and once again, a role that is challenged by the growth of online education. If there is no need to gather teachers in one place, where should research be conducted?

Professional Education

At the same time that research became a more central feature of some universities, so did professional education. For hundreds of years, professional education followed an apprenticeship model. Prospective lawyers, for example, apprenticed with a practicing lawyer and eventually took the bar exam to be licensed to practice law. While law had been taught at the College of William and Mary, Harvard University and the University of Virginia, with the addition of law professors to their faculties in the late 18th and early 19th Centuries, law was a subject taught in much the same way as history, with a focus on theory and doctrine. Professional training in the actual practice of law was assumed to come after graduation through an apprenticeship. In the late 19th Century, however, with the support of the American Bar Association, a newly formed national association for lawyers, the requirement of a university degree in law slowly became a requirement for admission to the bar. Eventually the requirement became three years of graduate study at a university (Barry, Dubin, & Joy 2010). The same pattern found in legal education was followed in medicine. In the 1870s, the president of Harvard began to reform medical education first by insisting that students were graded by faculty and ultimately that they required an undergraduate degree prior to admission to the medical school. In 1898, the Johns Hopkins Medical School, widely considered the first modern university-oriented medical school, began to require an undergraduate degree for admission (Flexner 1910). Over time, a degree from a medical school and passing board exams were required to practice medicine. In short, while the study of law and medicine had long been academic subjects, it was the reform that started in the 1870s that led to the requirement of a medical or legal degree as access to the profession. And while some initiatives in education, business, and journalism, among others, resulted in credentialing, other attempts did not.

The last great change in higher education occurred from the late 1940s through the 1960s. The driving force in this period was access. In 1944, the U.S. Congress passed the Servicemen's Readjustment Act to assist returning soldiers to reintegrate into civilian life. Commonly known as the G.I. Bill of Rights, one of the key provisions was to provide educational benefits. With so many solders returning from the war, there was a surge of interest in attending college, whereby millions of people were now eligible to attend. In 1947, veterans accounted for 49% of all college admissions (Department of Veteran Affairs n.d.). Broadening the eligibility to attend an institution of higher learning was the first step in the process in extending access. In the 1960s, women began to be admitted to colleges and universities in significantly larger numbers, both at the undergraduate and graduate levels, and institutions of higher learning responded in several ways. Both Yale University and Princeton University, for example, went co-ed in 1969. And between the years 1969 and 1980, scores of colleges and universities ranging from the U.S. Military Academy to the College of the Holy Cross opened their doors to women (Walsh 2012).

The increased demand to attend college led to an impressive expansion. As a result many teachers' colleges or normal schools became fully fledged universities. In 1960, in what was seen as a landmark in higher education, California passed a master plan to coordinate its community colleges, state universities and University of California campuses. Each level of the system would be charged with a specific task. The community colleges and state universities would be primarily devoted to instruction, while the University of California would be the state's primary academic agency for basic and applied research (University of California Office of the President 1960). The final factors in the drive to increase access were improvements in transportation and the general rise in wealth, which meant that more students could afford to attend colleges and universities away from home. The residential college experience became much more common and not restricted to the upper class. On the other hand, a much broader set of colleges and universities were in a position to recruit students nationally.

An analysis of the fundamental changes in higher education leads to three critical conclusions. First, virtually all colleges and universities reflect, to some degree, all the waves of change that have come before. Small colleges that have stuck closely to the liberal arts curriculum justify that approach by arguing that the critical thinking taught through the liberal arts is critical to professional success. The requirement to "publish or perish" is commonplace in many different types of institutions. Second, colleges and universities have responded to change in different ways, some successfully and some not. For example, Harvard incorporated many of the most significant changes—becoming a major research institution, establishing professional schools at the graduate level, admitting women—while maintaining a focus on a liberal arts education for undergraduate students. Swarthmore College and Amherst College have largely eschewed professional and graduate education to concentrate on their liberal arts undergraduate orientation. State colleges and universities have expanded their basic research activities. And many colleges and universities, ranging from state institutions to smaller private colleges that relied on commuter students, successfully transformed themselves into residential institutions. In the present state of disruption, many institutions, like your own, are going to have to make critical decisions regarding online education. While many institutions of higher learning have explored some of the possibilities of online education, most traditional colleges and universities have not yet studied, much less examined, what role online education should play. But you can no longer wait to start that process.

Many stakeholders in higher education have resisted addressing the role of online education. Faculty, administrators and staff often feel it is less risky to continue to do what they have experience with, and they feel they do well with the status quo rather than moving in a new direction. Colleges and universities are often deeply steeped in tradition, having clear identities that have been developed over long periods of time. Those identities help define what the various stakeholders including alumni and others expect the institution to do and what they find acceptable within the educational enterprise. Finally, in the way most universities and colleges are governed, very frequently nobody is truly empowered to be an agent of change and to facilitate an institution moving in a new direction, particularly if that new direction is substantially different than the current path. Some boards of trustees see their roles as stewards of the status quo, and in any case, trustees are too distant from the day-to-day operation of a university to smoothly assert influence. Presidents of universities are generally more focused on external constituencies and fund-raising rather than the day-to-day management. And too often, faculty do not trust administrators and ignore administrative efforts to do things differently. Many factors weigh against change in higher education and change will not take place until the forces driving change are greater than the forces maintaining the status quo (Diamond 2006).

Drivers of Change You Can't Ignore

The basic structure currently found in higher education has been in place for the past half century and overall diversity of higher education has been captured in the Carnegie Foundation for the Advancement of Teaching classifications that have remained intact for 40 years (Carnegie Classification of Institutions n.d.). Traditional and non-traditional students have a wide array of choices and degree opportunities. But the overwhelming number of choices requires going to campus and physically attending classes. The emergence of online education promises to change that. Five major trends are driving the demand for online education: cost, government support and intervention, assessment, a shift in credentialing and demographics. Each one is substantial and poses a significant threat to the way that many colleges and universities currently operate (Ordway 2013).

Cost and Government Support

The increase in cost of a college education has become a headline-grabbing issue in higher education. From 1985 to 2013, the cost of tuition for an undergraduate education jumped an eye-popping 538%, nearly twice the rate of the cost of health care. In contrast, the consumer price index has risen 121%. Tuition is only part of the expense of going to college. Many students also live on campus for which they pay room and board. And many institutions charge an assortment of other fees. In the academic year 2012–2013, at least 149 colleges and universities charged at least $50,000 for tuition, room, board and fees. Sarah Lawrence College was the first to break the $60,000 barrier (Yahoo Financial News 2013). Tuition and fees at state universities, which are a lower cost option, have also climbed sharply in the past decade, doubling in many states and tripling in Colorado. In 2013–2014, 14 states charged more than $10,000 in tuition and fees (Trends in Higher Education 2014), and that number does not include room and board, which can easily double the cost of attendance.

The response to the rising cost of higher education has been a sharp increase in financial aid, particularly from the Federal government, generally in the form of student loans, which accounted for 37% of the total of more than $181 billion of aid awarded to undergraduate students in 2012 (Trends in Higher Education 2012). The shift to financing a significant portion of undergraduate education has lead to three outcomes. First, many students leave college with large debts. According to The Project on Student Debt, an initiative of the Institute for College Access and Success, in 2012, 71% of graduating students had student loan debt averaging $29,400 per borrower (The Institute for College Access and Success 2014). And while college education is still highly valued, the evidence is growing that the cost of attending college can no longer go up at the rate it has over the past 20 years. The inability of colleges and universities to further raise tuition may be seen as partially good news for students but bad news for colleges and universities that depend primarily on tuition to fund their ongoing operations. Any shortfall in expected enrollment, which could be blamed at least in part for being perceived as too expensive, could lead to significant financial difficulties (Kiley 2013). In early 2013, Moody's Investors Service issued a report that questioned all of the traditional sources of revenues for colleges and universities, forecasting that for one-third of colleges and universities, tuition revenues would shrink or grow at less than the rate of inflation. Other sources of revenue, such as Federal support both for tuition and research, appropriations from state governments, endowments, and philanthropy, would all produce less revenue in the future than they had in the past. In short, the financial model that higher education has relied upon since the 1960s is no longer viable.

At the same time, public financial support for higher education is falling at both the state and Federal level. Although overall Federal student aid grew substantially over the past 20 years, aid has been generally flat from 2009 to 2014 (Trends in Higher Education 2014). The picture painted by examining the Pell Grants, the primary vehicle for direct student aid, is complicated. While the size of the Pell Grant program has grown, with more students getting larger grants, the grants cover a smaller percentage of the overall cost of a college education.

Moreover, about half of Pell Grant recipients were over the age of 24, or non-traditional undergraduate students (2014).

At the state level, support for higher education has dropped significantly since the recession of 2008. From 2007 to 2012, states cut the amount of aid they gave to colleges and universities by 17%, or more than $15 billion in total, while public colleges and universities have sharply increased tuition. The actual student cost of attending a public university has climbed more sharply than actual tuition increases (Clark 2012). By 2013, states were paying 28% less per student than they paid in 2008, and funding levels remained lower than they were prior to the recession. Thirty-six states cut funding by more than 20%, although the number of students rose by 12% from 2007 to 2012. In response to their inability to continue to raise tuition, public universities have cut faculty and staff, eliminating course offerings, reducing library hours and cutting other services, among other cost-saving measures (Oliff, Palacios, Johnson, & Leachman 2013). With the financial viability of many colleges and universities at stake, you have to find ways to cut costs without cutting quality. Because online education does not require the same investment in "bricks and mortar" and potentially increases the market for students, online education could theoretically result in an increase in revenue with only a marginal increase in cost, making it attractive to the business side of higher education.

Assessment

While overall public support for education has lessened, lawmakers have become increasingly interested in measuring the outcomes of the public investment in higher education. Assessment and outcome measures have become a major issue, with many states paying attention to degree completion rates and the time it takes students to complete a degree (Moore 2009). At the Federal level, the interest in assessment has moved beyond those typical measures. Citing the value of a college degree and the accelerating cost of higher education, the $220 billion the Federal government and the states invest in higher education along with rising student loan default rates, has resulted in an Obama administration plan to develop a ranking system for universities and colleges to enable students and families to identify which institutions provide the best value. The system would be based on three primary drivers— access, affordability and outcomes. Starting in 2018, according to the proposal, Federal financial assistance would be awarded on the basis of the ratings (The White House 2013).

In 2006, the U.S. Department of Education's Commission on the Future of Higher Education issued what is known as the Spellings Commission Report after Margaret Spellings, then the secretary of education, which noted the following: there was very little data to measure efficiency or productivity in higher education; graduation rates significantly trailed enrollment increases; and, many students at public two- and four-year colleges and universities graduated with only very basic quantitative and literacy skills. The report bemoaned the lack of commonly used assessment mechanisms to measure what students actually learn and that the information gathered and dissemination of the assessment by accrediting agencies was of little use to the public. Finally, the report noted the resistance in the academic community to assessment and recommended the evaluation and implementation of new testing regimes to measure effectiveness (Miller, & Malandra 2006).

Accrediting agencies and others have responded to the Spellings report by requiring universities and colleges to develop more comprehensive assessment measures. And several states have already begun to award funding based on outcomes rather than enrollment, with the state of Tennessee running one of the most ambitious experiments. In 2010, the state began to award as much as 80% of its total appropriations to higher education based on outcome measures (Lederman 2011). The Obama administration also proposed linking Federal financial aid and an overall ranking system leaving little doubt that colleges and universities were going to have to do a better job in assessing student outcomes.

Competency-Based Model

Cost, shrinking public support and a focus on outcomes has led to an interest in alternative or new credentialing. The idea is that rather than engaging in a long course of study that leads to a traditional degree simply by completing the course of study, students can take very focused courses and be awarded a certificate or digital badge once they demonstrated mastery of the subject. By demonstrating that mastery, students could help advance their careers. Once again, MOOCs have brought notoriety to this concept. In 2014 MOOC-provider Coursera launched a program it called Specializations in which students would complete a three to nine course sequence plus a capstone project to demonstrate their competence in a specific area of specialization. The first two Specializations, which Coursera likened to college majors, were Mobile Cloud Computing for the Android operating system sponsored by Vanderbilt University and the University of Maryland and one in reasoning and data analysis from Duke University. Eight additional Specializations were in development in conjunction with Johns Hopkins University, Rice University and others. Earlier, MIT announced it would offer certifications for students who had completed a sequence of six courses in computer science via its MOOC-platform edX (Kolowich 2014).

Other stakeholders in higher education and professional development have begun to offer alternative forms of credentials as well. Called badges, the concept is modeled after traditional continuing education units, licensing and other forms of professional development. Competency-based education strikes at the heart of the assessment issue in higher education. Critics argue that many students emerge with Bachelor degrees, yet they have trouble demonstrating their competencies for specific jobs. Badges would be awarded based on demonstration that the learner had mastered a specific set of skills rather than the amount of time invested in the learning process (Pearson Education Inc. 2013). But the competency model also narrows higher education by stripping away the idea that it offers more than skills. On the other hand, online education can provide an appropriate framework for competency-based education. Not uncommonly, online education can minimize the student–teacher interaction if a course or program is entirely focused on skills to be tested at its conclusion. Moreover, the self-paced nature of online education can make competency-based education more attractive to some learners.

Demographic Shifts

The final major disruptive force in higher education is demographics. Over the past decade, the make-up of both undergraduate and graduate student bodies has changed dramatically and that change is predicted to accelerate over time. Perhaps the most striking new factor is the rise of what used to be called non-traditional students; those who do not fall within the 18 to 24 year-old age group. According to a National Center for Education Statistics report, only 15% of the 17.6 million undergraduate students attending four-year colleges and living on campus fall into that age group. Of all the students who are enrolled in four-year colleges, only 36% graduate in four years. Nearly half of all undergraduates attend two-year colleges, and 37% are enrolled in part-time programs, while 32% of all undergraduates work full time. More than half of the undergraduates are not seeking Bachelor of Arts degrees, but are pursuing Associates degrees or other forms of credentials. Finally, 38% of all undergraduates are over the age of 25 and one-fourth are over the age of 30; those numbers are expected to rise significantly over the next decade (Hess 2011).

The rise of adult learners represents one side of the demographic equation. On the other side is the number of high school graduates. That number peaked in 2009 and the National Center for Educational Statistics does not project any growth in the number of high school graduates through 2020 (National Center 2011). In 2012, overall student enrollment dropped 1.8%, according to the National Student Clearing House Current Term Estimates report (National Student Clearinghouse 2012). Some observers argue that this demographic trend poses an existential threat to many institutions of higher learning, particularly residential colleges catering to traditional students that are heavily dependent on tuition as a source of revenue. One dire prediction is that as many as half of the 4,500 or so four-year colleges and universities will go out of business within the next 50 years (Harden 2012). Even more extreme, management and innovation expert and Harvard Business School professor Clayton Christiansen argued that half the colleges and universities in the country would be bankrupt within the next 15 years. In an analysis of 1,700 colleges and universities, the consulting company Bain & Co. found that fully one-third of colleges and universities were on an unsustainable financial trajectory, with operating costs growing faster than the sources of revenue available to them (Marcus 2013). Every college and university, from the Ivy League schools to the most obscure, has to craft a response to those trends right now. The risk posed by ignoring shifts in the marketplace of higher education is too great.

Online Must Go Mainstream

Online education has emerged as one of the ways even small private liberal arts colleges can respond to the changing landscape (Ordway 2013). In 2012, 70% of the chief academic officers polled by the Babson Survey Research Group indicated that online education was critical to their institution's long-term strategy. And only 10% of chief academic officers did not feel online education was important to their long-term strategy (Allen, & Seaman, 2013). The view that online education is a part of the solution is only the first step; the real challenge is how to integrate online education into the overall educational fabric and tradition of an educational institution. The goal cannot be just to learn how to deliver some subset of the curriculum online effectively. You must determine the role online education should play in supporting and perhaps expanding an institution's educational mission and footprint, and learn how to deliver online education effectively and appropriately.

The History and Growth of Online Education

As you consider the ways that online education can fit into your educational mission, you will find that online education has a significant history and a tradition of its own, a tradition that can be built upon. Its roots are in distance learning, and distance learning has always been driven by the introduction of new technology. The first correspondence courses were offered in Great Britain in the early 19th Century, once a reliable postal service was in place. In 1922, the Pennsylvania State University began to offer classes via the radio and by 1925, more than 200 colleges and universities had radio licenses. In 1958 the University of Wisconsin's Correspondence Study Unit reported that it offered 450 courses in 150 different areas of learning serving more than 12,000 students (University of Florida n.d.). And in 1965, the University of Wisconsin established an educational program based on the telephone and Stanford University set up the Stanford Instruction Television Network, primarily to address the needs of part-time engineering students (Straighterline n.d.).

Computer-based distance learning got its start in 1960 when scientists at the University of Illinois, Urbana-Champaign, created the Programmed Logic for Automatic Teaching Operations (PLATO) for computer-assisted instruction. Twenty years later, around 4,000 students per semester were using the PLATO-based learning program. While of interest as a general training platform, PLATO made few inroads into higher education, and as late as the mid-1980s, only approximately 100 systems were in place (Won n.d.). A more useable infrastructure for computer-based distance education—which began to be called online education, came into being during the 1980s. In the mid and late 1980s, in one of the earliest implementations of online education, Nova Southeastern University, a private university in Broward County, Florida began offering online degree programs in computer science and computer information systems (Nova Southeastern University n.d.). The Nova program used basic Internet services such as Telnet and FTP (file transfer protocol) available at the time. In the same period, the Electronic University Network (EUN) was established to help colleges and universities find and teach students online. Using proprietary software and servers, it offered its first course online in 1986. Over the next six years or so, EUN collaborated with a dozen universities including Washington State University and Quinnipiac University in offering courses online. EUN was incorporated into AOL in 1992 (Electronic University Network n.d.).

As the Internet exploded in the 1990s, interest in online education accelerated. As access to the Web became more routine, individuals became much more comfortable with using computer technology, and critical applications such as browsing, email and downloading files, made the technological infrastructure for online education more available and familiar. At the same time, for-profit institutions of higher education like the University of Phoenix, which catered to non-traditional students who often held full-time jobs, recognized the advantages that online education could offer. The University of Phoenix was founded in 1976 to serve the needs of working adults. In 1989, it established the University of Phoenix Online Campus and two years later its first online students graduated (University of Phoenix n.d.). In 2014, the University of Phoenix offered a huge array of online degree programs from the associate's degree to the doctorate.

Since the rollout of the World Wide Web in the early 1990s, the number of students taking online courses has climbed steadily. When the Babson Survey Research Group in 2002 began regularly conducting surveys about online education, the number of students taking at least one online course climbed by 300,000 to 900,000 students annually. In 2011, nearly 6.7 million students took at least one course online, a jump of 9.3% over 2010. At the same time, overall student enrollment in higher education dropped by 0.1%. By 2011, nearly one-third of all college students had taken at least one online course, compared to less than 10% in 2003 (Allen, & Seaman 2013). Online and hybrid classes are now a common feature in the higher education landscape.

The Platform is In Place

A robust technological platform for online education is now in place at most colleges and universities, and third-party vendors can provide a platform for those who believe their technology is inadequate to support online programs. One of the most significant developments was the creation of learning management systems in the late 1990s and early 2000s. Proprietary systems like Blackboard and open source systems like Moodle, among many others, provide opportunities for their wide adoption by colleges and universities. Some larger universities, such as the University of Michigan, created their own learning management systems. The proliferation of LMSs impacted higher education in two ways. First, as more functionality was added to the LMS, with the development of wikis, blogs and discussion boards for collaborative learning, and Youtube.com as a video content delivery system, the LMS could serve as a basic structure of the online classroom, significantly lowering the costs of creating and delivering new courses. Second, students became accustomed to using an LMS to access course material and interact with professors, as the LMS is not just for use in online courses. Over time, using a computer-based educational platform has become routine for most students.

The growth of broadband networks, coupled with technology that allows for the creation of low-cost video content, means that instructors can more easily incorporate video lectures into their online classes and create a better sense of social presence. Video conferencing tools allow video lectures to be streamed live to students in synchronous lectures, or recorded and accessed at the students' convenience. In addition to video, other kinds of rich content can be incorporated into online classes more efficiently and at a lower cost than before. Moreover, many students have easy access to broadband Internet connections, either at home or through libraries or coffee shops. Lack of Internet access is not a deterrent to participating in online education even for low-income students, although access can be more challenging for people without a suitable Internet connection at home. Students, particularly younger ones, are extremely comfortable interacting with each other through a device, often a smart phone. The cost of laptop computers, the primary end-user device of online education, has dropped significantly and is economically within reach for most people. Tablets and even smart phones are being adopted for use in online education. And, many of the tasks and applications associated with an online class are second nature to those who routinely utilize the Internet to chat online, post comments to blogs and discussion boards, download files, watch videos online, video conference and use other services and applications throughout the day.

The emergence of cloud computing and the huge storage resources the cloud offers means that students only have to download appropriate viewers to their computers and colleges and universities do not have to worry about installing new software onto individual computers. While downloading viewers and ensuring that they work correctly can sometimes require technical support, the process is much less complicated than installing client application software, which frequently was the case a decade ago. The cloud offers a huge amount of storage space at a reasonable cost, and many cloud services offer a generous amount of store without cost. This means that some colleges and universities can at least get started with online education without investing heavily in their technical infrastructure. And, in general, the cloud can provide the robust technical foundation for a richer online education experience. The technology needed for and used in online education will continue to develop, as will students' comfort levels using these tools.

What Online Education Means to You

Many stakeholders in the higher education community recognize that online courses and programs will be just one response to the myriad challenges they face. Viewed from a programmatic level, creating online programs as opposed to developing online courses creates a raft of obstacles that must be overcome. Online education is not just a matter of faculty putting their in-class material online. The establishment of online programs touches every part of the university, from student life to student development. It has an impact on the admissions process and procedures. And, a host of regulatory issues come into play. Over time, having students enrolled in online only educational programs could have an impact on alumni relations and advancement. At some level, moving into the online world of education requires that a college or university reflect on their primary mission, which is a difficult and painful process.

The push for and path to launching online programs is not straightforward and the process of establishing such programs will generally be distinct to each institution, as different stakeholders have different motivations. For example, in California, the state legislature has mandated that at least some state universities investigate the potential benefits of online education, particularly MOOCs, for some of their students (Meyer 2013). At the University of Virginia, the push to accelerate the university's entry into online education and MOOCs came from the Board of Trustees, which set off a fire storm on campus when the trustees removed the president for not moving quickly enough in that direction (Jaschik 2012). More commonly, units concerned with professional education and continuing education have pioneered the entry to online education. Sometimes deans or other administrators get interested in online education before faculty and academic departments. But more likely, in some cases, the impetus first comes from members of the faculty. Given the diffuse nature of governance in most colleges and universities, getting agreement from the various stakeholders for an online educational initiative is difficult and can take a long time. For example, although chief academic officers generally see online education as an important part of the future, college presidents are generally less enthusiastic, particularly about the potential of MOOCs (2013). And just because one set of stakeholders is interested in online education on one campus doesn't mean that the same stakeholders are interested on another campus. Online education does not have a single natural constituency pushing for its development and often faces resistance and opposition. The arrangement of proponents and opponents differs from campus to campus. At an institutional level, for online educational programs to succeed, they need a champion who can bring together the various constituencies. This may be your job. The champion has to recognize and address the interests and concerns of each of the stakeholders and reconcile their differences to craft an acceptable approach. The leaders of online educational initiatives have to be able to speak to faculty, to administrators, to trustees and even to alumni. The pioneers of online educational programs have to identify sources of resistance and reinforce the efforts of those who want to move forward.

Creating an appropriate institutional infrastructure to support online programs and online students is essential. But the goal is to deliver a high quality educational experience. Not only do most faculty members have no experience teaching online courses, but also most have never taken an online course. Developing an online course is quite different than developing a traditional course. And since faculty were students for a long time prior to becoming academics, they have a lot of implicit knowledge about traditional course development, knowledge that does not necessarily translate to online course development and delivery. Online education is a new adventure for faculty and many are more pessimistic about online education than optimistic and wonder if the online experience can match the learning outcomes of the traditional classroom (Kolowich 2012). Online course development takes time and patience to build and training to deliver. Online courses generally require new forms of collaboration with which many faculty members are not familiar or comfortable. Online courses require a new approach to learning and building a learning community. Simply put: online education is different, and therefore the challenges of developing and implementing online courses and programs are different. Students need to be prepared for and guided through their experience online if they are going to fully realize the benefits of this unique educational opportunity.

With the pressure to produce research at many institutions, faculty members may simply not want to invest their time in developing courses for online delivery. But colleges and universities simply can no longer wait to move at least part of their educational program online. The purpose of this book is to lay out the comprehensive range of issues involved in creating an appropriate infrastructure for online educational programs and the delivery of a high quality educational experience. This book serves as a guide for all of the constituencies involved across the institution, and it provides a common ground for different stakeholders to understand the requirements outside their domain. The book presents the development of online educational programs as an ongoing process. Colleges and universities that already offer some online educational programs have neither fully incorporated them into their core educational offerings, nor have they developed the entire scaffolding needed to support online education. In short, this book is designed to provide you with a roadmap to the future.

The crisis in higher education is acute. Many students can no longer afford its high costs. At state universities, students frequently can't get the courses they need to graduate in four years. The value of a liberal arts education is being hotly debated. Part of the discussion regarding the future of higher education includes the discussion of the place of online education. The road to incorporating online education into the mainstream of higher education is long and hard, and is an ongoing process. But you must start right now.

References

Allen, I. E., & Seaman, J. (2013). Changing course: Ten years of tracking online education in the United States. *Babson Research*, January. Retrieved from http://sloanconsortium.org/publications/survey/changing_course_2012

Atkinson, R. C., & Blanpied, W. A. (2008). Research universities: Core of the US science and technology system. *Technology in Society, 30*, 30–48.

Barry, M., Dubin, J. C., & Joy, P. A. (2010, August). *Legal education 'Best Practices' report*. Retrieved from http://www.pilnet.org/public-interest-law-resources/11-the-development-of-legal-education-in-the-united-states.html

Biemiller, L. (2014, February 13). QuickWire: Pearson offers a badge platform. *The Chronicle of Higher Education*. Retrieved from http://chronicle.com/blogs/wiredcampus/quickwire-pearson-offers-a-badge-platform/50469?cid=wc&utm_source=wc&utm_medium=en

Brinton, C., Chiang, M., Jain, S., Lam, H., Liu, Z., Wong, F., & Ming F., (2013). Learning about social learning in MOOCs: From statistical analysis to generative model. Under Review with *IEEE Transactions on Learning Technologies*. Paper presented at Workshop on Information in Networks, New York University, October 4–5.

Brooks, D. (2012, May 3). The campus tsunami, *The New York Times*. Retrieved from http://www.nytimes.com/2012/05/04/opinion/brooks-the-campus-tsunami.html

Bush, V. (1945). *Science the endless frontier*. A report to the President by Vannevar Bush, Director of the Office of Scientific Research and Development, July. Retrieved from http://www.nsf.gov/od/lpa/nsf50/vbush1945.htm#summary.

Carnegie Foundation (n.d.). *The Carnegie classification of institutions of higher education™*. Retrieved from http://classifications.carnegiefoundation.org/

Carrell, W. D. (1968). American college professors: 1750–1800. *History of Education Quarterly, 8*(3: Autumn), 289–305. Retrieved from http://www.jstor.org/stable/367429

Chafkin, M. (2013, November 14). Udacity's Sebastian Thrun, godfather of free online education, changes course. Retrieved from http://www.fastcompany.com/3021473/udacity-sebastian-thrun-uphill-climb

Christensen, C. (2013, February 2). In 15 years half of all universities will be bankrupt. *Silicon Valley Business Journal*. Retrieved from http://www.bizjournals.com/sanjose/news/2013/02/07/disruption-guru-christensen-why.html?page=all

Clark, K. (2012, October 24). Tuition at public colleges rises 4.8%. *CNN Money*. Retrieved from http://money.cnn.com/2012/10/24/pf/college/public-college-tuition/

Daniels Jr., M. E. (2014). An open letter to the people of Purdue, *Office of The President, Purdue University*. Retrieved from http://www.purdue.edu/president/email/2014/1401-med-openletter.html

Department of Veteran Affairs (n.d.). Education and training: History and timeline. Retrieved from http://www.benefits.va.gov/gibill/history.asp

Diamond, R. M. (2006). Changing higher education: Realistic goal or wishful thinking? *Trusteeship*, Nov/Dec. Retrieved from http://www.thenationalacademy.org/readings/hardtochange.html

Edwards, J. (2013, December 30). The largest class at Stanford right now will produce a new generation of 'machine learning' startups. *Seattle PI*. Retrieved from http://www.seattlepi.com/technology/businessinsider/article/The-Largest-Class-At-Stanford-Right-Now-Will-5101823.php

Flexner, A. (1910, June 1). Medical education in America: Rethinking the training of American doctors. *The Atlantic*. Retrieved from http://www.theatlantic.com/magazine/archive/1910/06/medical-education-in-america/306088/

Gillespie, I. (2104, January 23). The rise of brain machines. *Sydney Morning Herald*. Retrieved from http://www.smh.com.au/technology/technology-news/the-rise-of-the-brain-machines-20140122-317g3.html#ixzz2r9BAoJLs

Grimmelmann, J. (2013, December 26). MOOCs: Over already? [Commentary]. *Baltimore Sun.* Retrieved from http://articles.baltimoresun.com/2013-12-26/news/bs-ed-moocs-20131226_1_udacity-courses-moocs-great-courses

Friedman, T. (2012, May 15). Come the revolution. *The New York Times*. Retrieved from http://www.nytimes.com/2012/05/16/opinion/friedman-come-the-revolution.html

Friedman, T. (2013, January 27). Revolution hits the universities. *The New York Times*, http://www.nytimes.com/2013/01/27/opinion/sunday/friedman-revolution-hits-the-universities.html

Harden, N. (2012, December 11). The end of the university as we know it. *The American Interest*. Retrieved from http://www.the-american-interest.com/articles/2012/12/11/the-end-of-the-university-as-we-know-it/

Hess, F. (2011, September 28). Old school: College's most important trend is the rise of the adult student. *The Atlantic*. Retrieved from http://www.theatlantic.com/business/archive/2011/09/old-school-colleges-most-important-trend-is-the-rise-of-the-adult-student/245823/

High, P. (2013, December 31). Lessons from the CEO of the first ever MOOC. *Forbes*. Retrieved from http://www.forbes.com/sites/peterhigh/2013/12/31/lessons-from-the-ceo-of-the-first-ever-mooc/

Jamrisko, M., & Kolet, I. (2013, August 26). College costs surge 500% in U.S. since 1985: Chart of the day. *Bloomberg News*. Retrieved from http://www.bloomberg.com/news/2013-08-26/college-costs-surge-500-in-u-s-since-1985-chart-of-the-day.html

Jaschik, S. (2012, June 20). The e-mail trail at UVA. *Inside Higher Education*. Retrieved from http://www.insidehighered.com/news/2012/06/20/e-mails-show-uva-board-wanted-big-online-push#ixzz2u9zPA0yX

Jaschik, S. (2013, May 2). MOOC skeptics at the top. *Inside Higher Education*. Retrieved from http://www.insidehighered.com/news/2013/05/02/survey-finds-presidents-are-skeptical-moocs#ixzz2uA1pHlHL

Kiley, K. (2013, January 17). Nowhere to turn. *Inside Higher Education*. Retrieved from http://www.insidehighered.com/news/2013/01/17/moodys-report-calls-question-all-traditional-university-revenue-sources#ixzz2tPYZ9z5t

Kiley, K. (2013, July 12). Coming up short. *Inside Higher Education*. Retrieved from http://www.insidehighered.com/news/2013/07/12/loyola-new-orleans-enrollment-shortfall-will-mean-large-budget-cuts#ixzz2tPWMAqea

Kolowich, S. (2012, June 21). Conflicted: Faculty and online education. *Inside Higher Education*. Retrieved from http://www.insidehighered.com/news/survey/conflicted-faculty-and-online-education-2012#ixzz2uA6zEitJ

Kolowich, S. (2014, January 17). Credit-for-MOOCs effort hits a snag. Retrieved from http://chronicle.com/blogs/wiredcampus/credit-for-moocs-effort-hits-a-snag/49573?cid=wc&utm_source=wc&utm_medium=en

Kolowich, S. (2014, January 21). Coursera will offer certificates for sequences of MOOCs. *The Chronicle of Higher Education*. Retrieved from http://chronicle.com/blogs/wiredcampus/coursera-will-offer-certificates-for-sequences-of-moocs/49581?cid=wc&utm_source=wc&utm_medium=en

Kolowich, S. (2014, January 22). Completion rates aren't the best way to judge MOOCs, researchers say. Retrieved from http://chronicle.com/blogs/wiredcampus/completion-rates-arent-the-best-way-to-judge-moocs-researchers-say/49721?cid=at&utm_source=at&utm_medium=en

Kosner, A. W. (2013, December 29). Why is machine learning (CS 229) the most popular course at Stanford? *Forbes*. Retrieved from http://www.forbes.com/sites/anthonykosner/2013/12/29/why-is-machine-learning-cs-229-the-most-popular-course-at-stanford/

Lederman, D. (2011, July 25). Does performance funding work? *Inside Higher Education*. Retrieved from http://www.insidehighered.com/news/2011/07/25/study_examines_impact_of_state_performance_based_funding_on_graduation_retention#ixzz2tV6vUYA9

Lee, G. C. (1963). The Morrill Act and education. *British Journal of Educational Studies*, 12(1), 19–40. Retrieved from http://www.jstor.org/stable/3118919

Lewin, T. (2012, March 5). Instruction for masses knocks down campus walls. *The New York Times*. Retrieved from http://www.nytimes.com/2012/03/05/education/moocs-large-courses-open-to-all-topple-campus-walls.html?pagewanted=all

Lewin, T. (2013, May 3). Professors at San Jose state criticize online courses. *The New York Times*. Retrieved from http://www.nytimes.com/2013/05/03/education/san-jose-state-philosophy-dept-criticizes-online-courses.html?_r=0

Marcus, J. (2013, April 13). Why some small colleges are in big trouble: Money is tight. Competition is brutal. Are some Massachusetts schools on the road to ruin? *The Boston Globe*. Retrieved from http://www.bostonglobe.com/magazine/2013/04/13/are-small-private-colleges-trouble/ndlYSWVGFAUjYVVWkqnjfK/story.html

Markoff, J. (2012, April 18). Online education venture lures cash infusion and deals with 5 top universities. *The New York Times*. Retrieved from http://www.nytimes.com/2012/04/18/technology/coursera-plans-to-announce-university-partners-for-online-classes.html

Meyer, L. (2013, June 6). California bill allowing credit for MOOCs passes senate. Retrieved from http://campustechnology.com/articles/2013/06/06/california-bill-allowing-credit-for-moocs-passes-senate.aspx

Miller, C., & Malandra, G. (2006). A national dialogue: The Secretary of Education's commission on the future of higher education. Retrieved from http://www2.ed.gov/about/bdscomm/list/hiedfuture/reports/miller-malandra.pdf

Moore, C. (2009). Student profess toward degree completion: Lessons from the research literature. Retrieved from http://www.csus.edu/ihelp/PDFs/R_Student_Progress_Toward_Degree_Completion.pdf

Morrison, D. (2012, June 12). The next big disruptor – competency-based learning. *Online Learning Insights*. Retrieved from http://onlinelearninginsights.wordpress.com/2012/06/12/the-next-big-disruptor-competency-based-learning/

National Center for Education Statistics (2011). Projections of Education Statistics to 2020. Retrieved from http://nces.ed.gov/programs/projections/projections2020/tables/table_12.asp

The National Science Foundation (1994) A brief history. Retrieved from https://www.nsf.gov/about/history/nsf50/nsf8816.jsp

National Student Clearinghouse (2012, December 18). Current term enrollment reports 2012. Retrieved from http://www.studentclearinghouse.org/about/media_center/press_releases/files/release_2012-12-18.pdf

Nova Southeastern University (n.d.). FAQ http://www.scis.nova.edu/admissions/faq.html

Oliff, P., Palacios, V., Johnson, I., & Leachman, M. (2013, March 19). Recent deep state higher education cuts may harm students and the economy for years to come. Retrieved from http://www.cbpp.org/cms/?fa=view&id=3927

Ordway, D. -M. (2013, December 31). Small, private colleges fret over online classes. *Orlando Sentinel*. Retrieved from http://articles.orlandosentinel.com/2013-12-31/news/os-private-college-online-trend-20131227_1_least-one-online-course-online-learning-online-education

Our Documents (n.d.). Transcript of Morrill Act (1862). Retrieved from http://www.ourdocuments.gov/doc.php?flash=true&doc=33&page=transcript

Pangaea Network, Inc. (1999). Electronic University Network. Retrieved from http://www.pangaeanetwork.org/colleges.html

Pappano, L. (2012, November 2). The Year of the MOOC. *The New York Times*. Retrieved from http://www.nytimes.com/2012/11/04/education/edlife/massive-open-online-courses-are-multiplying-at-a-rapid-pace.html?pagewanted=all

Pearson Education Inc. (2013). Open badges are unlocking the emerging jobs economy. Retrieved from http://www.pearsonvue.com/sponsors/acclaim/open_badges_unlock_jobs.pdf

Penn GSE (2014, February 12). Penn GSE study shows MOOCs have relatively few active users, with only a few persisting to course end. Retrieved from http://www.gse.upenn.edu/pressroom/press-releases/2013/12/penn-gse-study-shows-moocs-have-relatively-few-active-users-only-few-persisti

Prescott, B. T., & Bransberger, P. (2012). *Knocking at the college door: Projections of high school graduates* (8th ed.). Boulder, CO: Western Interstate Commission for Higher Education, 2012.

Smith College (2011). The Futures Initiative 2010–2011. Retrieved from http://www.smith.edu/docs/president/FuturesInitiative.pdf

StraighterLine (n.d.). History of distance education [Infographic]. Retrieved from http://www.straighterline.com/online-education-resources/online-education-tools/infographic-history-of-distance-education/

Tagg, J. (2012). Why does the faculty resist change? *Change Magazine*. January/February. Retrieved from http://www.changemag.org/Archives/Back Issues/2012/January-February 2012/facultychange-full.html

The Institute for College Access and Success (2014). Project on student debt. Retrieved from http://projectonstudentdebt.org/state_by_state-data.php

Trends in Higher Education (2012). Total undergraduate student aid in 2012 (dollars over time). Retrieved from http://trends.collegeboard.org/student-aid/figures-tables/undergraduate-total-student-aid-nonfederal-loans-2012-dollars-over-time

Trends in Higher Education (2014). Tuition and fees by sector and state over time. Retrieved from http://trends.collegeboard.org/college-pricing/figures-tables/tuition-and-fees-sector-and-state-over-time

Turkle, S. (2012). Connected, but alone. [Ted Talk] Video retrieved from http://www.ted.com/talks/sherry_turkle_alone_together.html

University of California Office of the President (1960) A master plan for higher education in California 1960–1975. Retrieved from http://www.ucop.edu/acadinit/mastplan/MasterPlan1960.pdf

University of Florida (n.d.). History [Distance education at the University of Florida]. Retrieved from http://iml.jou.ufl.edu/projects/spring01/declair/history.html

University of Phoenix (n.d.). History of the University of Phoenix. Retrieved from http://www.phoenix.edu/about_us/about_university_of_phoenix/history.html

U.S. Department of Education, National Center for Education Statistics. (2011). The condition of education 2011 (NCES 2011-033), Indicator 43.

Walsh, C. (2012, April 26). Hard-earned gains for women at Harvard. *Harvard Gazette*. Retrieved from http://news.harvard.edu/gazette/story/2012/04/hard-earned-gains-for-women-at-harvard/

Webley, K. (2012, December 4). Planet of the MOOCS. *Time*. Retrieved from http://nation.time.com/2012/12/04/top-10-us-news-lists/slide/planet-of-the-moocs/#ixzz2sXfAfFaj

The White House (2013, August 22). Fact sheet on the President's plan to make college more affordable: A better bargain for the middle class. Retrieved from http://www.whitehouse.gov/the-press-office/2013/08/22/fact-sheet-president-s-plan-make-college-more-affordable-better-bargain-

Wladawsky-Berger, I. (2013, December 27). MOOCs: Inflated expectations, early disappointments. *The Wall Street Journal*. Retrieved from http://blogs.wsj.com/cio/2013/12/27/moocs-inflated-expectations-early-disappointments/

Won, M. (n.d.). History IT. Retrieved from http://people.lis.illinois.edu/~chip/projects/timeline/1960won.html#brief%20document%20history%20of%20PLATO

Yahoo Financial News (2013) Top 10 most expensive colleges in America 2013. Retrieved from http://finance.yahoo.com/news/top-10-most-expensive-colleges-in-america-180935227.html

Young, J. (2013, January 5). California State University will experiment with offering credit for MOOCs. *Chronicle of Higher Education*. Retrieved from http://chronicle.com/article/California-State-U-Will/136677/

2

Moving Online Programs Forward

The landscape for online educational programs largely developed over the last 20 years. And as the drive to move online learning to the center of higher education accelerates, the myriad of online programs currently in operation will serve as the foundation for what will come next. As the process of understanding the contours of online education unfolds, the goal is to develop a vision for what role online programs should play in your institution. Your challenge, therefore, is to determine how your institution will to get from here to there.

Colleges and universities have taken many different avenues in launching online educational programs. For example, in 1995, the Western Governors Association, now a group of 22 chief executives from states and territories ranging as far east as Kansas and as far west as American Samoa, met under the leadership of Mike Leavitt, the governor of Utah, to address what he saw as a pressing regional need: the population in the western states was growing rapidly, and investment in higher education was not keeping pace. His idea was to create a new university but a university with a twist. It would not have a physical campus. The Western Interstate Commission on Higher Education, the National Center for Higher Education Management Systems and the Western Governors Association, collaborated to bring that solution to fruition. The university would be based on five principles: make maximum use of distance learning technologies; be specifically geared to addressing economic and social needs; be competency based; geared to expanding access to higher education; and, it would not be expensive. Finally, the collaborators pledged to invest in the technological infrastructure needed to implement its mission—enabling working adults to improve their career opportunities and educational aspirations. Chartered in 1997, the Western Governors University launched its first Associate of Arts degree in 1999 and later that year inaugurated a Master of Arts degree in Learning and Technology. The following year, Genevieve Kirsch became WGU's first graduate when she earned her Master of Arts degree in Learning and Technology. In 2012, WGU had more than 30,000 students enrolled and more than 16,000 graduates from disciplines ranging from education, business and health sciences to information technology. Viewed by the governors as a success, the project required far less funding than building a new campus and could serve far more students. As an additional benefit, the model has been replicated and localized. In 2011, WGU partnered with Washington state to establish WGU Washington, which quickly became the most popular university to which community colleges graduates transferred. That same year WGU won a $4.5 million grant from the Bill and Melinda Gates Foundation to support WGU Indiana as well as WGU Texas and WGU Washington. The goal in establishing those entities is to give WGU a local imprimatur, according to Randy Spalding, the director of academic affairs and policy at the Washington Student Achievement Council, the state higher education coordinating board (Schrader 2013).

The apparent success of Western Governors University has inspired similar efforts. In 2007, the board of governors of the Colorado State University System set out to expand its educational reach. The system already had two traditional university campuses—one in Fort Collins and one in Pueblo. But the board was not interested in establishing a third campus. Instead, it created CSU-Global. The instruction would be completely online and be geared to the professional needs of working adults. The administration at CSU-Global views itself as market-driven, designed to meet the needs of the consumer, that is, its students. The school opened in 2008 with 204 students (Dixon 2013). By 2012, it had 6,500 students and more than 1,300 alumni, offering 15 Bachelor of Science degree programs in fields ranging from accounting and human services to public management, as well as ten master's programs.

Creating an entire online campus is one approach. Sometimes schools will put a high profile program online. For example, in 2013, the Georgia Institute of Technology announced that it would offer an Online Master of Science in Computer Science (OMS-CS) degree using a MOOC format. To create the courses, Georgia Tech's College of Computing partnered with Udacity, one of the pioneering MOOC providers. The courses would be available for free through Udacity's MOOC platform, but students would have to be accepted by Georgia Tech to receive credit. Students could pay either per course or for the entire program, which was expected to cost less than $7,000; the program was supported by a grant from AT&T. Georgia Tech was no stranger to online and distance learning. It has been offering online degrees for more than 30 years including master's degrees in Aerospace Engineering, Medical Physics, Operations Research and more. The OMS-CS initiative, however, had more ambitious goals than simply offering degrees via an online platform. According to Zvi Galil, the John P. Imlay Jr. Dean of Computing at Georgia Tech, the objective was to offer a high quality education in computer science to potentially hundreds of thousands of students, perhaps doubling the number of trained computer professionals within ten years (Georgia Tech 2013). The Georgia Tech experiment is an extremely important one. Georgia Tech has made a flagship program available to a much broader community at a sharply reduced cost.

In theory, if the program succeeds, it is likely to have an impact on programs around the country. While Georgia Tech has taken the online plunge with a core program, Brandeis University has focused its efforts in professional education. It offers online master's degrees in new fields such as Bioinformatics, Information Security and Virtual Management. The programs are not offered through its graduate school; rather, they are offered through the division of graduate professional studies, where the focus is on applied and innovative programs geared to working professionals who wish to enhance their skills in emerging industries. Professionals in the field generally teach the courses. And though the division historically offered on-campus classes, in the future all programs will be offered online.

While many efforts to build online educational programs are based on sound ideas, at the institutional level, many are not well planned. For example, in July 2012, a task force created by the Faculty Senate at the University of Virginia (UVA) reported the results of a survey of online education being offered. It found there were more than 200 courses being offered online and 11 online-only master's programs, primarily clustered in Engineering and Nursing. Moreover, the university offered seven hybrid programs that included both online and on-campus components. Despite what turned out to be significant activity in online education, there was no central authority at the university or any single office at any of the 11 schools that make up the university that catalogued, coordinated, supported or marketed their online educational efforts. In fact, those efforts were locally developed, driven by the interests of a specific faculty member or members, or driven by the interest of administrators in different departments and schools (UVA Faculty Senate Task Force 2012). Western Governors University, CSU-Global, OMS-CS at Georgia Tech, the Division of Graduate Professional Studies at Brandeis University and the online task force at the University of Virginia all represent different avenues in which non-profit universities have entered the online educational arena to provide degree and certificate-granting programs. In each instance, the initiative for launching the online educational effort initially came from a different stakeholder. In the case of WGU, it came from state government. For CSU-Global, the state university system itself was the prime mover. For Georgia Tech, the College of Computer Science played a lead role. At Brandeis, the division of graduate professional studies is the locus of online education. And the task force report at UVA documents a university in which the interests of individual faculty members have driven most of the initial forays into online education with little or no coordination at either the school or institutional level.

While the motivation for establishing online programs is different among these programs, each has certain similarities. The programs are aimed at working professionals and have as a centerpiece their convenience for the learner. In addition to eliminating the need for students to drive to a campus at a set time, many of the programs have changed their academic calendars, offering compressed semesters or allowing students to take as many credits as they wish per semester for a set fee, for example. Online programs are intended to increase access to higher education, and along the way—put into the business terms so frequently used when discussing online educational programs—increasing each institution's addressable market. And such online programs cost less than a comparable education at a traditional campus. In short, online programs can offer working adults a comparable education to the one that they would receive on campus more conveniently and at less cost. Earning a degree or certificate online will help them advance their career or otherwise meet their educational objectives. Few of the programs explicitly embrace the educational aims commonly associated with traditional undergraduate education, even though undergraduate education is one of the most significant areas to address in this period of change in higher education.

The New Competition

In many ways, public institutions of higher education arrived late to meet those promises identified above through the development of online programs. The lack of opportunity to study online at some public institutions has been at the foundation of the explosion of online programs at for-profit universities over the past several decades. The institutions of higher education with the greatest number of students enrolled online are all for-profit institutions, with the University of Phoenix the leader by a substantial margin with more than 300,000 enrolled students. Five of the top eight universities measured by number of online students enrolled are for-profit institutions including Kaplan University, Walden University, Devry University and Ashford University. Ashford is an interesting example of a for-profit university that has successfully blurred the lines between residential and online. In 2005, Ashford was a failing, regionally accredited college in Iowa, once known as the Franciscan University of the Prairies. That year it was sold to a for-profit company and currently has tens of thousands of online students, the majority of whom never receive degrees (Carroll 2014). Only Arizona State University, with more than 70,000 online students, and the University of Maryland, through the University of Maryland University College, have significant profiles both in online and traditional formats. Like Ashford, a growing number of formerly small local institutions are becoming major providers of online degree programs. Community colleges have been some of the most responsible institutions when it comes to establishing online programs; the smallest growth is in BA programs (Allen, & Seaman 2007). The 80-year-old Southern New Hampshire State University, for example, has about 2750 undergraduate students who attend school at its main campus in Manchester, New Hampshire and its regional centers in New Hampshire and Maine. But it has another 25,000 students enrolled online. In 2013, SHSU was expected to generate nearly $30 million in revenue from its online operation, enough to build a 308-student dorm and to begin work on a 50,000-square-foot library for its campus (Hechinger 2013).

Online Education: A Watershed Moment

Clearly, institutions are entering the online educational arena from all directions—elite universities like UVA, Georgia Tech and Brandeis as well as Stanford, Harvard, University of Pennsylvania and others via MOOCs. State systems like CSU Global Campus, the Pennsylvania State University World Campus, Arizona State University and University of Maryland University College enroll large numbers of students locally, regionally and internationally. Formerly local or regional universities like Post University, and Southern New Hampshire State University along with a host of for-profit universities like the University of Phoenix, Capella University, and Kaplan University extend the reach of online education. Finally, there are the non-profit start-up online universities like Western Governors University and the University of the People, a tuition-free online university launched in 2009 by Israeli entrepreneur Shai Reshef to support underserved students around the world.

Online educational programs are being launched at a fast and furious pace. In 2014, there may be as many as 2000 programs online, according to U.S. News and World Report, which began ranking online educational programs in 2012, in much the same way the magazine ranks graduate programs and schools. They evaluated more than 1,000 programs for their 2013 rankings. The names that have climbed to the top in the online rankings are far different than the leaders in on-campus education at both the undergraduate and graduate levels. For example, the top-ranked school for an online undergraduate degree is Central Michigan University. The best graduate education programs, according to U.S. News, are at Northern Illinois University. The rankings have two important implications. The competition posed by online education to traditional colleges and universities is significant and the field is still largely unsettled. Even Harvard is not the "Harvard" of online education.

The plethora of online programs is like an arms race; however, the exponential growth is accompanied by hit-and-miss experimentation. For example, in the fall of 2012, CSU-Global announced that it would accept credits from students who completed a MOOC offered by Stanford University. This announcement looked like it could demonstrate the value of a MOOC and point to the potential flexibility of online education of being inclusive and lower cost. The greater implication is that CSU students could get the benefit of a Stanford education. Even better, students who took advantage of this opportunity would only have to pay $89 compared to the $1050 that Colorado State would charge. If the collaboration worked, one could imagine a future in which a set of relatively standard courses in a given area would be offered online by a group of elite schools and other schools would be relegated to teaching specialized courses or be forced from the arena altogether.

But the experiment did not work. After a year, not a single CSU student had attempted to transfer credit. In a similar vein, as MOOCs burst into wider public view, the Council of Adult and Experiential Learning, which helps students create a portfolio of outside-the-classroom learning for which some universities will award credit, anticipated that many students would seek their help to receive college credit for completing a MOOC. As of 2014, the Council had not had a single request (Kolowich 2013).

The Critical Institutional Players

One marker of the significance in the emergence of online education is that virtually every major stakeholder in higher education has a perspective and opinion about the suitability of online education and each stakeholder will play a significant role in determining its shape. Online programs are not just a pedagogical endeavor and certainly have not emerged only under the supervision of the faculty. They potentially represent a fundamental change in the structure of higher education and most stakeholders are fighting to shape that change.

Perhaps the most unexpected drivers of online programs are state governments such as California. In cases where government gets involved, the legislature generally is responding to news reports and public discussion about the need to reduce the cost of a college education, and online appears to be one way to achieve that goal. But state interest in online education is not completely reactive. Many states, including Michigan, Alabama and New Mexico, are requiring students in the K-12 levels to take at least some courses online (Davis 2013). And while no other states have replicated California's experiment in compelling university campuses to accept online credits, according to a policy brief published by the American Association of State Colleges and Universities, online and competency-based education are among state legislatures' top higher education legislative priorities. AASCU analysts noted that the 14 universities of the Pennsylvania State System of Higher Education had collaborated with LearningCounts.org and the Council for Adult and Experiential Learning to facilitate the awarding of credit for completing MOOCs. States, the briefing pointed out, see online education as a way to lower overall costs for students (AASCU 2013). State governments are not standing still. The California State Assembly passed a bill mandating that any student attending any campus of the California State University could enroll in any online course being offered by any other CSU campus. And the Florida House of Representatives approved legislation that required the State Board of Education and the Board of Governors to craft rules for students to earn academic credit for online courses, including MOOCs, prior to initial enrollment at a postsecondary institution (Weeden 2014). Online education is clearly on the agenda of state legislatures and minimally state colleges and universities will have to respond to mandates issued from state houses around the country.

In some states, the governing boards of university systems and boards of trustees have also embraced online education. Following the path set by Colorado State University Global Campus, the Florida State Legislature appropriated $15 million in start-up funding and the university system's Board of Governors approved the University of Florida to start the nation's first fully online-only BA program. Supporters of the measure said the move signals an aggressive approach to online programs in higher education in Florida, where high school students already can attend elementary school and high school fully online (Cotterell 2013). For in-state students tuition was set at no more than 75% of the tuition rate for traditional students. Moreover, students can save on room and board, as they do not have to live on campus, as do many University of Florida students. Within ten years, officials anticipate that UF Online will enroll 24,000 students, offer 35 majors, generate $77 million in revenue and produce a profit of $15 million. The main campus of the University of Florida enrolls approximately 6400 first year students, drawing from a pool of close to 30,000 applications. UF Online will adhere to the same admission standards as the residential campus, according Joe Glover, the UF provost. Many Florida students were qualified to attend the university, but were turned away because of a lack of space, and UF Online could be a good alternative for those students (Stockfisch 2013).

Mandates for online education programs from state legislatures or university system governance bodies represent a top-down approach to program development. The decisions about what majors to offer and other aspects of the program are decided at levels far removed from where those decisions are actually carried out. In fact, those decisions are made prior to faculty being recruited and oftentimes before an administration is even in place. And while these top-down initiatives are often couched in terms that suggest that the motive is to increase access to higher education—and certainly the potential is there to do so—they are also intended to reduce costs while generating increased revenue. At some level, such efforts represent a lessening of support for higher education as a public good and are driven largely by market considerations.

Where is the Faculty?

Historically, the drive to create new educational programs has been in the hands of the faculty and the administration of a particular institution. A school or department sees an opportunity or an area that can be successfully taught through online education and crafts a program to do so. The motivation may be to increase the reach of a particular program, or it may be to offer a program with new subject material or content. Not infrequently online programs developed from the ground up are interdisciplinary in nature or reflect an innovative approach to an existing discipline. But many faculty and academic departments are not racing to develop online programs and in many cases feel very little motivation to do so. To a great extent university curricula have been largely static for decades, and faculty feel very little urgency to change. Academic departments are largely silos and tenure and tenure-track faculty have major responsibilities in addition to teaching, including producing high quality research and participating in university governance structures, among other duties. Making the kind of sustained investment in time and effort needed to craft and implement an online program is not high on the priority list for faculty. Furthermore, many faculty members perceive online education as a risk rather than an opportunity.

Sitting on the sidelines, however, poses a significant risk to faculty. New program launches such as UF Online and CSU-Global required rapidly assembling a new faculty and new administrative staff. Moreover, those projects and other top-down initiatives in higher education called for rapid growth. Many of the efforts target accessibility and affordability as key aims, expanding enrollment to populations that have not been well served by traditional campus-based education. In those cases, traditional faculty hiring practices cannot, or simply are not, being followed. In many instances, newer online programs hire no tenure/tenure track or even full-time faculty at all. For example, in 2014 Southern New Hampshire State University hired the first full-time faculty members associated with its online programs. At the time it had more than 25,000 online students. The same pattern holds true when universities and colleges focus their online efforts in the areas of continuing and professional education, professional master's degrees and remedial education. In many cases, the idea that courses are taught by working professionals with "real world" experience is marketed as an advantage to the working adults who represent the student body these programs wish to attract. Staffing online programs with affiliate and part-time faculty is part of a larger trend in higher education. Likewise, the composition of the faculty in online education may have a significant impact on higher education overall.

As a top-down approach to online educational programs seems to diminish the faculty's stewardship of the educational project at colleges and universities, many other stakeholders in higher education are eager to pursue online education for a myriad of seemingly non-academic reasons. As a result, online program development often takes place within a sea of resistance and acrimony. Faculty often resent intrusion into the curriculum by other stakeholders and efforts to offer lesser, perhaps less rigorous programs and, in the view of some, questionable outcomes. On the other hand, if administrators or other stakeholders are not interested in aggressively pursuing online education, it may be difficult for faculty to garner the resources and support they need to craft a successful program. Investing time and effort on the part of faculty, can lead to significant career risks when it comes to balancing the development of new initiatives against research productivity, for example.

Ideally, incorporating online education into the ongoing education project of the college or university requires the entire campus community to come to an understanding regarding the role online education can and should play given the history and mission of the institution. Online educational programs may be crafted to support the mission and vision of the institution or the mission and vision of the institution may be enlarged to incorporate online education. But the issue is really more fundamental. Online education drives right to the heart of what a college or university will be in the future. Unfortunately, most colleges and universities are not equipped to conduct that kind of introspective dialogue, and even if they could, reaching a consensus among the different stakeholders would be difficult.

Why it Matters

The impetus for an institution to move into online education will vary greatly from institution to institution. And, while one of the primary goals of establishing online programs is simply to extend the market reach to attract new students there are many other reasons as well. For example, in 2005 Hurricane *Rita* devastated Lamar University in Beaumont, Texas. As a result, more than 10% of its 11,000 students never returned to campus. In response, the university moved many of its programs online, and in 2014, around 35% of its now 14,000 students were enrolled online. After the University of Texas Arlington moved its nursing program online, enrollment in the College of Nursing went from a little under 2000 students to nearly 9000 (Howard 2014). Some institutions have either opted out of simply moving existing programs online, or they are constrained, for various reasons, from moving existing programs online. For example, the university system of North Carolina insists that new online programs have no adverse impact on existing programs at the system's 17 campuses, and there is a requirement that new programs fit the strategic plan for higher education in North Carolina, and be appropriate for the specific region or campus it serves. That requirement has lead to the creation of innovative programs like a BA program in neurodiagnostics and sleep science and interdisciplinary programs like health informatics. Because they cannot just move existing programs online, the campuses in the North Carolina system have begun to collaborate on new offerings. The University of North Carolina at Chapel Hill and UNC Charlotte, for example, collaborated on the program in sleep sciences.

Opportunities for Innovation and Collaboration

With the drive toward online programs begin fueled by legislatures, boards of trustees and administrators, responding to what could be described as market forces, and with the faculty in many institutions largely absent from the conversation or resistant to online education, what has largely been left out of the conversation are the positive ways in which online educational programs could help remake the future of higher education. In some respects, virtually every college and university could not only benefit from putting at least some courses and programs online but perhaps should be required to do so. Learning online is a skill that students will need after they graduate and they should gain experience how to learn online while there are undergraduates. Many students arrive on campus with some experience in online education during their high school years. But as in many cases, colleges and universities should build on the skills students already have and learning online is no exception. Moving at least some classes online would allow colleges and universities to better utilize their physical space. Online educational programs allow colleges and universities to experiment with and explore new formats for educational experience. For example, online programs are not necessarily tethered to the rhythms of the campus, so planners of online programs can think creatively about the academic calendar. Many for-profit colleges and universities geared toward adult learners have pioneered the use of shorter semesters with purported more intense learning experiences. Not only can classes be of variable length, but also the number of classes that a student takes in a given period of time is open to adjustment with online programs. Instead of full-time students taking four or five classes a semester spread over a 15-week period, which is the most common structure now, a full-time load could be four one-month courses, for example. Of course, the length of time a course requires will have an impact on the way the content is delivered and the way student performance will be assessed.

With regard to scheduling, traditionally students start an academic program in September. As online programs are often predicated on being more convenient than campus-based learning, many online programs allow students to start at different times of the year. Some opt to allow online learners to begin their program at the start of any semester—fall, spring or summer. For-profit universities that do not use a semester or quarter-based structure frequently allow their students to start at virtually any time. Although most campus programs currently adhere to a semester-based structure in which students meet one to three times a week for approximately three hours per week for 14 or 15 weeks, that structure is not set in concrete. Some universities still adhere to a quarter system. Many MBA programs geared to working adults meet for full days on the weekend. Some colleges and universities offer "mini-mesters" in which students can complete a course between semesters in several weeks or a month. But online educational programs allow for much more flexible formats.

Online education could have a huge impact on admission. As noted earlier, one of the goals of the University of Florida Online is to enroll students who were qualified to attend the campus but were not offered a place because of space constraints. Because many online programs currently are geared primarily to working adults, many programs do not require standardized tests for admission and the further away a person is from their undergraduate experience, the less relevant their academic performance may be to their ability to succeed in an online program. Indeed, in the case of MOOCs, there are no admission requirements. By definition they are open admission and credit toward a degree— if a degree is to be awarded, this comes upon successful completion of the course and a demonstration of competency. This competency-based approach calls into question the need for admission requirements at all. If admission requirements are only in place because of space limitations on campus, since online classes and programs theoretically can accommodate many more students, perhaps anybody who meets the baseline requirements should be accepted. On the other hand, part of the cachet of a degree is driven, at least in part, by its exclusivity. Would a degree from Harvard have the same panache if hundreds of thousands of students could earn their degree by demonstrating competency in Harvard-sponsored MOOCs? What a specific institution hopes a degree or certificate will signal is driven by the overall vision for the online program.

But the most important reason why colleges and universities should explore online options is the creativity online programs can unleash. The most obvious possibility, which is being explored in the University of North Carolina System and elsewhere, is the opportunity to create new interdisciplinary programs and fostering collaborations between departments and even institutions. As a new way to deliver education, online programs do not have to be locked into traditional academic departments or single campuses. Expert faculty can be recruited from across the country or even the world to participate in a highly focused educational experience. While continuing and professional education have already proven to be fertile ground for experimentation in online education, there is far more that could be done by broadening offerings to postgraduate learners, particularly alumni.

Done correctly, online educational programs can challenge many of the assumptions upon which higher education rests today. The vision and goals of each program and the overall vision for the online effort for a particular institution will drive the projected content, including how the program is staffed and who will be admitted to the program. Each of those will indelibly shape the character of the program and its position in the academic enterprise. The entry into online educational programming should stimulate a burst of creativity in many different areas of the university and in many different academic departments. The potential for change and creativity enabled by online education should fit within the expanding mission statement or strategic plan of the institution. Colleges and universities must investigate and assess the new directions most appropriate for them and incorporate those efforts into an overarching framework that can guide and stimulate innovation. For many colleges and universities, online education should not be seen as a threat but as an opportunity to reshape and invigorate their educational effort.

The Approval Process

The need to develop a comprehensive vision for online education is essential. But the overall online effort will be implemented through specific programs and embodied in specific classes. With that in mind, virtually all institutions have defined processes through which new programs and courses are approved. These processes may vary depending on whether the programs and courses are at the undergraduate or graduate level: whether they are housed in one of the traditional academic units; in a division of continuing or professional education; or, perhaps a special unit focusing on a particular aspect of education such as degree-completion. In most cases, new courses or programs have to pass through multiple levels of approval. They have to win faculty approval at the department and school level and often at the university level as well. Faculty approval generally comes through various curriculum committees representing different constituencies. Most programs will also need some sort of administrative approval, minimally at the level of the dean or in some cases the president of the university. Moving online course and program approvals through the standard channels is essential to ensure the credibility of the proposals. Credibility is important to faculty not involved or interested in online education that often looks suspiciously at the whole idea of online education. And it is important to potential students, who want to be assured that the quality of the courses they take online match the same quality as those delivered by traditional methods.

Most online programs and courses have to pass through two internal approval procedures and both processes are not always well coordinated. The first is the standard process with which most faculty and administrators are long familiar. The second is a new process designed to ensure that the quality of the online educational experience meets institutional standards and expectations. This second approval mechanism requires faculty to interact with online educational specialists who generally are not faculty members themselves. While many schools have instituted peer evaluation of teaching programs in which colleagues visit each other's classrooms and evaluate their teaching, few have outside experts guide instructors in ways to effectively teach their classes. Nonetheless, drawing on outside resources and establishing productive collaborative relationships between faculty and online education support personnel can be critical to a program winning internal approval. As an example, at Bowling Green University if a faculty member wants to move a course online, the first step is to contact the university's Center for Online and Blended Learning (COBL) and discuss the proposal with the director. The next step is to have the idea approved at the appropriate administrative level and then to file a course modification form (Center for Online and Blended Learning n.d.). The Office of the Provost has the final approval. Once a faculty member gets the green light to develop a course, the syllabus must conform to the guidelines and checklist developed by COBL and reviewed by the COBL director. Once the syllabus has gotten the okay, faculty members teaching online for the first time must be trained in online pedagogy. They then work with instructional designers to actually upload their course materials to the learning management system. In many cases, universities will have developed a set of standards to ensure that all courses follow the same online format so students can become familiar with navigating different courses. Some institutions require that courses meet external standards as well. For example, the University of West Florida requires faculty members to assess their online courses via the Quality Matters course review process. Faculty can also be certified as online instructors via a Quality Matters training program (Academic Technology Center: Quality Online Instruction). Course development must be facilitated by a number of people beyond the instructor, and courses must be approved by administrative units within the university. This course development and approval process requires a substantial amount of time. A year is not an unreasonable amount of time required to develop an online program.

External Approvals

In most cases, online programs face three levels of external approval. Like other programs, regional accrediting agencies must review and approve an online program. In most cases, the state in which the institution is located must give its stamp of approval. And, colleges and universities must be authorized to provide online education in each state in which students are enrolled. The requirements for state authorization vary greatly and are different if a college or university has a physical presence in a state such as a remote campus or even an administrative office. Approval by the regional higher education accrediting agency is the most significant external approval needed. Colleges and universities are generally not allowed to provide online education without their approval and programs that are not approved by the accrediting agency are not considered legitimate.

External regional accrediting agencies are responsible for certifying that a program is appropriate, the content is appropriate and that the institution proposing the program has the capacity to deliver the program with acceptable quality. With the growth of for-profit institutions whose students receive tens of millions of dollars in Federal financial aid but have very low rates of graduation, the accrediting agencies' standards have come under scrutiny, with critics contending the agencies have failed in their three most basic responsibilities—determining what programs are sufficiently rigorous to allow institutions to issue credits toward a degree; guiding the Federal government in its allocation of financial aid to higher education, and providing a peer review and improvement process for colleges and universities. The critics have focused on outcomes of student learning, highlighting studies that purport to show that nearly half of all students show little improvement in writing, critical thinking and analytical reasoning in their first two years, and furthermore that verbal and mathematical literacy rates even decline during the time a student is in college, coupled with low graduation rates even in some traditional non-profit colleges and universities (Brown 2013).

Accrediting agencies have responded to their critics by trying to make their work more transparent and more responsive to governmental policy concerns. They are exploring how to respond to innovation in higher education appropriately, particularly with the development of online courses and educational experiences being offered either outside or in addition to traditional colleges and universities. And they have renewed their focus on examining learning aims and learning outcomes (Easton 2013). The accreditation process for online education focuses on four key areas: curriculum, faculty, student support and assessment. The first is curriculum and instruction. In general, the substance of online programs and courses should not vary significantly from those taught in the traditional classroom. Programs must go through the standard internal review process and be supervised by the appropriate academic unit. The second key area is faculty support. Faculty must be trained to teach online and other issues surrounding faculty involvement such as compensation and ownership of intellectual property must be resolved. The third key area is student support. The institution must demonstrate that it has the services in place to facilitate students successfully completing classes and programs online and can provide the same services to online students as it does to on-campus students. The final key area is evaluation and assessment. This area reflects the overall trend to put procedures in place to measure learning outcomes and institutional effectiveness. The outcomes must be appropriate to the institution's mission and strategic goals (Morgan State University n.d.).

In summary, the accrediting agency is charged with ensuring that the institution has an appropriate plan for an online program; can reasonably execute the program pedagogically, and can measure if the program has achieved its learning objectives. The regional accrediting agencies must judge if a college or university has the expertise and training to deliver a high quality education online. An accrediting agency may give provisional approval for an institution to offer online education the first time an institution proposes an online program, and it may give permanent approval only after the second program is up and running. Regional accrediting agencies are involved in any substantive change in an institution's educational line-up. New online programs, and even offering online courses for the first time, are considered substantive changes and must be submitted to a regional accrediting agency for review and approval.

In addition to accreditation by the appropriate regional commission on higher education, most online programs—as well as other educational programs—have to be approved by a state board of higher education. The purview of the state board is wider than that of the regional accrediting agency and at least in some cases the same application to the state board can be used as the application to the accrediting agency as well. Regional accreditation, however, usually comes before state approval. In addition to the quality of the educational program, the state board is charged with determining if there actually is a market or demand for the program in the state. This requirement is paradoxical for online programs, which may be offered regionally, nationally, or perhaps globally, but institutions of higher education are still regulated on the state level. In any case, institutions that want to create a new online program may have to complete a competitive survey to ensure that the new program will not undercut existing programs offered by other institutions in the state. Institutions may also have to do market research to demonstrate there is sufficient demand for the program, and they need to demonstrate that the program is consistent with the educational needs of the state. In addition to the program itself and the market impact of the program, the state agency for higher education expects the institutional resources available to support an online program to be accessible at the same level as resources for traditional programs. That stipulation means, for example, that online students must have access to technology support during the same hours that traditional students do. So if tech support is available on campus from 7 a.m. to 8 p.m., it must be available the same hours regardless of which time zone a student resides.

Beginning in 2010, the U.S. Department of Education, with the goal of maintaining program integrity, announced regulations that require online programs to be approved in each state in which students enrolled in the program reside. Although a portion of the regulations were struck down for not following appropriate procedures, the regulations focused attention on the need for institutions that offer online programs to adhere to state laws regarding program approvals. State by state approval can be a long and laborious process. Each state has different requirements: determining who may apply; different standards and regulations that must be met to be approved; and, different fees. Some states have mandated that if a college or university has a physical presence it must apply for approval and other states insist that institutions that operate in the state meet state regulations for online learning. And, there is a separate approval process for authorization to enroll international students. The difference between "physical presence" and "operating" varies from state to state as do the fees charged to operate. In some states, out-of-state institutions do not need special authorization to operate. In others, every out-of-state institution needs to apply to be allowed to offer an online course or program. Some states do not charge out-of-state institutions anything to offer online programs. In contrast, it will cost institutions that want to offer online education in Massachusetts $10,000. And the type of authorization an out-of-state college or university receives can vary. In some cases, the institution receives approval to deliver online education in a state in which it is not primarily located. In other cases, each specific program must be approved. Finally, programs that lead to state licensing, such as nursing programs, may need additional approvals.

The regional accrediting agencies for higher education have recognized the huge burden placed on colleges and universities in obtaining state-by-state approval for online programs. In response, they have created a voluntary process called the State Authorization Reciprocity Agreement (SARA), which establishes national standards for offering distance and online learning. SARA is intended to be a consistent and transparent method to obtain state authorizations. In 2014, Indiana became the first state authorized to join the National Council for State Authorization Reciprocity Agreements (NC-SARA). Despite its promise, the SARA process is not easy to navigate and will likely take several years to implement fully. States must designate a lead agency to manage the process of authorizing online programs and that step might require legislative action. Once a state has joined NC-SARA, institutions of higher education may apply for approval of their online programs in that state and they will automatically be approved to operate in other states participating in SARA (NC-SARA n.d.). As not all the regional accrediting agencies have joined the SARA effort, and it will be quite some time before all the states will be in a position to join NC-SARA, colleges and universities wishing to market online programs outside of their home states will face a myriad of rules and regulations.

Although critics argue that state accrediting agencies have failed to protect consumers, ensuring that institutions of higher education provide a quality education or reasonably guide the Federal government in its appropriation of aid both by direct grants and guaranteed loans not available to non-accredited institutions, a countervailing argument has emerged. In this view, accrediting agencies have been too slow to embrace change and have unreasonably stood in the way of online education and other innovative efforts to broaden the scope and reach of higher education (Shalin 2013). As a response, alternative accrediting mechanisms have emerged. For example, when the University of the People, an innovative, tuition-free online university founded by Israeli entrepreneur Shai Reshef, announced that it had been accredited just before its first class of students graduated, the accreditation had come from the Distance Education and Training Council (Lewin 2014). The Distance Education and Training Council is the successor to the National Home Study Council, which was established in 1926 to promote best practices for correspondence courses. It established accrediting standards and procedures in the 1950s and was recognized by the Federal government in 1959 as a nationally recognized accreditor. Currently, the U.S. Department of Education, the Council for Higher Education Accreditation (CHEA), which was established by college and university presidents to strengthen the accreditation process, recognizes DETC. DETC is authorized to accredit programs ranging from those that do not offer a degree to professional doctoral degrees, and its accreditation is considered on a par with the regional accrediting agencies. DETC's accreditation of the University of the People demonstrates the challenge online education poses to the accreditation process. Founded four years ago, it currently has

700 students from 142 countries majoring in business administration or computer science. While the first graduating class in 2014 had only seven people, interest in the university is very high as it has more than 1.2 million followers on Facebook. The University does not charge tuition, and classes, which are ten weeks long, are taught by volunteer faculty. Students take proctored exams, for which there is a fee of $100 and students must complete 40 exams to receive a degree. The cost of exams, however, can be covered by scholarship or by other means (Parr 2014).

Managing the Process

Shepherding a program though the approval process takes patience and skill. Responsibility often reflects the top-down or bottom-up impetus for establishing an online program. Currently, in many scenarios, program creation and the approval process is handled at the administrative level. A dean or other administrator may see the opportunity to move online and then recruits faculty and others to capitalize on that opportunity. A specialist in the Academic Affairs office may serve as a guide to the external approval process. In institutions where the push for online education comes from an academic department or individual faculty member, the champions of a particular proposal may also have the responsibility for moving the program through the approval processes. This strategy involves a sharp learning curve for faculty, who otherwise have little contact with of the stakeholders outside of their department who must be involved, and they will likely have had even less contact with external agencies required to approve programs. Some institutions have established new program offices to assist stakeholders who want to start online programs. These administrative offices gain the expertise needed to manage all the technical and administrative details involved in the approval process, both internally and externally. Faculty members can then focus on developing the program and the content of individual courses. The new program office can be affiliated with a center for online teaching or perhaps attached to the office that generally monitors regulatory affairs at the academic level.

Conclusion

In many ways, the University of the People epitomizes the strengths and weaknesses, the promises and potential pitfalls of online educational programs. The University of the People's founder has a clear vision for the global university and a clear rationale why online education is the appropriate vehicle to achieve that vision. He has enlisted other stakeholders, both inside and outside the academy to support that vision. And he has found students who are willing to take the chance on a new delivery structure for education, and there is evidence that he can apparently succeed within that global online learning environment.

Moreover, many of these students would otherwise not have access to higher education.

But the University of the People also has several obvious shortcomings; perhaps the most glaring is that course delivery rests on the shoulders on volunteer faculty. Traditionally, the centerpiece of any institution of higher education is the faculty. The faculty is responsible for the content and the quality of the courses and the program. And the faculty should be responsible for the vision of the program. Moreover, universities are not just collections of instructors and students distributed across the globe, as novel as that is. Correspondence schools were never seen as the equivalent of the traditional college experience. University education is at its most powerful when it sparks people's imaginations and gets them to see the world in a new way. The students at the University of the People may acquire a functional skill set in computer science or business administration, but does the educational experience deliver the intangibles in intellectual inquiry potentially found in other educational opportunities?

New online-only universities can potentially compete with traditional institutions, but will more likely supplement traditional schools by serving hard-to-reach populations; only one factor presented by the growth of online educational programs. More pressing is the need for campus-based colleges and universities to determine the ways in which online education fits into their overall educational enterprise. Does the college or university want to support the development of MOOCs, which could potentially allow the institution to touch tens of thousands of students in a single class and raise its public profile, but is it willing to tolerate very low completion rates? Does it want to put programs online primarily as a vehicle to lower tuition costs or to generate more revenue by broadening the geographic reach of its programs? Does the institution want to use online education to allow it to be more nimble in creating new programs that are more targeted and niche-oriented or perhaps cut across disciplinary lines? Or is the university's goal in moving into online education designed to further its role in professional and continuing education?

The reasons colleges and universities create online educational programs are different and those differences can have a significant impact on every aspect of the development of the program. The first step in building an online program is establishing a vision. Ideally, all the stakeholders in the university would share a vision for the appropriate role of online educational programs, and development would take place within that vision. In practice, at least in the early stages of online education program development on most campuses, the specific stakeholders most interested in promoting online educational programs will need to articulate a vision that is compelling enough that other stakeholders will not block or impede their progress. As every constituency in an institution of higher learning has a stake in the progress of online education, each constituency can potentially inhibit the growth of online educational programs. An overall vision is important to minimally engineer acquiescence to online education in many settings if not generating enthusiastic support. Once a vision has been articulated, the hard work of developing an online program begins either through a campus-wide conversation that generates broad support or in the corner of the campus where the people interested in promulgating online education are to be found. The nature of the program including the length of the program, the individual courses, the faculty associated with the program and an overview of the various services required for the program will have to be determined along with several other factors including a proposed budget.

With a preliminary planning document complete—using the same form that will be required to earn approval from regional accrediting—a prospective online program must go through a series of internal and external reviews. The program must go through the standard approval process plus a series of approvals designed to gauge the institutional and pedagogical capacity to provide an acceptable online educational experience. In some cases, these approval processes can run in tandem and in other cases they must run sequentially. The set of approvals—those authorizing a program to be run in individual states—often can be pursued as the institution is marketing the program but must be completed before a student can enroll from a specific state. The formal approval processes for a new online program will run from one to two years after the initial idea has been crafted. If a program requires extensive training of the faculty, that period may be even longer. Moreover, the less experienced an institution is with online education, the longer the preliminary processes are likely to take. Of course, program approvals are only the first, albeit arduous, step. Implementing the program entails another set of processes that will be taken up in the remainder of this book.

References

AASCU State Relations and Policy Analysis Team (2013). *Top 10 higher education state policy issues for 2013*. Retrieved from American Association of State Colleges and Universities Web site: http://www.aascu.org/policy/publications/policy-matters/topten2013.pdf

Academic Technology Center (n.d.). *Quality online instruction*. Retrieved from University of West Florida Web site: http://uwf.edu/atc/index.cfm

Allen, I. E., & Seaman, J. (2007, October). *Online nation: five years of growth in online learning*. Retrieved from http://sloanconsortium.org/publications/.../online_nation.pdf

Brown, H. (2013, September 27). *Protecting students and taxpayers*. AEI Report. Retrieved from http://www.aei.org/files/2013/09/27/-protecting-students-and-taxpayers_164758132385.pdf

Carroll, C. (2014, March 1). The innovation solution. *Townhall*. Retrieved from http://townhall.com/tipsheet/conncarroll/2014/03/01/the-innovation-solution-n1801043

Center for Online and Blended Learning (n.d.). *Online course approval process, Bowling Green State University*. http://cobl.bgsu.edu/howto_get_course.php

Cotterell, B. (2013, April 23). Florida to open first online-only public university in U.S. *The Huffington Post*. Retrieved from http://www.huffingtonpost.com/2013/04/23/florida-online-university_n_3135328.html?view=print&comm_ref=false

Davis, M. (2013, October 19). States, districts move to require virtual classes. *Education Week*. Retrieved from http://www.edweek.org/dd/articles/2011/10/19/01required.h05.html

Dixon, A. (2013, January 14). Practicing what they preach: How Colorado State University-global campus utilizes the best business practices from its courses for the university's own operational success. Retrieved from the ICOSA Web site: http://www.icosamedia.com/2013/01/

practicing-what-they-preach-how-colorado-state-university-global-campus-utilizes-the-best-business-practices-from-its-courses-for-the-universitys-own-operational-success/

Easton, J. (2013). The changing role of education: Should it matter to governing boards? *Trusteeship Magazine*, November/December. Retrieved from http://www.chea.org/pdf/Eaton-Changing_Role_Accreditation.pdf

Georgia Tech (2013, May 14). Georgia Tech announces massive online master's degree in computer science. Retrieved from http://www.news.gatech.edu/2013/05/14/georgia-tech-announces-massive-online-masters-degree-computer-science

Hechinger, J. (2013, May 9). Southern New Hampshire, a little college that's a giant online. *Business Week*. Retrieved from http://www.businessweek.com/articles/2013-05-09/southern-new-hampshire-a-little-college-thats-a-giant-online

Howard, C. (2014, February 12). No college left behind: Randy Best's money-making mission to save higher education. *Forbes*. Retrieved from http://www.forbes.com/sites/carolinehoward/2014/02/12/no-college-left-behind-randy-bests-money-making-mission-to-save-higher-education/

Kolowich, S. (2013, July 8). A university's offer of credit for a MOOC gets no takers. *The Chronicle of Higher Education*. Retrieved from http://chronicle.com/article/A-Universitys-Offer-of-Credit/140131/?cid=at&utm_source=at&utm_medium=en

Lewin, T. (2014, February 13). Free online university receives accreditation in time for graduating class of 7. *The New York Times*. Retrieved from http://www.nytimes.com/2014/02/14/education/free-online-university-receives-accreditation-in-time-for-graduating-class-of-7.html?_r=0

Morgan State University (n.d.). *Middle states expectations for distance education*. Retrieved from http://www.morgan.edu/academics/morgan_online/administrative_links/middle_states_expectations_for_distance_education.html

NC-SARA (National Council for State Authorization Reciprocity Agreements) (n.d.). *FAQs*. Retrieved from http://www.nc-sara.org/content/faqs

Parr, C. (2014, March 2). University of the people gains accreditation. *Times Higher Education*. http://www.timeshighereducation.co.uk/news/university-of-the-people-gains-accreditation/2011702.article

Schrader, J. (2013, December 22). Western Governors University's education revolution. *The Olympian*. Retrieved from http://www.theolympian.com/2013/12/22/2897668/education-revolution.html#storylink=cpy

Shalin, J. (2013, November 21). *Time to decouple accreditation from federal funding*. The John William Pope Center, November 21. Retrieved from http://www.popecenter.org/commentaries/article.html?id=2934#.Ux5KVV5heJE

Stockfisch, J. (2013, September 29). University of Florida to offer bachelor's degrees online. *The Tampa Tribune*. Retrieved from http://tbo.com/news/education/university-of-florida-to-offer-bachelors-degrees-online-20130929/

UVA Faculty Senate Task Force (2012). Overview of significant programs in online education at the University of Virginia. Compiled by The Faculty Senate, July 17.

Weeden, D. (2014, January 8). Higher education legislation in 2013. National Conference of State Legislatures. Retrieved from http://www.ncsl.org/research/education/higher-education-legislation-in-2013635247670.aspx

Western Governors University (2012, July 14). Commencement. http://alumni.wgu.edu/s/1110/images/editor_documents/commencement/2012_final_edit_p.pdf

Western Interstate Commission on Higher Education (2013). 2010 federal regulations on state approval of out-of-state providers. Retrieved from http://wcet.wiche.edu/advance/state-approval

Western Governors University (n.d.). *The WGU story, overview*. Retrieved from http://www.wgu.edu/about_WGU/WGU_story

3
Faculty Engagement in Online Programs

In 1854, John Henry Newman, who would eventually be named a cardinal in the Catholic Church and vicar of what has become University College in Dublin, the largest university in Ireland, wrote a seminal book titled *The Idea of the University*. The book was written at a time in which the practices and forms of higher education were changing. Newman argued that a university consisted of professors and students assembled in one place. The faculty and students would be involved in what he called every department of knowledge. He was suggesting that a university, in essence, is a place for circulation of thought through interpersonal communication (The National Institute for Newman Studies 2007). Newman's description of the university has long held a strong emotional appeal. Faculty gather on campus to interact both with students and each other in pursuit of the creation and dissemination of knowledge. But the growth of online education has called into question the very character of universities, at least as Newman described them. Faculty members no longer have to gather in one place, nor do their students. Online education changes the interactions among colleagues that can alter fundamental student–teacher relationships and theoretically eliminates the need for a campus at all.

The development of online educational programs requires that faculty fundamentally revise the way they create, teach and assess their courses. The processes through which courses are organized and content is developed for online classes cannot easily be applied to online learning: teaching techniques that work in the classroom do not necessarily work online; and, online learning often requires a much broader set of assessment measures than do standard courses. Online educational programs pose significant challenges for faculty, particularly with traditional faculty who have been responsible for creating, monitoring and managing the academic enterprise at a college or university. Online educational programs can generate pressure to "unbundle" faculty responsibilities. If faculty traditionally controlled curriculum design, instruction and curriculum quality and assessment, in online education those functions may be divided among several different job functions. Curriculum designers and subject matter experts may design courses. The instructor's main responsibility may be to deliver the course content to the students. Graders can assess quality and instructional designers can align technology with course design (Neely, & Tucker 2010). In short, individual faculty members may no longer control every aspect of their courses.

At the same time, the rise of online education has coincided with the rise of part-time adjunct faculty. The National Center for Educational Statistics (2011) reported that half of all faculty in degree-granting institutions were part-time instructors. The increase of part-time and affiliate faculty has raised questions in higher education. The working conditions for part-time affiliate faculty are such that they often work in an environment that leads to high quality teaching and learning. However, constraints on their time may encourage them, for example, to utilize less time-consuming, but also less effective, teaching methods (Schmidt 2010). Paradoxically, as part-time faculty members' primary responsibility is teaching, they are often recruited to teach in online programs, particularly those programs geared to continuing and professional education. Having working professionals as opposed to regular faculty teaching courses in online continuing and professional educational programs is often seen as an advantage as they have additional professional credibility. Moreover, an adjunct faculty member's sole responsibility is instruction. And, as in other parts of the university in which they are employed, adjunct faculty represent a low-cost, flexible workforce. As many online educational programs are geared to generating surplus revenue, the use of adjunct faculty can be seen as adding to the bottom line of a college or university. For their part, adjunct faculty have different motivations for teaching than do full-time faculty, and many of those faculty members are willing and eager to teach in online programs.

This chapter will review the critical issues online educational program development raises in relation to the faculty and faculty development. It will explore the challenges in recruiting and retaining faculty for online programs. Finally, this chapter will describe the ways in which faculty members have to interact effectively with other stakeholders in the university to build high quality online educational programs.

The Challenge in Recruiting Faculty

The relationship to teaching over the past several decades of faculty in colleges and universities has been complex (Zemsky, & Massey 1990). Writing a quarter of a century ago, Zemsky and Massey noted that since the huge expansion of higher education following World War II began to slow in the late 1960s and early 1970s, teaching loads for faculty have generally fallen as other demands, particularly the ongoing requirement to publish original research, have risen. Over time, while faculty have been required to teach fewer classes than their predecessors did, permanent faculty have been able to focus their teaching activities on courses in their areas of expertise rather than on general courses, and they have been able to develop courses geared to students with academic interests closely aligned to their own.

The combination of a reduced teaching load, the ability to concentrate to a greater degree on highly specialized courses, the pressure to devote more time to research, and the reward system associated with the faculty's changing responsibilities, Zemsky and Massey argued, loosened many faculty members' commitment to their own teaching and their role in developing the department curriculum (1990). The goal for many faculty members was to gain more discretionary time to pursue what the faculty member defined as purposeful work—often research or raising their profile in their academic discipline at the expense of teaching. Many faculty members think of themselves as "independent contractors not bound by institutional needs or constraints" (p. 6). The trends that Zemsky and Massey identified 25 years ago have deepened, becoming more entrenched within the university system. The key tension for faculty members is the competition for time between research, which has become increasingly important in the overall faculty assessment in many institutions, and teaching. Most institutions underestimate the time needed for course development and preparation to teach the course, and consequently faculty members have an incentive to try to minimize their teaching responsibilities to free up more time for research.

The tug of war between the time needed to conduct quality research and the time needed for high quality instruction and mentoring students is deeply rooted in many institutions and in most faculties. The tension between research and teaching poses a significant problem in institutions with an interest in expanding into online education. For many faculty members, teaching online is new, requiring a considerable amount of start-up time to develop a course or adapt a course for delivery online, participate in training to become well-versed in technological delivery of course material, and adjust to the rhythms of course meetings, participation and assignments that are different than a traditional course. Many faculty members have come to believe that teaching online requires much more time than teaching in a conventional classroom (Lazarus 2003). Even if conducting an online class does not necessarily require more time than teaching in a conventional setting (and anecdotally it is clear that many faculty members do invest much more time into their online classes), developing an online class inevitably requires an extensive time commitment. Integrating online instruction into an ongoing program or developing an entire program online is a time consuming process, and many faculty are leery about investing their time, taking them away from their research, or they believe that they will not be fairly compensated or recognized for their commitment or time investment to online education (Hiltz 2007).

Other systemic constraints block recruiting faculty to teach. First, given the way governance in most universities operates, it is not clear what would be an appropriate mechanism for recruiting faculty to teach online. Moreover, since the impetus for developing online educational programs varies from institution to institution, the mechanism for recruiting faculty to participate varies. And given the growth of many faculty members' sense of independence from the other stakeholders in the university, unless the drive to teach online comes from the faculty itself, faculty recruitment will present a significant challenge.

The challenge is magnified, as faculties in higher education are deeply conflicted and ambivalent about online learning. A 2012 study by the Babson Survey Research Group revealed that professors feared the growth of online education more than they were excited by it (Allen, Seaman, Lederman, & Jaschik 2012, p. 5). Approximately two-thirds of those surveyed felt that the educational outcomes attained by online education were inferior to those possible through traditional, face-to-face teaching methods (Allen, Seaman, Lederman, & Jaschik 2012, p. 9). Only a little more than 5% felt that online educational techniques could produce outcomes superior to traditional methods. In fact, there is a strong and ongoing skepticism about the quality of online education, even among faculty who have taught online, although the attitudes of people who have taught online are more positive than those who have not taught online (Lederman, & Jaschik 2013). While administrators hold a significantly more positive view about the potential efficacy of online education, from a faculty perspective, the reason to invest a considerable amount of time to produce results that will be generally inferior and at best equal to current methods is not immediately clear.

A third constraint to recruiting faculty to teach online is perhaps the most deeply rooted: many faculty members understand the pressures on higher education to include online courses and programs, but they are not convinced that the change is inevitable or if the change will be good (Zemsky 2013). To some degree faculty in general have cast themselves in opposition to change being driven by other stakeholders in the university, and there is no mechanism within current structures of faculty governance in which the faculty can engage in constructive interaction with other stakeholders to manage change processes. As a result, in an area as close to the center of the mission of the university as teaching, too frequently, faculty members are reactive and resist exploring the benefits of online education rather than exploring how it can enhance an institution's overall educational footprint.

Building a Faculty Team for Online Programs

Despite faculty bias against teaching online, as online education has grown and as the number of online students has climbed, the number of faculty who have experience teaching online presumably has grown as well. Although exact numbers are not readily available regarding the increase in the number of faculty members with experience in teaching online, according to some estimates, between 25 and 33% of all faculty involved in post-secondary education have taught at least one course online.

Many different reasons can motivate faculty to teach online (Chapman 2014). The primary motivation for tenured and tenure-track faculty members teaching online is the perceived flexibility that online teaching affords. Given the demands on faculty time, flexibility in teaching is highly valued. Other strong motivators for tenured and tenure-track faculty members to teach online are the personal satisfaction of teaching online, the opportunity to use new technology, in some cases, the financial rewards, and finally, the intellectual stimulation of teaching online (2014). The opportunity to share knowledge with others can also be a motivating factor (Green, Alejandro, & Brown 2009). Finally, Ko and Rossen observed that some faculty teaching online are motivated by their awareness that they are entering a global network of educators interested in issues related to teaching online (2010). To date, the primary motivations for faculty to teach online are personal or intrinsic. Generally speaking faculty face little pressure from their colleagues, department chairs, or institutions to move their classes online. For the most part, faculty who teach online are those who have raised their hands, so to speak, and volunteered to do it.

Having faculty volunteer to teach online, however, is not sufficient to build an online educational program. In that situation, courses must be delivered on a regular basis online. When faculty volunteer to teach online, they can stop teaching online at a time of their own choosing. When online classes are being offered on an ad hoc basis, the class can simply no longer be offered online. But if the class is an integral part of an online program, or even a key online element in a blended program, simply offering the class in a traditional format is not an attractive alternative. Moving a class that has been routinely offered online to a traditional format can clash with student expectations and disrupt their educational experience. The problem of continuity becomes more complex if the online class is taught by a tenured or tenure-track faculty member and cannot easily be transferred to an adjunct or affiliate faculty member. Building a faculty to teach in an online program or a blended program that has an ongoing online component places several new demands on staffing. First, incentives to retain online faculty must be put in place. Second, since faculty teaching online, by definition, do not have to be on campus as frequently as those who teach online do, structures and processes to support faculty-to-faculty interaction, and in that collegiality, need to be developed.

Several strategies can be employed to improve the retention of experienced online faculty (Green, Alejandro, & Brown 2009). Perhaps the most important factor is to provide ongoing institutional support and recognition. Commonly, once a faculty member has completed the initial course development and training, institutional support can fall away. Teaching online, however, can place demands on faculty that traditional courses do not: the underlying technology of the course management system or other useful instructional technology can change; and, the kind and quality of appropriate content available online and required in an online class may be more fluid than in a traditional classroom and need more ongoing revision. For example, if a faculty member has recorded several lectures for an online class, revising those lectures will be more burdensome and time consuming than simply revising lectures delivered in a face-to-face setting. Faculty need ongoing support to ensure they can use the most appropriate technology and that the courses they teach remain fresh.

This ongoing support can be provided in many ways (Thompson 2006). One approach is a formal mentoring or support process in which faculty can be assigned staff in a central support unit to work with on an ongoing basis. A structured process with defined responsibilities and anticipated outcomes characterizes this type of support. Alternatively, at institutions in which formal mentoring procedures are not in place, informal mentoring can be employed. With informal mentoring, more experienced faculty pair with less experienced colleagues to develop a co-learning environment. Given the myriad motivations faculty have for teaching online, including the desire to share knowledge and intellectual stimulation, informal mentoring can be effective. But formal and informal mentoring each has pitfalls. An understanding of the instructional technology used in online education does not guarantee that a person will be an expert in sound pedagogical practices or be able to determine the correct mix of technology and pedagogy to support specific learning outcomes or content.

To address those pitfalls, supporting faculty who teach online to attend professional development conferences in which issues associated with online education are explored can also provide incentives for faculty members to continue teaching online over a significant period. Ideally, over time, all faculty would be trained in developing online or hybrid courses and they would be trained to teach online, making online classes just one more delivery option in the same way that a class can be conceptualized as a lecture class, discussion class or a seminar. In the interim, however, online faculty need ongoing support. Involving faculty teaching online in both formal and informal mentoring programs, as well as providing professional development opportunities, can have the added benefit of helping build a sense of community. A sense of community can both help retain faculty teaching online as well as recruit new faculty to online teaching as it reduces the uncertainty and risk in teaching online. Ongoing support is only one tool (Green, Alejandro, & Brown 2009). Other effective retention measures include defining how teaching online fits into tenure and promotion considerations, ensuring that online students are adequately supported so they can succeed in an online environment, and developing strategies so the instructor does not have to supply all sorts of non-educational related support. The final issue is compensation. At different points, teaching online does require an extra investment in time and attention and faculty are more likely to continue teaching online if that investment is recognized.

Developing a tenured and tenure-track faculty team that teaches online on an ongoing and continual basis can have an unintended consequence. When all or a significant portion of a faculty member's teaching load is online, that faculty member is likely to spend an increasingly smaller percentage of time on campus (Kroll 2013). The lack of faculty presence on campus can be troubling in many ways. In fact, the idea that the university once was a place where teachers and learners from all the branches of knowledge gathered to engage in scholarly communication is giving way to a new paradigm. With online education, neither instructors nor students gather in one place. Faculty may still engage in conversation with their students, but opportunities for informal engagement among faculty members is reduced. The lack of personal interaction has long been a challenge posed by the growth of the use of affiliate faculty. But affiliate faculty are not expected to participate in department governance. As online teaching becomes more commonplace, the informal ties among faculty members than help facilitate effective governance are weakened.

As departments and institutions develop more online programs, they must also develop new mechanisms to ensure faculty-to-faculty communication and interaction. These communication structures must be created both so online faculty can learn and support each other, but also to provide opportunities for colleagues to interact and communicate with each other appropriately. Not surprisingly, the routine absence of faculty on campus can also have an impact on the student experience. In addition to teaching, faculty serve as advisers, role models and mentors for students. It is much easier for students to arrange to meet with faculty and to interact with faculty members informally when faculty are on campus. In addition, meeting face-to-face with faculty can be more informal and less driven by a specific agenda or need to resolve specific questions or address concerns. In *Making the Most of College*, a book geared to helping students maximize their college experience, Richard Light suggests that students try to get to know at least one of their instructors personally each semester (Light 2004). When faculty teach primarily online, they may spend less time on campus and that makes building those informal interpersonal relationships harder to initiate and sustain. As more faculty teach extensively or exclusively online, new modes of communication have to be developed to ensure that students have the opportunities to develop relationships with the faculty outside the formal teaching–learning setting. In programs in which the instruction is exclusively or predominately online, students still need the opportunity to network with faculty and build the kinds of relationships that will allow faculty members to serve as mentors and references for the students as they move into the workforce or go on to graduate school.

The character of courses within an online education program impacts the recruitment and retention of faculty to teach online. In terms of faculty recruitment and retention, online courses must be developed in a way that new instructors can replace departing instructors while maintaining the essential character of the course. Faculty members have fluid schedules and do not teach the same courses every semester. They go on sabbatical and from time to time are relieved of their teaching responsibilities. In the same way that teaching, for example, British Literature in an English program is not completely idio-syncratic to an individual instructor, but has some relatively large degree of commonality regardless of where the course is taught and by whom, online classes cannot completely reflect the idiosyncratic leanings of the course devel-oper. Courses for online delivery have to be created with the idea that other instructors will teach those classes at some point in time. New online instruc-tors cannot be expected to recreate a specific ongoing course anew for online delivery. The process is too labor intensive and the need to always recreate a course prior to a new person teaching it would discourage faculty from taking the leap to teaching online.

Developing online educational programs requires institutions and depart-ments to actively work to recruit faculty to teach online. Programs require continuity through a cadre of instructors willing and ready to teach in the program. Efforts to recruit faculty can be based on the primary reasons they have typically volunteered to teach online—emphasizing the flexibility of teaching online, the intrinsic rewards of intellectual stimulation, and financial incentives among other factors. Retaining faculty requires that appropriate ongoing support mechanisms are in place, including ongoing professional development opportunities, among others. At the same time, as the number of faculty teaching online grows, institutions and departments will have to create new ways for faculty to communicate with each other and to build ongoing, formal and informal relationships with students. If new channels of ongoing communication among and between faculty and students are not developed, faculty-to-faculty and faculty-to-student ties may be significantly weakened. The former could have an impact on faculty governance and other faculty-specific issues. The latter can lead to a less robust overall educational experience for students.

Developing an Online or Hybrid Program

From a faculty or departmental perspective, developing an online educational program, as opposed to developing online courses, has to focus primarily on five elements. First, the objectives and outcomes of the program have to be clearly defined, as do the individual courses associated with the program. Second, the structure of the program must be created. Third, ongoing admin-istrative and governance processes must be put into place. Fourth, the needed resources for the program, including participating faculty, have to be identified and assembled. Fifth, the program has to be integrated in the university-wide infrastructure. From a departmental perspective the first step in creating an online educational program is defining its goals or objectives and outcomes. Even if the project is simply to move an existing traditional program online, clarifying the specific goals, objectives and outcomes of the program can be a useful exercise. In many ways, every established program that moves online should be considered a new program, and the move online should be seen as an opportunity to rethink and reimagine existing programs.

The differences between goals and objectives are very nuanced. Goals are broad and general, whereas an objective is the desired end-state of the program. In theory, objectives can be grouped into three broad areas. Cognitive objectives define what students will be expected to know when they complete the program. Affective objectives are what students are expected to care about or feel once they have moved through the course of instruction. And behavioral objectives are those that describe what students should be able to do and how they should act once they graduate. In practice, objectives do not necessarily fall neatly into one category or another. For example, an objective in a career-oriented M.A. program may be that students will have the requisite skills to find a mid-career position in a specific profession. Similarly, in a remedial program one of the objectives could be that the students have the background and skills to enter more advanced educational programs. These kinds of objectives can be seen as being both behavioral and cognitive. A more specific and ambitious objective may be that graduates will actually find a position within the given field. Other objectives may be that students graduate within a defined timeframe or conduct themselves ethically as they prepare for careers, and so on. Outcomes are more specific than goals or objectives, as they describe the specific competencies students will have that support attaining the desired objective. Outcomes describe both what students will know and how they will be able to demonstrate what they know. For example, if the objective of a remedial program is for a student to be prepared for upper division undergraduate study, an outcome may be the ability to write a research paper with footnotes. An outcome in an engineering program might be for the students to be able to apply engineering principles to real world problems. Defining the objectives and outcomes of an online educational program are essential for several reasons. Most importantly, desired objectives and outcomes will serve as the basis of a program assessment over time. Assessment is becoming increasingly important throughout higher education and in some ways is now a national priority (Miller 2006). As online educational programs become a more integral part of higher education generally, the ability to assess those programs becomes more urgent. Given the skepticism among many faculty and other stakeholders about the quality of online education, having the necessary foundation—goals, objectives and outcomes—for an appropriate assessment of an online program is vital.

The program's established objectives and outcomes will form the basis of objectives and outcomes in each course. As with the traditional approach to higher education, each course does not have to embody every programmatic objective or outcome. But the objectives and outcomes of each course should in some way support and further the program aims. As assessment has become more important generally, many departments and programs have gone through the process of determining objectives and outcomes and then mapping individual course objectives and outcomes to their program aims for their legacy programs. This process is even more critical for new online programs, hybrid programs and moving existing programs online, because the mode of delivery and the technological tools employed in online programs can have an impact on the ways those objectives and outcomes are achieved. For example, if one of the objectives is for students to learn how to work collaboratively, the online program developers will have to ensure that adequate collaboration tools are in place and that students, as well as faculty, are trained on those tools.

In addition to laying the groundwork for assessment and driving the goals for individual courses, establishing program objectives and outcomes will provide the framework for the program structure. Completely online and hybrid programs represent an opportunity to do something new, even if the new program largely consists of moving an existing program online. Having carefully considered and crafted outcomes provides the scaffolding for constructing the new program. For new programs, the number of courses and credits and the sequence in which courses may be taken is open for discussion, although whatever form the program takes it will have to meet defined standards devised by state higher education regulatory agencies and higher education accrediting bodies. For hybrid courses, which courses will be taught online and which will be taught on campus or in residence elsewhere is an area for deliberation. Even if a legacy program is simply moving online, its structure should be reconsidered, as online programs offer the possibility of creating dramatically new program structures.

Certainly for the past 50 years, and generally long before that, academic programs have been shaped primarily by the traditional academic calendar and the need for students to be on campus for instruction. Those factors have led to a fairly standard undergraduate academic calendar in which classes run in the fall and spring generally around 3 hours a week during a 14 or 15 week semester. Students receive three or four credits for each class in most cases (and an additional credit for a lab). In most traditional institutions of higher education, the undergraduate academic calendar provides the primary rhythm for the campus as a whole.

Of course, there is some variation. Some schools use a trimester system. Mini-mesters between semesters still exist. Classes run during the summer can vary in length and the number of class hours per week required. Professional programs frequently meet for full days on Saturday and so on. With online programs, however, the entire calendar can be revised and reorganized. The primary operational metric is no longer how many hours per week a student studies and how many weeks the course runs. The key statistic is that the course has the requisite number of hours and those hours can be spread over many different units of time. In fact, for-profit universities have been pioneers in running individual courses for one month only. Instead of full-time students taking four or five classes per semester, they take one course at a time. Once the need to come to campus is eliminated, the academic calendar and course meeting schedule are not constrained.

As online courses, along with hybrid courses and traditional in-class courses become part of the regular mix within the schedule, institutions will have to make clear to students the differences between those modalities. It cannot be assumed that students do know the difference between an online and hybrid course. Perhaps new course designations will have to be incorporated into the course numbering system in order to distinguish one type of course from another. Institutions will have to educate students regarding what is meant by an online or a hybrid course and how those courses will differ from traditional courses. Even the definition of a hybrid course, or flipped course, may vary from institution. Shaping the structure of the program requires careful deliberation and the needs of students, faculty and the other stakeholders in the university including the registrar, academic records and other functions have to be considered. Nevertheless, creating online programs opens up opportunities for experimentation. For example, with many graduate hybrid programs, the residential courses run only one or two weeks. Students attend those residential classes for 40 to 45 hours per week. That compacted schedule provides a very different educational experience than going to class for 50 minute sessions three times a week over an extended period of time, 14 or 15 weeks. Although creating an online education program has the potential for developing new and experimental structures both for individual classes and the overall program, online programs can also revive older forms of educational interaction by making them logistically more feasible. For example, higher education in Great Britain long had a tutorial component in which students periodically meet one to one with a professor. With video conferencing technology in place, students and instructors can conveniently participate in a tutorial-like learning structure.

Administration and Resources

With regard to online programs, different administrative and governing structures have emerged. In many continuing and professional education-only programs, a central office may administer the programs. In some cases, a single faculty member will serve as an academic director to review and monitor the quality of the instruction. Affiliate and adjunct faculty often teach in many online programs, and the programs themselves are housed in a separate academic unit focused on continuing or professional education. This kind of administrative structure reflects the separation of professional and continuing education from the primary academic efforts of many traditional non-profit colleges and universities. While continuing and professional education may be well established at many universities, associated online programs have often been launched as a satellite, relatively marginal enterprise (Toombs, Lindsay, & Hettinger 1985). Admissions standards are different. Expectations of the students may vary, and the way that students move through a program may be different than traditional or typical university enrollment. The marginal nature of continuing education to the main project of many universities has opened up opportunities to experiment with online educational programs. Not surprisingly, many for-profit universities also have a governing structure driven by the administrative staff and courses taught by part-time instructors. This structure has allowed them to move quickly into online education.

Successfully moving online educational programs more to the institution's administrative center requires the creation of several different levels of bureaucracy. Centralized administrative services, critical to online programs, will be discussed in Chapter 6. At the program level, each online program should have an academic director and an administrative director along the same lines of traditional graduate programs. The academic director should be responsible for recruiting and training faculty, monitoring overall program quality, representing the program at appropriate venues including the department with which it is associated and elsewhere, and generally ensuring that the program develops academically appropriately. This can be a time-consuming task—a full-time position—that will draw the director away from other academic responsibilities and should be compensated according to the amount of time it requires.

The administrative director of an online program plays a very complicated and multifaceted role. As expected, the administrative director is the liaison between the department and all the other stakeholders in the program such as admissions, marketing, records, student life and so on. However, for online students, the administrative director will also be the primary and initial point of contact with the student for any problem or issue that may occur. Student support plays a large part of the administrative director's role. Online students are not as connected to the campus and the campus-based functions of the university as traditional students. In addition to the specific faculty member teaching a course that a student is taking at that moment, the administrative director is the first point or sometimes the only point of contact.

The administrative director will undergo training to be able to execute the student support role. The director will maintain contact with other offices in the university to get answers quickly, and the director will be empowered to intercede on behalf of online students with various stakeholders. The student support component and the responsibility to solve problems may be different than the administrative roles in many academic departments. Furthermore, depending how the channels of communication have been established between individual faculty members and students, the administrative director may have to serve as an intermediary between the professor and the student. As so many instructors in online programs are adjunct and affiliate faculty or working professionals, they often are not in a position to respond to urgent student concerns in a timely fashion. The administrative director will establish strong lines of communication not only with the academic director but also with the individual faculty members teaching in the program. Depending on the size of the program, a single administrative director may not be sufficient for an online educational program and additional support personnel may be needed. The critical point is that students have the support they need to progress through the program appropriately. Building staff capacity to support an online educational program can be very challenging (Mallinson, & Krull 2013).

In addition to the administrative structures, universities and colleges have to determine how online programs will be governed. Increasingly, colleges and universities want to establish online programs within their existing academic infrastructure. With that in mind, the role and the responsibility of the department and the department chair has to be determined. Moreover, there is the question as to whether faculty who actually teach online have a larger say in shaping an online program than those who do not. The answer to that question may not be difficult to answer, but the discussion is necessary to avoid confusion or dissension. Steps need to be taken so that all needed resources are in place. Perhaps the most obvious and most important resources are the computer technology—hardware and software—that will be needed to conduct the course. In developing an online program, the technology team must assess the following: the interaction tools and technologies that are available; which tools are appropriate for the students; and, which tools the instructors can master. Generally speaking, most universities have learning management systems (LMS) that have wide ranging functionality, and when individual faculty move individual courses online, the faculty member chooses the level of functionality with which they are most familiar, the functions they feel most comfortable with, and the functions that do not have a steep learning curve. Too many tools or the use of complex tools may not be the best approach when designing an online program. Students cannot be expected to master a huge array of technologies or have the technology toolbox, so to speak, as they move from course to course. Within reason, the same set of applications should be used across classes in the program so as the students progress toward their degree the technology itself will fade into the background in much the same way that students know how to behave in a traditional lecture class or seminar. Consistency and continuity are key when it comes to adapting technologies to online learning environments.

Online programs require other resources as well. For example, departments must devise structures to deliver effective advising services. Student advising is different than the general provision of student services, which will be discussed in Chapter 6. Successful advising has three dimensions—conceptual, informational and relational (Starks 2014). While some of the informational aspects of advising can be effectively delivered online and through tailored social media, the relational and conceptual aspects are more difficult to execute online. Academic advising implies a relationship between a faculty member and a student in which the faculty member can help guide the student's academic journey, pointing out potentially fruitful directions and helping the student overcome challenges and barriers to academic success. Perhaps it goes without saying, but academic advising should be tailored to the needs of the individual student; advising provides that student learner with an additional point of contact. Advising within the online context presents conceptual, structural and time management problems. Commonly in educational settings, advising is a departmental responsibility that is spread to a great extent across the faculty. Students make appointments with their advisers and presumably over time, establish some rapport with the adviser. In many cases, a student restricts their interaction with the adviser to course selection but that is not always the case. That standard model does not work in online educational programs, or for programs that rely heavily on part-time instructors for that matter. In a distance learning setting, advising is often positioned as a student retention operation (2014). As student retention is a component of advising, in traditional settings that is only one of the goals and perhaps not the most significant. The objective in advising in online programs is to replicate the same sort of relationship that can be developed through face-to-face communication. Student retention is one goal of effective advising, along with building a multifaceted relationship that can potentially help guide a student's career.

Traditionally, advising is seen as a generalized faculty responsibility and advisers are assigned accordingly. In online programs, however, only a small subset of the faculty may ever actually interact with students. Moreover, not all faculty members are equipped to advise distance learners. In response, several different models for advising have emerged. In some cases, a single faculty member will serve as the academic adviser for all the students. Obviously this approach can only work in small programs, and designating a very few faculty members to serve as advisers, can be workable. Another solution is to enlist the entire faculty who teach online to serve as academic advisers. Finally, some programs simply offload academic advising to staff. The upside to this approach is that in some aggressive and well-heeled programs, staff that work with students in the admission process will stay in contact with the student throughout the program (Varney 2009). While that approach may be effective for retention, it diminishes the academic component of advising. Advising in an online program requires initiative from the adviser to establish a fruitful relationship. Distance learners may not know who their adviser is or understand the benefits of engaging in the relationship. Faculty members may have to reach out to students to identify any problems or concerns and to help find solutions. Faculty have to be trained to make that kind of effort, which also can take a considerable amount of time. If the faculty member and the students feel comfortable with the appropriate technology, faculty members can set up virtual office hours in which students can video conference. Face-to-face video conferences can help build a close enough relationship, but they can require training and outreach.

The final broad area of faculty concern in developing an online program is establishing working relationships with the other stakeholders in the university.

Historically, faculty have had little need to interact with admissions, records management, marketing, financial aid and so forth. But with online programs, the most obvious first stop for students with problems is the instructor or the administrative director. Simply referring the student to an appropriate office may not be sufficient in many cases and the administrative director, adviser or faculty member will have to take extra steps to resolve the issue. Academic departments and faculty may have to build new relationships with other departments in the university for other reasons as well. If in the development of the online program a decision is made that breaks the traditional mold for course delivery, taking advantage of the flexibility that online education offers, those changes or challenges will have to be negotiated with many other stakeholders. Online academic programs cannot be developed in a vacuum. Many offices in the university will have a voice in shaping the program.

Conclusion

The rise of online education has the potential to completely redefine the college or university and the role of the faculty. If an institution of higher learning was once conceived as a gathering of faculty and students in one place to engage in intellectual dialogue, with online education neither the faculty nor the students need to gather face to face. Teaching and learning online is a qualitatively different experience.

As online education, both courses and entire programs, has proliferated, full-time faculty have been suspicious of its impact, as teaching online alters the role of the instructor. Faculty believe teaching online will add to their workload in ways that will not be recognized. In some settings, despite the professed interest of administrators in online education, the availability of technical and administrative support is not always apparent (Clay 1999). And many faculty members do not believe that online courses can achieve the same outcomes as face-to-face learning that has long been at the heart of the higher education enterprise (Windes, & Lesht 2014). Faculty wariness about online education has meant that online efforts have largely been implemented at the margins of the university, largely in professional and continuing education programs, and among institutions that hope to expand their marketing footprint. Given the inevitability of online and hybrid courses and programs at institutions of higher learning, faculty will play a vital and central role in the development of online educational programs.

References

Allen, I. E., Seaman, J., Lederman, D., & Jaschik, S. (2012). Conflicted: Faculty and online education. A joint project of the Babson survey Research Group and Inside Higher Ed. Retrieved from http://www.insidehighered.com/sites/default/server_files/survey/conflicted.html

Chapman, D. (2014). Contingent and tenured/tenure-track faculty: Motivations and incentives to teach distance education courses. *Online Journal of Distance Learning Administration*, Spring. Retrieved from http://www.westga.edu/-distance/ojdla/fall143/chapman143.html

Clay, M. (1999). Development of training and support programs for distance education instructors. *Online Journal of Distance Learning Administration*, Fall, 2(3). Retrieved from http://www. westga.edu/~distance/clay23.html

Green, T., Alejandro, J., & Brown, A. (2009). The retention of experienced faculty in online distance education programs: Understanding factors that impact their involvement. *International Review of Research in Open and Distance Learning*, June 10(3).

Hiltz, S. R., Kim, E., & Shea, P. (2007). Faculty motivators and de-motivators for teaching online: Results of focus group interviews at one university. *Proceedings of the 40th Hawaii International Conference on System Sciences*.

Ko, S., & Rossen, S. (2010). *Teaching online: A practical guide*. New York: Routledge Publishers.

Kroll, K. (2013, May 9). Where have all the faculty gone? *Inside Higher Ed*. Retrieved from http://www. insidehighered.com/views/2013/05/09/faculty-who-teach-online-are-invisible-campuses-essay#ixzz2xORSDUKj

Lazarus, B. D. (2003). Teaching courses online: How much time does it take? *Journal of Asynchronous Learning Networks*, September, 7(3). Retrieved from https://www.utdallas.edu/elearning/instructors/materials.html

Lederman, D., & Jaschik, S. (2013, August 27). Survey of faculty attitudes on technology. *Inside Higher Ed*. Retrieved from http://www.insidehighered.com/news/survey/survey-faculty-attitudes-technology#ixzz332Md8bqU

Light, R. (2004). *Making the most of college: Students speak their mind*. Cambridge: Harvard University Press.

Mallinson, B., & Krull, G. (2013). Building academic staff capacity to support online learning in developing countries. *Journal of Asynchronous Learning Networks*, July, 17:2.

Miller, M. (2006). Assessing college level learning. *Policy Alert: The National Center for Public Policy and Higher Education*, May. Retrieved from http://www.highereducation.org/reports/pa_aclearning/Assessing_College-Level_Learning.pdf

National Center for Educational Statistics (2011) Digest of education statistics: 2011. Retrieved from http://nces.ed.gov/programs/digest/d11/ch_3.asp

The National Institute for Newman Studies (2007). Newman reader: Works of John Henry Newman. Retrieved from http://www.newmanreader.org/works/historical/volume3/universities/chapter2.html

Neely, P., & Tucker, J. (2010). Unbundling faculty roles in online distance education programs. *The International Review of Open and Distance Learning*, May. Retrieved from http://www.irrodl.org/index.php/irrodl/article/view/798/1543

Schmidt, P. (2010, November 30). Conditions imposed on part-time adjuncts threaten quality of teaching, researchers say. *The Chronicle of Higher Education*. Retrieved from http://chronicle.com/article/Conditions-Imposed-on/125573/#comments

Starks, S. (2012, May 31). Online student retention strategies. Distanceadvising.com. Retrieved from http://distanceadvising.com /2012/05/online-student-retention-strategies/#more-1716

Starks, S. (2014). Distance advising: A personalized approach. *The Evolllution*, April. Retrieved from http://www.evolllution.com/distance_online_learning/distance-advising-a-personalized-approach/

Thompson, D. (2006). Informal faculty mentoring as a component of learning to teach online: An exploratory study. *Online Journal of Distance Learning Administration*, Fall, 9(3). Retrieved from http://www.westga.edu/~distance/ojdla/fall93/thompson93.htm

Toombs, W., Lindsay, C., & Hettinger, G. (1985). Modifying faculty roles to institutionalize continuing professional education. *Research in Higher Education*, 22-1, 93–109.

Varney, J. (2009). Strategies for success in distance advising. NACADA Clearinghouse of Academic Advising Resources. Retrieved from http://www.nacada.ksu.edu/Resources/Clearinghouse/View-Articles/Distance-advising-strategies.aspx#sthash.HFeYu3ib.dpuf

Windes, D., & Lesht, F. (2014). The effects of online teaching experience and institution type on faculty perceptions of teaching online. *Online Journal of Distance Learning Administration*, March, 17:1. Retrieved from http://www.westga.edu/~distance/ojdla/spring171/windes_lesht171.html

Zemsky, R. (2013, September 30). How to build a faculty culture of change. *Chronicle of Higher Education*. Retrieved from https:/chronicle.com/article/How-to-Build-a-Faculty-Culture/141887.

Zemsky, R., & Massey, W. (1990). The lattice and the ratchet. *Policy Perspectives: The Pew Higher Education Research Program*, June, 2(4), 5–8.

4

Online Course Development and Implementation

Online course development could be reduced to a series of steps, like planning the course, producing content, building course components and trying it out. But we know that is an oversimplification of a complex process that takes considerable time and effort. Even creating the course materials for online delivery does not imply that you know how to teach online, even if you have experience teaching traditional courses. Online course development has two distinct phases. In the first, the faculty member determines the content or essence of the course. In the second, the faculty member works with instructional designers and other technologists to move the content online. Because the second part of the process is seen to be as important as the first, sometimes when the second phase of the process kicks in, the faculty member is referred to as the "subject matter expert," borrowing the language of professional training, a field in which online education is deeply rooted. At this point, many schools have a centralized resource, often called the Center for Online Learning or the Center for Distance Learning that has been established to help faculty develop online courses. But there is also an additional phase to course development: learning how to teach online. This may require attending in-service workshops at the university, workshops offered by external organizations, like Sloan-C, among others, or reading about best practices for online teaching and attending webinars to hone your online teaching skills.

This chapter will explore the processes for online course development and strategies for course management. It will review approaches to faculty training and it will examine assessment strategies for faculty from several different perspectives. Finally, it will describe the ways in which faculty members have to effectively interact with other stakeholders in the university to build high-quality online educational programs.

The first phase of the online course development process, what might be called the course plan, is not much different than developing a traditional course. The faculty member has to determine the learning goals and outcomes, the competencies to be mastered, the material to be used, the activities to facilitate learning, and the assessment strategies. The difference is that the process has to be more structured and transparent when developing an online class. All the implicit knowledge about developing courses accumulated through the years of teaching experience or being a student no longer applies. All aspects of the course, including learning outcomes and assessment, have to be packaged in a way that can be translated into effective delivery online. Even if an instructor wants to record lectures and use presentation slides to convey content, the experience for both the teacher and the student is completely different than if you deliver a lecture face to face. Consequently, the planning for those lectures has to be different if they are going to be delivered online. A standard approach to the first part of online course development is to use a fairly standard methodology common among high school teachers in lesson development. The first step is to develop a set of learning objectives, learning aims, and outcomes. As with the program overall, the learning objectives are the broad goals that students should achieve by completing the course. The learning outcomes are a more focused statement about what students will be expected to be able to do. A learning objective for a course in American literature, for example, may be to explore the development of literary genres in American literature in the 19th Century. A learning outcome would be to demonstrate knowledge of the key works of 19th Century American literature.

As with a standard course, once the major objectives and outcomes are determined, the course must be divided into sub-units. At this point in the process, the development of an online course begins to diverge from standard practices. The point of divergence is the division into sub-units. The traditional sub-unit of instruction in a course is the class session. Dividing a course into three sessions per week, for example, which is a common unit in many college courses, does not translate well in an online environment. In many cases, students want to pace themselves when learning online and dictating a highly rigid and fixed schedule can make it more difficult for students to manage their work appropriately. Additional issues students face in managing their time in online courses will be discussed in Chapter 5. More common, online courses are sub-divided into modules, each of which can be completed over a fixed period of time, often a week or two weeks. Each module should have its own set of learning aims and outcomes. Once the course materials are assembled, an assessment processes should also be established. Both of these—materials and assessments—will be different for online courses than for traditional courses. For example, frequently in a traditional college course, most of the course material is outside reading; face-to-face interaction takes place in the classroom. Although it is generally not always viewed this way, the face-to-face interaction provides balance to the reading. Ideally, course materials for online courses should be varied and balanced to help engage the learner more completely. Along the same lines, as students are not physically in the classroom to be challenged and observed, some assessment tools, particularly short answer tests, may not be appropriate without careful modification. While there are many different options for assessment in online classes that are not available in face to face—grading each contribution to a discussion board, for example—options must be carefully thought out and appropriately weighted. Another aspect of online courses that differs from in-class courses is the threat of cheating online—this subject will be discussed in Chapter 6.

Perhaps the most challenging part of creating an online course is devising the learning activities that support the objectives and outcomes. While difficult, planning learning activities is one of the more interesting aspects of developing an online course. Since most faculty have a lot of experience as students in traditional classrooms, they frequently know what classroom techniques they want to use such as a lecture, whole class discussion, group work and so on. While these kinds of activities can be translated into an online format, the translation requires planning and additional effort. The appropriate technology tools have to be in place, and the instructor has to be comfortable teaching with those tools and students have to be comfortable learning within these new modalities. Moreover, thought has to be given about whether a learning activity should be synchronous, i.e. a real-time online chat, or asynchronous, i.e. a discussion board. If the instructor wants students to engage in peer assessment, commenting on each other's work, the most appropriate tool needs to be considered. If Turnitin.com is utilized their "Peermark" assessment may be appropriate, or commenting on a course wiki might be selected depending on the nature of the activity and the type of assessment the instructor prefers. The learning activities used should be selected in ways that support effective online learning. While effective teaching online is a complicated endeavor, Graham, Cagiltay, Lim, Craner, and Duffy (2001) suggest, at a minimum online teaching should embody several critical elements: encourage both student–teacher and student–student interaction; involve active learning and foster student cooperation; provide prompt feedback and employ strategies to help keep students working consistently through the semester by providing milestones; and, apply suitably rigorous activities while respecting different learning styles. Beyond student–teacher and student–student interaction, another consideration to be made is student–technology interaction. This latter type of interaction is unique to the online learning environment, and course planners need to be mindful of such interactions as they develop their courses. In short, devising the learning activities for online courses requires extensive planning, which can be substantially different than the planning that goes into a traditional class. The activities, however, play a key role in achieving the course objectives and outcomes as well as the program objectives and outcomes.

To some extent, the exact mix of learning activities will be driven by the class size, which can be very elastic in online courses. At one end of the spectrum are MOOCs, which enroll thousands and perhaps tens of thousands of students. On the other end of the spectrum, online technology is great for one-to-one tutorial learning situations as well. Generally speaking, however, for classes that are designed to have a lot of student–teacher and student–student interaction, around 20 students per class is considered optimal (Orellana 2006). MOOCs offload student–student interaction to discussion groups that may or may not be facilitated by teaching assistants, and they rely heavily on student–technology interaction. The instructor of record rarely interacts directly with particular students in a MOOC.

In addition to constructing a broad range of learning activities and having technology in place to support those activities adequately, planning an online course involves another component. As regulatory agencies have become increasingly involved in scrutinizing online courses, the need to document that online courses embody the same amount of instructional and learning time as traditional courses has been put onto the agenda. The United States Department of Education requires that each institution develop a written credit hour policy that conforms to the definition of a credit hour as defined in the Federal Register. These regulations define a credit hour as "An amount of work represented in intended learning outcomes and verified by evidence of student achievement that is an institutionally established equivalency that reasonably approximates not less than one hour of classroom or direct faculty instruction and a minimum of two hours of out of class work each week for approximately fifteen weeks for one semester or trimester hour of credit, or ten to twelve weeks for one-quarter hour of credit, or the equivalent amount of work over a different amount of time; or an equivalent amount of work for other activities as established by an institution, including laboratory work, internships, practica, studio work, and other academic work" (U.S. Department of Education 2010).

The concept of a credit hour has been in place since the late 19th Century, when Charles Eliot, the president of Harvard University, introduced the unit (Kamentz 2013). These regulations historically have not been closely monitored. While classes may be scheduled to meet for 2 hours and 30 minutes a week, nobody truly monitors individual faculty members' classroom activities. An athletic scandal at the University of North Carolina revealed that for years, students received credit for classes that never actually met (Barrett 2014). Teachers and administrators have very little insight in how much homework students actually complete.

This laissez-faire attitude is not sufficient for online courses. Since online courses do not meet by the hour, when an online course is being developed, care must be taken to assemble a pool of learning activities that will approximate the required instructional time. One approach is to assign a time to different instructional activities. For example, writing a discussion post may be intended to take 10 minutes, and so on. Of course, there are no set external standards for the length of a discussion post so it is impossible to tell a priori how long it will take to write one. Consequently, instructors must determine how much time they expect students to devote to asynchronous tasks such as posting to a discussion board or commenting on a blog and communicate those expectations to the students.

Meeting regulatory requirements is not the only reason for assigning times to the various learning activities incorporated in an online course. The instructor needs to strike a balance between assigning too much work in an online course and too little. For example, one of the most common activities in an online class is for students to write blog posts and then require other students to comment on those posts. But if there are 15 students in a class and the teacher requires each student to write a 400-word blog post for a given module and then a 200-word response to each of the other posts, that represents 3000 words of writing just for that one activity. A ten-page term paper, often the centerpiece assignment of an undergraduate Humanities class, is approximately 2750 words. It is very easy to overload the work in an online course and going through the new and often tedious task of assessing how much time the teacher anticipates each task to take and communicating that expectation to the students can have a fruitful result.

Although it has been slow to be adopted by online programs, learning management systems contain a great deal of data that can help determine levels of student engagement in an online course (Romero, Ventura, & Garcia 2007). There is a paradox between the availability of data and the reluctance of faculty to utilize that data for assessment purposes. As data that is available in the LMS is in some ways similar to the data that is available to marketers on the Internet, there is little understanding for the most part regarding what data exists, its accessibility, the need to massage the data in order to develop meaningful assessments, and an accompanying fear that such data may be used to evaluate an instructor's performance based on this little understood and unwieldy deep set of data that can consistently be updated during the course of a semester. As a broad understanding of the usefulness of such data is developed, it is anticipated that LMS-based data assessments will become not only a standard practice in assessing student engagement in courses, but also such data will be essential for student retention in online courses and programs.

Instructional Design

Crafting compelling learning objectives and outcomes, identifying appropriate materials, constructing appropriate learning activities, and gauging the length of times each will take to complete and then developing and implementing assessment tools are time-consuming and labor-intensive tasks. Additionally, the course must be put online in a way that students will be able to easily navigate and negotiate the LMS. The learning should be focused on the objectives and outcomes and student time should not be wasted trying to find their way around the course Web site. In many institutions, the instructor or course developer will work with an instructional designer to present and in other ways implement the course online. Sometimes instructional designers or course designers will help faculty create content for the course, particularly video content. The concept of instructional designers originated in the online training industry, where subject matter experts would work with designers and technologists to devise online training programs. To some degree, this professional training model has been incorporated into higher education. Instructional designers are expected to understand the functionality of the underlying technologies used in online courses. They are able to anticipate the experience that instructors and students will have using specific tools, and they offer expertise in building the course platform to ensure that the user interface is suitable and functional. In some cases, an instructional designer may aid in identifying appropriate instructional materials and provide insight for faculty into learning theories associated with online learning. In short, in higher education, the instructional designer can serve as support staff, guide, instructor, co-creator and/or manager of the course development process (Moskal 2012). While instructional designers provide invaluable services in creating online courses, their relationship with faculty members is not always friction free. First, faculty members are generally not accustomed to negotiating how to develop their courses with third parties and may bristle at the advice or suggestions of the instructional designers. Interestingly, instructional designers frequently do not have specific training in the area but have gravitated to industrial design through careers as K-12 teachers or trainers in industry, so instructors may question their credentials or resist their advice. For their part, since in most academic settings a small cadre of instructional designers work with a larger set of faculty members, the instructional designers may have a set way in which they like to develop courses and that template may not be appropriate for every course. And there are other complications. While most universities require faculty who want to teach online to consult with instructional designers, instructors who make extensive use of educational technology often do not have to work with third parties and the expectations of both the faculty and the instructional designers are not always clear. Instructional designers are generally located in an administrative unit that is external to academic departments, such as a Center for Online Learning or an Instructional Technology group within an academic computing group. Faculty may not, in some cases, be clear exactly what value instructional design provides. Finally, as instructional designers are likely to work with faculty teaching online and faculty making extensive use of educational technology, frequently there are too few instructional designers to work exclusively or extensively with one faculty member for an extended period of time. With those institutional and psychological barriers in mind, cajoling a faculty member to work with an instructional designer may take a financial or some other incentive.

Despite potential problems, a productive relationship between faculty members and instructional designers and other educational technologists is essential. Synthesizing online courses into an online program places additional demands on the course design. Since students take all or most of their courses online, the LMS sites for each course must be consistent. The more time students spend learning how to navigate through the LMS, the less time they have to spend learning. In addition, student frustration with the technology can have a negative impact in their overall participation. Along the same lines, it is most efficacious for courses in an online program to share the same technology tools to accomplish the same tasks. For example, each course should use the same video conferencing platform, even though institutions may support multiple tools to accomplish the same task. Ideally, faculty members teaching in the online program should communicate with each other and decide together the standard user interface for their courses and the set of technology tools they will use for each activity. Instructional designers can play an important role in facilitating those discussions and communicating those decisions when appropriate. Finally, when developing courses that are going to be part of an online program, the faculty member and instructional designer who assists in creating the course initially must be aware that the course may be taught by other instructors over time. Courses should have some standard components in terms of both content and function that will allow them to be taught by different instructors over time without an undue amount of revision.

In short, developing online courses that are integrated into online programs must go through three distinct stages. In the first stage, individual faculty members create or select the content of the course starting with the course objectives, which should support the learning objectives of the program. Online course development is generally more and less granular than course development in traditional settings in higher education. On the one hand, courses usually are not divided into individual class sessions, and as such the learning activities have to be carefully thought through and appropriately applied. Both the array of course materials and the assessment tools used may change when a course moves online. Second, online courses have to be implemented appropriately. Instructional designers frequently assist in this process, which can require a degree of negotiation between the instructional designer and the faculty member. To assist in building a fruitful collaborative relationship, individual faculty members and the instructional designers working with them need to clarify their expectations when they embark on a common project. Third, the look, feel and functionality of the LMS for all the courses in an online program should be similar if not identical. The sites for the individual classes in an online program are, in some ways, the equivalent of a physical campus. As students move through the program, they seek a degree of familiarity and continuity in the same way that students enjoy the sense of knowing their way around campus. Moreover, the courses should be designed with the idea that the faculty who creates the course may not teach it in perpetuity. This third goal of making sure that each course is developed in a way that accounts for the needs of the program requires ongoing communication among the faculty members teaching in the online program, as well as follow-up communication with the instructional designers who work with them. Developing an online course is a collaborative process that involves different team members with various skill sets and interests. Team members often play multiple roles and the process requires a higher degree of flexibility than standard course development, and the process requires a new organizational structure that facilitates the work of all the team members (Hixon 2008).

As could be anticipated given the complexity of the process, the length of time needed to create an online course varies depending on a wide range of factors. The e-Learning Center at Northern Arizona University estimates that it should take between 120 and 180 hours to develop a fully online course and about half that amount for a hybrid course. Adding documents and media elements to the course may demand more time. Creating original content extends the development period even further. NAU's e-Learning Center suggests that faculty allow at least 6 months for course development (Northern Arizona University n.d.).

Faculty Training

One of the noteworthy aspects of higher education over the past 50 years is that faculty generally received little or no formal training in teaching. In most fields, graduate programs are geared toward the production of new knowledge. And while many colleges and universities have established support centers to help instructors improve their teaching skills or have even provided financial incentives to engage in faculty development, participation in those activities is often voluntary. In fact, an international survey found that less than half of the colleges and universities polled had training centers to support the improvement of teaching quality and less than a quarter provided financial support to teaching improvement (OECD 2009). The situation is reversed with online education. A 2011 survey found that 94% of institutions provide training for online teaching and that training is frequently mandatory prior to a faculty member being authorized to teach online (Allen, & Seaman 2011). Several different models for preparing faculty to teach online have been developed (Testori 2012). The most common is for a specialized team to be established to support faculty through the entire process of transitioning online, including course development and pedagogical training. The support group many be based in a specialized center, be associated with a center charged with teaching enhancement in general or be a part of the academic computing team. These teams generally develop a systematic program that addresses the design, delivery and facilitation of online courses. Faculty must complete their training prior to engaging in their first online class.

Training programs can take several forms. A standard approach is to craft an asynchronous online program for faculty. For example, the University of Wisconsin-La Crosse (UW-L) instituted an online instructor-training program (OIT) in 2010. Prior to that, teachers of online classes were not trained. Their program focuses on three competencies: first, participants gain an understanding of the design, delivery and review stages of teaching courses online; second, instructors are guided in the effective use of the university's LMS, including how to organize the interface to facilitate student learning; and third, the development of strategies to help instructors better understand the student experience by engaging them in the same kinds of tasks that students engage in online such as discussion boards and other interactional activities (Koepke, & O'Brien 2012). The OIT approach used at the UW-L represents a standard model of training for online instruction. But within some general parameters the actual implementation of faculty development training varies widely. Some training lasts for a day, some for a weekend, a week or an entire summer (Meyer 2014). While some programs start and conclude with face-to-face sessions, emulating a hybrid approach used in many online programs, delivering the bulk of the training program online makes intuitive sense. While engaging in formal course development and the associated activities and gaining more in-depth knowledge of the learning management system is helpful, most faculty have had little or no experience learning online.

While very significant, formal programs are one aspect of a comprehensive faculty development program, in many cases, training programs are aimed at faculty when they are first starting to teach online. But as the educational technology and learning management systems improve, student expectations and technological capabilities change, and new and different course structures are developed. Hence, there is a need for ongoing training to update and upgrade online teaching skills. Unlike the face-to-face classroom, in which the use of technology is primarily a vehicle to enhance and deepen the interpersonal interactions between student and teacher, in the online classroom, technology mediates virtually every aspect of teacher-to-student and student-to-student communication. And the technology keeps changing, which is among the reasons why it is important to consider student–technology interaction. When online education first began to proliferate in the 1990s, email was a primary form of communication. For the past ten years, discussion forums were central and they still play a key but perhaps no longer a primary role. Chat rooms are now frequently used. The production of video content is becoming easier and less expensive to produce and will play an increasingly larger role in online education in the future. Finally, video conferencing technology is becoming more widely available, as platforms become more stable, and video conferencing software is easy to use.

The model of charging a specialized center or team with planning and implementing faculty development for online training also has its limitations.

In the same way that many schools have developed peer evaluation of teaching programs that are supplemented with mentoring to help younger teachers improve their teaching, departments with online educational programs sometimes establish mentoring programs, in which teachers experienced in online teaching work with new faculty. While mentoring should not replace the more formal training, it does have several advantages. First, many of the facilitators in the formal training program will not, in fact, have taught college students online. The trainers may come from a corporate or K-12 background or may have no formal training in teaching online themselves. Second, when the training is conducted through a centralized facility, the nuances of teaching in different disciplines may be lost. One size does not fit all in online education in the same way that it does not fit all in traditional learning. And while individual instructional designers work one-on-one for specific courses, the other aspects of teaching online including the expected student–teacher interaction can vary from discipline to discipline, department to department and even instructor to instructor. Experienced faculty mentors are in a better position to address those variations. Pairing new faculty with experienced online faculty in their discipline can help build the newcomer's enthusiasm and motivation to teach online as well. In general, instructors who have already taught online are more positive about the overall experience than those who have not (Allen, Seaman, Lederman, & Jaschik 2012).

Informal and department-based mentoring programs can also help address another challenge presented by the emergence of online educational programs. Not uncommon, particularly in continuing and professional educational programs, online courses are taught by affiliate and adjunct faculty. In fact, many online educational programs have no full-time faculty members. Affiliate and adjunct faculty need to be trained in teaching online and in some cases, institutions provide an additional training stipend when an adjunct faculty member teaches a course for the first time online; undergoing training is a condition of being appointed. At some point, the regular faculty in a department have to take responsibility for programs being offered under their aegis and mentoring faculty is one method that can be utilized to do so. Many faculty development programs are aimed at new faculty teaching online for the first time. The programs devote a lot of time and effort to guiding instructors in developing online courses and developing content for the LMS. But as online programs, as opposed to stand-alone online courses become more commonplace, a wider range of faculty training programs will have to be developed. In particular, training programs may in the future focus largely on effective techniques for teaching online, as in many cases, a course will have already been moved online, and the objectives, material and even the structure of the LMS interface will be largely in place. With this in mind, faculty development programs geared to faculty who will be teaching online but not necessarily creating new courses online have to be developed. A considerable amount of research aimed at recognizing the factors associated with successful teaching online has been conducted, and there is widespread agreement that instructors have to facilitate active learning, provide timely feedback and be socially present in the course, effectively manage the class, and have a handful of other skills and competencies linked directly to guiding students through their online experience (Bigatel, Ragan, Kennan, May, & Redmond 2013). Developing these competencies is critical to the implementation of successful online educational programs as well successful online courses.

Faculty development is a pressing issue in the creation of online education programs. In general, faculty development has been geared toward instructors teaching online for the first time and also engaged in course development. As online education matures and spreads, a more varied set of training programs will be developed that focus more comprehensively on teaching and course management issues. These programs will address the particular challenges faced by affiliate and adjunct faculty. And training programs have to be integrated in some way into the ongoing activities of academic departments.

Course Management

From a faculty perspective, course management is probably the most challenging aspect of online education. Almost by definition, faculty are expert learners. Not only can faculty be trained to develop online courses, but also many find that under the right circumstances, the techniques used in training to teach online can be usefully deployed in their face-to-face courses (Scagnoli, Buki, & Johnson 2009). Indeed, faculty development for online education introduces instructors to a tested course development model of which many are not aware. However, few faculty members have experience as online learners and it can be hard to envision students' learning experiences. In addition, the skills and techniques with which instructors are comfortable using in face-to-face settings will not necessarily translate to online courses. For example, online lectures, no matter how skillfully produced, will generate a different kind of experience than in-class lectures. The potential for spontaneity and a degree of informality are lost online. Synchronous discussions via chat rooms or video conferences are qualitatively different than discussions in the classroom. Those differences are significant. In traditional classroom settings, positive student evaluations are frequently correlated with the enthusiasm a teacher demonstrates for the subject matter and for being able to gear the course at the correct level of difficulty for the students (Palmer 2001; Centra 2003). Communicating enthusiasm about the subject material and judging exactly how difficult a course should be are difficult to gauge in an online learning environment.

But perhaps the greatest fear faculty face as they approach getting involved in online education is that teaching online is going to consume all of their available time (Cavanaugh 2005). While most effective instructors manage their teaching load along with their responsibilities in a face-to-face setting, the first cohort of faculty who have pioneered teaching online reported that teaching online demands more time than traditional teaching (Seaman 2009). One of the reasons that teaching online can potentially require more time than traditional teaching is that in moving a class online, the role of the teacher changes considerably. On the one hand, in an online class, the teacher does not command center stage in the same way as in a traditional classroom. Instead the instructor serves as a facilitator of a multi-faceted and multi-dimensional educational experience, a mentor and first point of contact for technical and other problems (Easton 2003).

In many ways, the most challenging element in management of an online course is negotiating the shift from holding the center stage in a course to becoming a course facilitator. For example, in a traditional class structure, a teacher may decide to devote a class session to a discussion of a specific topic. The students do the requisite reading; the faculty member prepares some prompts and the discussion is initiated. In a spirited discussion, perhaps half the class makes at least one contribution, and perhaps the teacher intercedes a half a dozen times. At the end of the class period, the discussion ends. Translating a similar kind of discussion to an asynchronous discussion forum can potentially require a lot more time, and an entirely different effort on the part of the students and the instructor. As before, the students prepare themselves and the teacher offers a prompt to start the discussion. In an asynchronous setting, the discussion may last for a week or more. The instructor has to check in periodically to monitor the activity, and the instructor needs to be careful not to dominate the discussion. Some instructors feel the obligation to respond to every single post, in essence turning the discussion into a one-to-one interaction with perhaps 20 or 30 students. Moreover, during the asynchronous online discussion, students may rely on others to participate. If they don't participate, students are in a sense not present. Participating in an online discussion is reminiscent of text messaging on a mobile phone. Individuals like to be able to control when they respond to a text message, and they like to think about what they want to say before sending a text message. Similarly, in an online discussion, responses are likely to be more considered than the spontaneous responses one is likely to garner in an in-class discussion. This example illustrates both the benefit and a potential pitfall of online discussions. There is the potential for the online discussion to be richer and fuller than a classroom discussion. More students can participate and their posts and responses can be more thoughtful than in class. The content of the discussion is available for testing later in the semester and is an ongoing resource for students. For many, participating online can be a less stressful experience. But for the faculty member, reading, monitoring, facilitating and responding to the discussion posts can take a lot of time, particularly if the faculty member chooses to respond to a lot of the students' posts.

Simply being less involved in the online experience is not a good solution to the course management challenge. One of the critical elements in teaching successfully online is creating what is called social presence, which in turn helps build a sense of a learning community among the students (Shea, Li, Swan, & Pickett 2005). For an online course to succeed, students want to feel that the instructor is involved in the learning process, but not too involved. This constitutes a balancing act as instructors have to decide in which discussion to participate and when to participate. One option is to provide a summary at the end of the discussion period. Feeling the presence of the teacher is critical to building an online learning community and developing the students' sense of connection to course. Creating social presence requires a conscious effort for the instructor to manage the course time commitment. As with any instructional enterprise, students will have course-related questions and concerns, and in response it is not unheard of for instructors to make themselves available all day, every day, which is certainly not a good practice. A student may not fully understand a particular assignment, or the student may have other difficulties with the assignment. A student may need an extension or a deadline. Perhaps a student would like to request a recommendation. Or an individual may just want to get to know the faculty member more personally. This kind of interaction usually takes place at the beginning or the end of the class, or in the instructor's office in a traditional setting, and such discussions can be dispensed with in a few minutes. For online classes, each student many require a personal and immediate response, as with the growth of texting and email, people come to believe their messages should be answered very quickly. Given this impatience, some faculty members feel they have to be available to their students on a round-the-clock basis.

Another component of online teaching that can serve as a draw on faculty time is that for many students, the instructor is the first point of contact. In many cases, online students are only taking one or two courses per semester. They are not familiar with the campus. Their only contact with the university may be the learning management system, and they are rarely likely to use the university's general Web site. Even for non-academic questions, students will often turn to their instructor first for guidance. Despite the potential time demands, properly managed, teaching online courses does not have to require more time than teaching in traditional settings. Several strategies are available to keep time demands consistent with the demand on faculty time generally. One strategy involves the design of the course interface. Students must be able to navigate through the site and easily find the materials they need to complete the assignments. Therefore each interactional tool needs to have a set of instructions about its use for students who are not confident about their technical skills or who have not used the tool very frequently, or perhaps not at all. This is where instructional videos may be quite helpful.

Besides the course modules, detailed descriptions of the assignments, course policies and other material normally found in a syllabus are essential. As well, students benefit from a separate detailed schedule that is displayed in the LMS and available as a PDF download. In addition, links to other key offices in the university may be displayed on the course site or on a program orientation site within the LMS. As online courses rely entirely on the use of technology, the most important link is the one that directs the student to technical support. The overall requirements for technical support will be discussed in Chapter 6. From the faculty perspective, when students have technical difficulties associated with completing an assignment, the instructor is advised to be flexible—either offering a solution or directing the student to an office that can support their technical needs. Providing clarification by posting course policy will mitigate anxiety when technical problems arise.

A well-designed LMS site is essential for effective course management. Standard course interfaces breed comfort; links to key support staff minimize anxiety; and, knowing what to expect beforehand with regard to course parameters and expectations will go a long way to create a smooth relationship between the student and instructor. For example, teachers can establish times by which they will respond to email—perhaps within a 24-hour period or maybe by certain days in the week. Or, they may hold virtual office hours by having Skype on during set times of the day or days of the week. In establishing ground rules, the instructor must be clear that there may be a gap between when students submit questions and when those questions may be answered. Something that needs to be taken into consideration is that flexibility will be required when teaching across time zones.

Instructors may consider proactively communicating with students. Sending an email at the beginning of each week detailing what students are expected to complete that week helps keep students on track as well as cutting down on the number questions that may arise. Along the same line, establishing a discussion board that can be used for general class questions—a virtual water cooler—can alleviate the need to respond to individual students, as general questions are likely to be on the minds of other students in the course.

Online classes have the reputation of requiring more of the instructor's time than traditional classes for several reasons. First, this is a new way of teaching and faculty have little or no experience developing course management strategies. Second, the first generation of teachers who migrated online were interested in the technology and pushing the boundaries. Third, as with social media, the easy accessibility of communication technology has created a pressure to be always available. As experience with teaching online grows, so will the instructor's ability to manage the time needed to conduct online classes. In many cases, on a per-student basis, teaching online takes no more time than teaching face to face (Van de Vord, & Pogue 2012).

Disabilities and Online Students

As online education has grown, so has the number of students with various kinds of disabilities that must be accommodated. Obviously, when developing online courses and programs, it is important to keep in mind government requirements for accommodating students with disabilities. Beyond the government's requirements, course and program developers need to go beyond compliance to ensure the success of all of their students in the online learning environment. Online education may be particularly attractive to students with disabilities, especially when viewed within the three categories of disabilities developed by the U.S. Bureau of Census. Those categories include communication, mental and physical disabilities. With regard to communication disabilities, course designers must provide accommodation for those that are sight or hearing impaired. Videos, for example, will need to include captioning at the bottom of the screen. For students who are sight impaired, screen readers and voice recognition software will need to be made available. For students with speech difficulties, online discussion forms, blogs, and wikis may be quite efficacious as forms of expression. Online programs and courses may be quite attractive to students who have some mobility issues. According to the Americans with Disabilities report of 2010, more than 30 million American adults had at least one form of disability. Because disabilities may be multiple, it is impossible to list all of the possible ways in which online education may aid in disabled students' success. Betts et al. (2013) provide a thorough review of the issues facing those developing online courses and programs as they strive to accommodate students with various kinds of disabilities. There are various resources available to those interested in subjects like developing online content for students with disabilities (Cannect 2014).

Assessment

Assessment represents a major trend in higher education generally. Accrediting agencies, both for higher education and professional standards organizations, state legislatures and the Federal government, are pressuring colleges and universities to develop clear learning aims and demonstrate that their programs meet those aims. This drive has led to the mandate for academic departments to create measurable program and student outcomes and gather data to prove that the programs meet those goals. Colleges and universities are under increasing pressure, to establish formal processes of assessment that clearly show that defined aims are being met at the classroom, program, departmental, and institutional level. These data collection processes require another level of bureaucracy, as the task of data collection alone is onerous (Lesboprof 2011). Given the general climate of assessment in higher education, the need to develop effective measurement tools for online educational programs is even more acute than in the other areas of the educational enterprise, as online programs for many institutions of higher learning are still considered a stepchild. Teaching online is still relatively new and despite the evidence to the contrary, many people including faculty members, administrators and the general public are suspicious about the quality of online education (Bidwell 2013). Online instructors need data to show that classes and programs meet established goals. In addition to being a new venture for many institutions of higher learning, online education is new for most students as well. Consequently, student evaluations can help faculty better understand what works and what does not work when teaching online. Finally, the technology used in online education changes regularly. Those responsible for administering online programs need to be able to monitor the effectiveness of the technology.

There are four levels of assessment for online programs: teaching, technology, course and program. Assessing the teaching, the technology and the course is clearly within the domain of the purview of the faculty, though, given the current administrative structure of online education, responsibility for those assessments may be shared with a centralized center for online learning or its equivalent on campus. The requirement for program reviews generally comes from the institutional level and will be discussed in Chapter 6.

Identifying appropriate tools to evaluate teaching has been an ongoing point of contention throughout higher education and the debate about what data should be used and in what ways has heated up as assessment moves toward the top of the agenda. Historically, student evaluation surveys have been the major piece of information for assessing teaching, but even as external stakeholders look more closely at student survey data, others have contested their significance (Thompson 2013). The problematic nature of student evaluations and their relationship to the assessment of teaching effectiveness has been well documented. As colleges and universities vary widely in terms of size, orientation, mission and student population among other variables, and in many academic disciplines student outcomes have not been specified, it is very difficult to determine what the data gathered by student evaluation surveys actually reveals. Furthermore, student evaluations are rarely analyzed, controlling for factors within the instructor's control, including the race, class and gender of the students, the starting time of the course, the demonstrated interest in the course, the specific content, and the mode of delivery (Otani, Kim, & Cho 2012).

While the use of student evaluations raises issues across the university, their application in online educational programs poses additional problems. First, some of the questions used on standard student evaluation forms are not relevant to online education and many of the teaching techniques that are important to student success in an online setting are not as critical in traditional settings or they are implemented in very different ways. For example, it is not uncommon for a standard student evaluation form to ask students to indicate if a teacher encouraged classroom participation. This question poses problems on many different dimensions but in an online class, motivating people to engage in some sort of interactional activity is central to the entire experience. Moreover, "discussion" in an online class can be conducted in several different ways—via a discussion board, a chat room, a video conference or comments on a blog. The whole concept of "student engagement" and how it can be measured is different in an online environment.

In many cases, the form commonly used for student evaluations is inappropriate for use in online education. But discarding the standard form raises a host of serious questions. First, who will be responsible for creating a new form? And second, if the questions asked and the data elicited on the student evaluation form for online classes varies greatly from the questions and data gained through a standard form, how should the results be compared for purposes of annual evaluation and ultimately tenure and promotion? In most settings, the data gathered through student evaluation surveys is used in a comparative way, often within a department or across an academic unit. But not only is comparing data generated by different forms difficult, most academic departments and universities do not have the equivalent historical knowledge about how good teaching online is reflected in student surveys, as they do about how good teaching in a traditional classroom is revealed through student surveys. Over time, experienced faculty and administrators can simply glance at student evaluations of teaching and get a good sense of the meaning of the data. This is not the case with online teaching. The knowledge base is not developed enough.

Creating an appropriate new student evaluation form for online educational programs is difficult and raises additional problems to be resolved. In the same way that faculty cannot rely on their experience to quickly evaluate the data, often students do not have a lot of experience taking online classes and do not know what to expect. Some researchers have argued that meeting student expectations is perhaps the single significant factor in positive student evaluations (Wachtel 1998). Since students may not have many points of comparison as to what constitutes effective online teaching, the meaning of their responses on surveys may be murky and open to interpretation.

In many, if not most cases, online educational programs require the development of new student evaluation forms. But even if departments or appropriate academic units can agree upon methods to reconcile and compare the data generated by the new forms with the data gathered by the existing student evaluation forms, other obstacles emerge. By definition, evaluation surveys for online courses and educational programs must be delivered online. While many universities have already moved to online delivery of student evaluations, this mode of delivery has well-understood shortcomings. While students indicate a preference to complete evaluations online, if the evaluation is not mandatory, response rates can fall. Second, each student completes the evaluation in an uncontrolled environment, which may have an impact on the responses (Donovan, Mader, & Shinsky). For colleges and universities that still administer student evaluations during class time, developing an appropriate way to deliver online evaluations so the data is comparable to other data can be complex.

Of course, as the assessment of teaching has grown in importance, many colleges and universities have moved away from relying solely on student surveys as the only data point. A common alternative has been to use what is called a peer evaluation of teaching process (PET). In the peer evaluation process, designated faculty members collaborate with a colleague to construct a meaningful evaluation process that incorporates extensive qualitative data and a qualitative final report. Actual classroom observation is generally a central activity in this process (Osborne 1998). While some of the measures used in the peer evaluation process can be easily applied to online education, others cannot. For example, evaluators can review the syllabus for a class, analyze the course objectives and outcomes, and perhaps comment on the appropriateness of the material selected. But online education does not present an analogue to direct observation in a classroom to gauge how a teacher interacts with students. The notion of a lesson plan is different online. And most importantly, the explicit standards with which a peer reviewer may assess a colleague's performance conducting an online course have not been broadly articulated and standards may not be commonly shared. While developing new approaches to evaluating teaching for online learning is a knotty issue, the move online, over time, will open up access to a new array of data and new methods of measurement. For example, many current student evaluations ask a "time on task" question. With online education, data detailing how long students spend online, how frequently they access the course and how long it takes them to complete certain tasks is captured by the learning management system. The increased use of learning management systems coupled with emerging technology such as data analytics will give new insight into student behavior online and instructors' ability to influence and shape that behavior. Incorporating the new data available into faculty evaluation processes, however, has to be managed at a college or university-wide level.

The evaluation of teaching is clearly a faculty responsibility. Historically, the development and implementation of faculty evaluation methods and standards has been a parochial activity decided by each college or university. With that in mind, as online programs grow, departments have to invest time in exploring how faculty conducting online classes should be evaluated. These deliberations will inform a university-wide audience to develop standards and methods to judge performance. At the same time, the faculty and the administration will need to find agreement on the ways that the evaluation of teaching online classes can be compared to the evaluation of teaching in more traditional settings.

Assessing teaching is a standard university process. However, since online education is still new, many universities and colleges have begun to implement processes to assess the design of online courses as well. There are several different approaches to judging the quality of the course. Quality Matters is an international consortium dedicated to developing research-based rubrics that lead toward best practices for the evaluation of online education. Informally founded by a group of community colleges in Maryland in 2002, more than 700 colleges and universities now participate in its activities. More than 23,000 faculty and instructional design staff have been trained in QM (Maryland Online 2013). The Quality Matters rubric is a faculty-centered, peer-reviewed process to assess the quality of the course design for online courses. It consists of eight broad sections with a series of granular elements in each section. For example, the first heading is Course Overview and Introduction, and the first granular task in the 2006 public domain version of the standards, is to make sure that the navigational instructions make the organization of the course easy to understand (Temple University n.d.). The current rubric (which is not available in the public domain) has 41 tasks associated with the different sections. The Course Overview section, for example, has eight tasks, while the section on Accessibility has four tasks. Tasks have different weightings as well. The task that calls for faculty to insure that the tools and media used in the course support the learning objectives, has a score of three. That the tools used are current and up to date is only worth one. In the 2008 standards, a total of 68 points can be accumulated. The Quality Matters rubric can be used in three ways. First, it provides a guide for design of online courses. Second, it can be used to evaluate existing online courses, and finally, it is a measure that can lead to ongoing course improvement. In the Quality Matters process, a course is developed through a collaboration involving faculty and other stakeholders. The course is then peer-reviewed, taking into account the rubric, the appropriate literature and other input. Based on the feedback, the course is judged to be of sufficient high quality or in need of revision (Shattuck 2007).

The Quality Matters approach primarily intersects with course development and improvement in two places—during the initial course development and during the peer-review process. If faculty and designers are alert to the QM standards, those standards can be integrated into the course from the beginning. Nonetheless, the review process is a critical component of the QM structure. QM offers a two-week course through which faculty or course designers can become a certified peer reviewer. Quality Matters represents a sustained effort to facilitate the development of online courses with sound instructional design. As could be expected, it is implemented differently at different institutions. The length of time institutions require for learning the QM rubric varies, as does the method of delivery. In some cases, the training is delivered online. In other cases, training requires some face-to-face meeting, but the overall course length is compact. Some institutions have opted to extend the training for a longer period of time. Moreover, the way course reviews and assesses changes from university to university, and perhaps most important, the course assesses the ways shortcomings are rectified if they are not consistent. In general, the QM approach benefits both faculty and staff (Roehrs, Wang, & Kendrick 2003).

QM raises significant issues including who has the ultimate authority for the look and feel of the course—the faculty, the reviewers, or the instructional design staff. Moreover, faculty report that they may not have the time to engage deeply in the review process and may need the assistance of the instructional design staff to implement changes.

There are costs associated with utilizing the Quality Matters rubric; however, there is a free rubric for online instruction from Cal State Chico. The Cal State Chico rubric offers a guide to the developmental process of online courses. The rubric helps to enhance the expertise of faculty and to provide support for faculty. The rubric may be utilized in three ways: as a self-evaluation tool, a course design tool, and as a means to reward high quality instruction (Cal State Chico, n.d.).

The final piece of the puzzle for online educational programs is assessing the effectiveness of the technology. As with other elements of online education, the technology is a shared responsibility. Specifying and supporting the underlying platform itself is usually the responsibility of Information Services or the Academic Computing team. In most cases, faculty have very little input into the selection of the platform. Along the same lines, faculty cannot determine how the platform will be supported, both for themselves and for the students. Also, individual faculty members should not completely control the interface of the different course sites so all of the courses in an online program have a relatively standard look and feel. This enables students taking several classes in an online educational program to become familiar with the interface and invest less time learning to navigate the site to access the content and tools they need. More-over, as students become more accustomed to the site design, their comfort level and sense of familiarity could help connect them better to the program in the same way that students feel more connected to a university after they learn how to find their way around campus. In theory, when an online program is first launched or classes first start to move online, the interface should reflect collaboration between the faculty and the instructional designers associated with the online initiative. The precise nature of the collaboration between faculty and the designers in creating the interface will be determined by the local conditions.

The aspect of the technology infrastructure for which faculty assessment is critical is in the use of the different interactional and content creation tools. Instructors have access to three sets of online tools—the basic tools available in the learning management system (LMS), more advanced tools that can be easily plugged into the LMS and other tools that reside outside the LMS completely, social media, for example. Along the same lines, original content for online courses, particularly audio and video content, can be created using a wide range of tools. Different content creation tools, however, may require different playback viewers that would have to be downloaded by the students.

Specifying which tools should be used in an online educational program is a balancing act. As a general rule, the more the tools integrated into the LMS are used, the easier it should be for students to access and master those tools. A discussion board hosted internally in the LMS should be easier for students to access and use than a discussion board residing in a third-party platform. But the general rule is often violated. While LMSs provide basic functionality, many of the more advanced tools they use are plug-ins and may not represent the best version of that functionality. For example, the blog tool in an LMS may not be as good as an external blog tool. The faculty associated with a specific online program should have a significant say in determining if internal LMS capacity meets the needs of the program. In the same way, content creation tools and content creation processes vary widely. Perhaps the most striking contrast is in the creation of video. In developing MOOCs and other large-scale online courses, universities can invest hundreds of thousands of dollars producing slick videos. The courses created by the MOOC platform Udacity, for example, can cost $200,000 to $400,000 to produce (DeLong 2013). Videos are produced in dedicated studios and edited using professional-level editing equipment. But a wide range of low-cost video creation tools exist that can be plugged into the course site. Faculty can record video on their computers and upload the content directly to the course site via a plug-in. A third option is for faculty to record video, upload it to Youtube.com and then provide a link to the video. The faculty participating in an online program should assess the approach or approaches to be used in their program but there should be some consistency across classes. Leaving the choice to individual faculty members can potentially hinder the student experience. Instructors can play an important role in identifying new tools and technology that could enhance their online programs. While specifying and acquiring new educational technology is generally the responsibility of the academic computing group, in some cases faculty can better spot new technology that can be useful and actually applied in their courses.

In online programs, assessing technology should be a part of the student evaluation. Students should be queried about ease of use; the adequacy of support and their overall user experience. As with other technology projects, the key is to establish goals and benchmarks for the use of technology and then develop the indicators and methods of data collection that can measure to what degree the goals and benchmarks are being met. Faculty are not likely to control the technology environment in which an online program is conducted. In many settings, the faculty do not even have a significant voice in making decisions about the infrastructure. Faculty members do have a role to play in assessing the technology used. They should determine which tools meet the needs of their program. That determination should set up processes to measure the student experience and qualitatively examine the faculty experience with different tools as well.

Conclusion

More programs directed at non-traditional students and at institutions in which access is central to their missions such as community colleges have been open to implementing online educational programs. A growing body of research indicates that under the right circumstances, online education can achieve the same educational outcomes as traditional classes (Wagner, Garippo, & Lovaas 2011). And the widespread attention generated by the emergence of MOOCs coupled with the other factors driving change in higher education means that online educational programs are on the road to becoming an ongoing part of higher education—faculty must find a role in guiding and shaping online programs. It is a complicated task and the changes that online education will bring to faculty will unfold over time. In fact, whether or not a specific faculty member teaches online, online educational programs will influence in some way every aspect of every instructor's teaching responsibility. Not only do online educational programs change the way courses are developed, implemented, and assessed, but also those changes have led to the need for faculty to be trained to teach online. The changes engendered by the emergence of online are potentially more profound than the obvious differences in class creation and delivery. The growth of online education will force faculty to reconsider their relationship to each other and the university at large. As a result, academic departments may have to modify their communication and governance structures to accommodate online educational programs.

References

Allen, I. E., & Seaman, J. (2011). Going the distance: Online education in the United States. Retrieved from http://sloanconsortium.org/publications/survey/pdf/goingthedistance.pdf

Allen, I. E., Seaman, J., Lederman, D., & Jaschik, S. (2012). Conflicted: Faculty and online education, a joint project of the Babson Survey Research Group and Inside Higher Ed. Retrieved from http://www.insidehighered.com/sites/default/server_files/survey/conflicted.html

Barrett, P. (2014, February 27). In fake classes scandal, UNC fails its athletes—and whistle-blower. *Business Week*. Retrieved from http://www.businessweek.com/articles/2014-02-27/in-fake-classes-scandal-unc-fails-its-athletes-whistle-blower

Betts, K., Welsh, B., Pruitt, C., Hermann, K., Deietrich, G., Watson, T. L., Trevino, J. G., Brooks, M., Cohen, A. H., & Coombs, N. (2013). Understanding disabilities & online student success. *Journal of Asynchronous Learning Networks*, 17(3: October), pp. 15–48.

Bidwell, A. (2013, October 15). Americans doubt the rigor and quality of online education. *U.S. News and World Report*. Retrieved from http://www.usnews.com/news/articles/2013/10/15/americans-doubt-the-rigor-and-quality-of-online-education

Bigatel, P., Ragan, L. C., Kennan, S., May, J., & Redmond, B. F. (2013). The identification of competencies for online teaching success. *Journal of Asynchronous Learning Networks*, 16(1).

Cal State Chico, (n.d.). Rubric for online instruction. Retrieved from http://www.csuchico.edu/roi/

Cannect (2014). How-to guide for creating accessible online learning content. Retrieved from http://projectone.cannect.org/

Cavanaugh, J. (2005). Teaching online: A time comparison. *Online Journal of Distance Learning Administration, Spring, 3(1)*. Retrieved from https://www.westga.edu/~distance/ojdla/spring81/cavanaugh81.htm

Centra, J. A. (2003). Will teachers receive high student evaluations by giving higher grades and less coursework? *Research in Higher Education, October, 44(5)*, pp. 495–518.

Donovan, J., Mader, C., & Shinsky, J. (2007). Online vs. traditional course evaluation formats: Student perceptions. *Journal of Interactive Online Learning*, Winter, 6(3), 158–180. Retrieved from http://www.ncolr.org/jiol/ussues/pdf/6.3.2.pdf

Easton, S. (2003). Clarifying the instructor's role in online distance learning. *Communication Education*, April, 52(2), pp. 85–105.

Graham, C., Cagiltay, K., Lim, B.-R., Craner, J., & Duffy, T. (2001). Seven principles of effective teaching: A practical lens for evaluating online courses. *The Technology Source Archives*, March/April. Retrieved from http://www.technologysource.org/article/274/?utm_content=buffere64be&utm_source=buffer&utm_medium=twitter&utm_campaign=Buffer

Hixon, E. (2008). Team-based online course development: A case study of collaboration models. *Online Journal of Distance Learning Administration*, Winter, 11(4). Retrieved from http://www.westga.edu/~distance/ojdla/winter114/hixon114.html

Inside Higher Ed (2013) The 2013 *Inside Higher Ed* survey of faculty attitudes on technology: A study by *Inside Higher Ed* and Gallup. Retrieved from http://www.insidehighered.com/news/surveys_faculty_and_technology

Kamenetz, A. (2013, October 29). Are you competent? Prove it. Degrees based on what you can do, not how long you went. *The New York Times*. Retrieved from http://www.nytimes.com/2013/11/03/education/edlife/degrees-based-on-what-you-can-do-not-how-long-you-went.html?pagewanted=all

Koepke, K., & O'Brien, A. (2012). Advancing pedagogy: Evidence for the role of online instructor training in improved pedagogical practices. *Journal of Asynchronous Learning Networks*, March, 16(2). http://sloanconsortium.org/jaln/v16n2/advancing-pedagogy-evidence-role-online-instructor-training-improved-pedagogical-practice

Lesboprof (2011, October 2). Assessment in higher education: On the train or under it. *The Chronicle of Higher Education*. Retrieved from http://chronicle.com/blognetwork/lesboprof/2011/10/02/assessment-in-higher-education-on-the-train-or-under-it/

Maryland Online (2013). About us. Retrieved from http://www.qualitymatters.org/about/

Meyer, K. (2014). An analysis of the research on faculty development for online teaching and identification of new directions. *Journal of Asynchronous Learning Networks*, 17(4). Retrieved from http://sloanconsortium.org/jaln/v17n4/analysis-research-faculty-development-online-teaching-and-identification-new-directions

Moskal, T. M. (2012). Instructional designers in higher education. Digital Commons. Retrieved from http://digitalcommons.unl.edu/cgi/viewcontent.cgi?article=1125&context=cehsedaddiss

Northern Arizona University (n.d.) e-learning center FAQs. Retrieved from http://www2.nau.edu/d-elearn/faq/answers_327

OECD (2009). Learning our lesson: Review of quality teaching in higher education. Retrieved from www.oecd.org/edu/imhe/44058352.pdf

Orellana, A. (2006). Class size and interaction in online courses. *Quarterly Review of Distance Education*, 7(3), pp. 229–248. Retrieved from http://itecideas.pbworks.com/f/22941927.pdf

Osborne, J. (1998). Integrating student and peer evaluation of teaching. *College Teaching, ProQuest Education Journals*, Winter 46(1).

Otani, K., Kim, B. J., & Cho, J. I. (2012). Student evaluation of teaching (SET) in higher education: How to use SET more effectively and efficiently in public affairs education. *Journal of Public Affairs Education*, Fall, 18(3), pp. 531–44.

Palmer, P. (2001). *The courage to teach: Exploring the inner landscape of a teacher's life.* San Francisco, CA: Jossey Bass.

Roehrs, C., Wang L., & Kendrick, D. (2013). Preparing faculty to use the quality matters model for course improvement. *MERLOT Journal of Online Learning and Teaching*, March, 9(1).

Romero, C., Ventura, S., & Garcia, E. (2007). Data mining in course management systems: Moodle case study and tutorial. *Computers & Education*, submitted. Retrieved from http://maxwell.sju.edu/~jz570129/CSC792/ICWL/reference/data-mining-in-course-management-system-moodle-case-study-and-tutorial.pdf

Scagnoli, N., Buki, L. P., & Johnson, S. D. (2009). The influence of online teaching on face-to-face teaching practices. *Journal of Asynchronous Learning Networks*, 13(2).

Seaman, J. (2009). Online learning as a strategic asset: Volume II: The paradox of faculty voices – views and experiences with online learning. Babson Survey Research Group: Babson College, August. Retrieved from http://www.aplu.org/document.doc?id=1879

Shattuck, K. (2007). Quality matters: Collaborative program planning at a state level. *Online Journal of Distance Learning Administration*, Fall, 10(3). Retrieved from http://www.westga.edu/~distance/ojdla/fall103/shattuck103.htm

Shea, P., Li, C. S., Swan, K., & Pickett, A. (2005). Developing learning community in online asynchronous college courses: The role of teaching presence. *Journal of Asynchronous Learning Networks, December, 9*(4).

Temple University (n.d.). Guide to online course design and quality standards. Retrieved from https://www.temple.edu/tlc/resources/handouts/course_design/QualityMattersRubric.pdf

Testori, P. (2012). Orientation, mentoring and ongoing support: A three-tiered approach to online faculty development. *Journal of Asynchronous Learning Networks, March, 16*(2).

Thompson, S. (2013, March 1). The unnecessary agony of student evaluations. *The Chronicle of Higher Education.* http://chronicle.com/blogs/conversation/2013/03/01/the-unnecessary-agony-of-student-evaluations/

U.S. Department of Education (2010, June 18) Federal Register, *75*(117). Retrieved from https://www2.ed.gov/legislation/FedRegister/proprule/2010-2/061810a.html

Van de Vord, R., & Pogue, K. (2012). Teaching time investment: Does online really take more time than face-to-face? *The International Review of Research in Online and Distance Learning, June.* Retrieved from http://www.irrodl.org/index.php/irrodl/article/view/1190/2212

Wachtel, H. (1998). Student evaluation of college teaching effectiveness: A brief review. *Assessment & Evaluation in Higher Education,* 02602938, *June, 23*(2).

Wagner, S., Garippo, S., & Lovaas, P. (2011). A longitudinal comparison of online versus traditional instruction. *Journal of Online Learning and Teaching, March, 7*(1).

Windes, D., & Lesht, F. (2014). The effects of online teaching experience and institution type on faculty perceptions of teaching online. *Online Journal of Distance Learning Administration, March, 17*(1). Retrieved from http://www.westga.edu/~distance/ojdla/spring171/windes_lesht171.html

5
Challenges for Students in Online Programs

As the poet T. S. Eliot wrote, "April is the cruelest month," especially for high school seniors who have applied to the top tier of colleges and universities across America. In 2014, for example, the acceptance rate for undergraduates at Stanford University was 5%. And the numbers were no better at other elite schools. The acceptance rate at Harvard and Yale universities was 6%. Columbia and Princeton were at 7%, and acceptance rates at Massachusetts Institute of Technology and the University of Chicago were 8%. Ten years ago the acceptance rate at the University of Chicago was 40%. Among public colleges, the number of applications at the University of California, Los Angeles jumped to more than 86,000 for 6000 open places (Perez-Pena 2014). At a time when some visionaries have suggested that the emergence of MOOCs could place a Stanford-quality education within reach of hundreds of thousands of people around the world, actually getting admitted to Stanford as an undergraduate is more difficult than it has ever been.

And the picture at the graduate school level is not much brighter. For example, in 2012 the acceptance rate for the graduate schools of business at Stanford and Harvard was 7%, and the acceptance rate at the top ten graduate schools of business was under 15%. The overall acceptance rate for graduate schools of business was under 50% (Sheehy 2012). The average acceptance rate at the top ten law schools generally is around 15%, and the acceptance rate at the top tier engineering schools is roughly 20%.

The question is: Why, with the promise of greater accessibility that online educational programs offer, would students subject themselves to such high rejection rates knowing that if they are the lucky ones to be accepted, they will face significant tuition, often more than $50,000 a year? The answer, simple as it may seem, is that a college education represents much more than just the classes you take. A college education is a complete experience; schools they have attended shape part of a student's identity. On campus, they encounter and interact with a wide range of students, professors and professionals, among others. For example, Harvard Law promotes that it has students from more than 160 undergraduate institutions and 12 countries. In this respect, the student body is diverse. More than 40% of Harvard's students are non-white. Moreover, Harvard offers a range of experiences outside the classroom including working in law clinics or working closely with faculty on research or other projects. Harvard Law graduates enter an unparalleled professional network stemming from contact with the students in their classes, the general student population on campus and the alumni. And, of course, a Harvard law degree carries a great deal of prestige. In other words, there are many other social aspects of a Harvard Law education that extend beyond the classroom.

One of the challenges for online educational programs is how to deliver what can be considered a full higher education experience, beyond the classroom (McKeown 2012). How can online educational programs be designed so that students who enroll in them not only benefit from the formal academic experience, achieving the program's learning outcomes, but also that they receive the informal benefits associated with higher education, including generalized knowledge and skills learned outside the classroom, social growth, networking and other advantages? This chapter will discuss the components needed to promote a successful formal academic experience for participants in online educational programs. The institutional components including support services and student life programs that can help enrich the online educational experiences are discussed in Chapter 6.

Who is the Online Student?

The first step in understanding how to create a successful and enriching online education program from the student perspective is to understand who students are and what their motivation is for taking online courses. While the numbers of students taking online courses is steadily growing, this growth has largely come from specific groups such as non-traditional students including adult learners. Online educational programs are largely clustered in community colleges, continuing and professional educational programs, and professional master's degrees. The U.S. Department of Education estimated that in 2012 approximately 5.5 million students took at least one online course (a figure lower than the more commonly used figures from the Babson Research Group Survey) (Kolowich 2014). Currently, online learners have a very distinct demographic profile. According to a 2012 study conducted by The Learning House, a company that designs online learning programs and has partnered with 100 colleges and universities and the Aslanian Market Research company, which conducts market demand studies for institutions that desire to increase their online and adult enrollments, around 60% of all students in online educational programs were 29 years old or older; for-profit institutions having a larger percentage of older students than non-profit institutions. About 70% of those students are women. The Learning House survey was based on a national sample of 1500 respondents who were recently enrolled, currently enrolled, or plan to enroll in a fully online undergraduate or graduate degree, certificate, or licensure program. Estimating that between two and three million people meet those parameters nationally, the survey had a plus or minus 3% margin of error at a 95% confidence level (Aslanian, & Clinefelter 2012).

The survey revealed several other interesting characteristics of that pool of people enrolled in fully online programs as well. About 65% of the respondents were attending online programs in traditional non-profit institutions, both public and private, with the remainder at for-profit colleges and universities, a much higher percentage than in the wider universe of higher education. In undergraduate programs, more than 80% had prior college credits, typically around 35 credits, but around 25% had more than 60 credits. And 25% of all online undergraduate students had already earned a bachelor's degree earlier, and 35% of all graduate students had already completed a prior graduate degree. Almost half of the undergraduate students and nearly three-quarters of the graduate students reported working full time. Not surprisingly, around 60% of the undergraduate students reported studying full time while the same number of graduate students reported that they were working full time. About one-third of online learners entered their programs with a goal of switching careers most often to health care and other professional services careers. In short, The Learning House survey describes the typical student in a full-time online educational program as a 33-year-old Caucasian woman who is not the first in her family to attend college.

The typical profile for full-time students in online educational programs promises to evolve due to several factors. First, although the students interested in online education skews to an older population, in many ways, online education is more popular among younger students. In fact, a study conducted by researchers at the Applied Learning Technologies Institute at Arizona State University, in which data mining techniques were used to determine who was taking courses online, found that contrary to conventional wisdom, younger students are more likely to take online courses than older students. Moreover, younger students are most likely to take online courses in education and fine arts (Ho Yu, Digangi, Jannasch-Pennell, & Kaprolet 2008). Arizona State University has aggressively recruited students for its online offerings since 2007 and has estimated that by 2020 online revenues will represent around 10% of tuition (Fishman 2013). In their research, the ASU researchers suggested that given the surprising demographics of the online student population, the structure of ASU courses, which frequently run for 8 weeks instead of a standard 14 or 15 weeks, based on the assumption that shorter course lengths are more suitable for working professionals, may not be appropriate. Not only are younger students more likely to opt for online educational opportunities when given the choice, but also more students are gaining experience with online education in high school. In the academic year 2011–2012, 620,000 students in kindergarten though 12th grade took at least one course online, up 16% from the prior year. Moreover, several states including Florida, Michigan, Virginia and Idaho have made taking at least one online course a requirement of graduation (Sheehy 2012).

The final trend that will change the general demographics of the student population for online educational programs is the rising comfort level with technology itself. While younger students have always been more comfortable with technology, the technology needed to deliver high quality courses online continues to improve significantly. In fact, the emergence of Cloud computing with its massive storage capacity is one of the enabling technologies for MOOCs. As the cost for producing video drops and the speeds at which video can be transmitted across the Internet increases, the overall quality of online courses will increase. At the same time, the playback ability of the devices at the edge of the network such as smart phones and tablets will improve as well. Once tablets and smart phones become the primary device through which students can participate in online classes, those classes will be accessible to a wider community of potential learners (Bolkan 2013).

Motivations for Studying Online

As the student population for online education changes, the motivations for enrolling in online educational programs change, as does the motivation for taking online courses in general. Although it often gets lost in the analysis, the primary reason that students enroll in online educational programs is that they have an educational goal in mind; educational aspirations come first. The motivation to pursue that goal online follows, and it is often driven by the person's particular circumstance and options at that moment.

Flexibility

By far, the most commonly cited reason that students choose to study online is flexibility (Aslanian, & Clinefelter 2012). But the flexibility associated with online education can reflect different attributes of online learning; just because students say they want flexibility does not mean their reasons for taking courses online are the same. The most common interpretation of the word flexibility in this context is the idea that a student can fit the class around the other parts of their life, such as their family, social life, work and so on. The flexibility of online education can be seen in other ways as well. In many cases, students can also study at the time and place of their choosing. Of course, even in face-to-face courses, students can study in ways of their own choosing. However, since the schedule of online classes is often not as structured and rigid as traditional classes, and the overall time frame of many courses is shorter than traditional courses, students feel as though they have an additional measure of control.

The third element under the umbrella of flexibility for online courses is that students can take whatever course they want. In traditional settings, course-scheduling conflicts are not uncommon so a student may have to choose one course over another and not be able to take both. In the online learning environment, students are not faced with that kind of choice. The notion of flexibility has one other distinct element as well. Online education potentially provides students with access to a wider array of programs since they are not bound by offerings in their immediate surroundings. In theory, students can enroll in educational programs from whomever those programs are offered regardless of where the student actually resides.

While undoubtedly attractive, each of those aspects of flexibility poses significant challenges for students. The idea that students can schedule their classes so the classes do not interfere with other aspects of their busy lives creates the possibility that students will have trouble prioritizing their responsibilities and their participation in their online courses will be secondary to more immediate and pressing concerns (Herbert 2006). Being able to study at any time in any place means that students have to have the discipline to actually set aside the time and find the place to complete their coursework. And, although students potentially can enroll in online programs offered by any college or university in the world, there are many virtues to enrolling in programs offered by universities closer to home. Studying online is more than simply taking courses. In many cases, students will need technical support, access to the library holdings and other forms of student services. Being in the same time zone can help with those non-class processes. Moreover, students often build a stronger sense of identification with colleges and universities in their area, which can have a significant impact on their experience both during and after their participation in the program. The impact to alumni relations of studying online will be discussed in Chapter 6. In short, although the ability to enroll in any program anywhere may be a motivation for students online, most choose programs from universities within a 150-mile radius of their home (Aslanian, & Clinefelter 2012).

Admission to Study Online

The same factors that motivate students to choose online programs also can create significant barriers to their success. More than with traditional students, because online students have consciously opted for an educational experience with less formal structure, they have to be more self-motivated and be able to build their own learning environment in which they can succeed within the course, and develop a structure in which to manage their time to read and complete assignments, among other things. Moreover, they must be able to use the technology platform through which the program will be delivered. With that in mind, many online programs include short self-assessments to judge whether potential students are ready for online education. Those assessments generally consist of approximately ten questions, asking if the student is comfortable with computer technology, can read at the proper level, express themselves in writing, are willing to participate in online discussion groups, and are willing to finish assignments a few days in advance (ALCTS, the Association for Library Collections and Technical Services n.d.).

While these are valid questions, it is hard to imagine that people who wish to enjoy the benefits that online programs have to offer will review them and then opt out. Students expect that they will be able to succeed online even if they are not the most computer-savvy or have had trouble succeeding in a more traditional learning environment. The formal application process for online programs frequently does not have a separate set of criteria than those used for traditional programs. Even the criteria utilized by online only universities do not necessarily try to assess students' readiness for online education (Western Governors University n.d.). Despite the self-assessments, it is not surprising that there are no specific additional skills required and evaluated in the admission process for online students. In traditional educational settings, many students are admitted who are in need of remedial work, particularly in community colleges that have invested heavily in online education. College readiness in general is a significant problem (Shulock 2010). Readiness for online education poses several additional dilemmas. In addition to not having the expected academic preparation, it is difficult if not impossible to really know if a student has the necessary study habits or computer skills to succeed in learning online. Frequently, there are few if any processes in place to assess online students' readiness once they are admitted, and since instructors cannot as easily observe students online as they can in face-to-face settings, students who are unprepared to succeed may be harder to identify.

Exacerbating the situation, in many institutions, online learning is still associated with non-traditional students, and non-traditional programs often have relaxed admission standards. Even Harvard University, Columbia University and the University of Pennsylvania offer degrees through their extension programs that have a healthy sampling of online courses. Admission to those programs is dramatically different than admission to other schools and programs at these universities. For example, to be admitted to the M.A. in Liberal Arts at the Harvard Extension School, a student has to enroll and pass a "gatekeeping" class. There are no acceptance standards to be admitted to the first course. Students who pass the course are enrolled in the degree-granting program (Johnson 2013). The admission standards at for-profit institutions are lower. As the admission process for online programs is dramatically different than those in most traditional programs, the abilities and experiences of the student body can vary widely. Students and faculty can have low expectations about the potential level of academic performance. The variation in quality can have an impact on the educational experience, particularly when a class makes heavy use of unmonitored discussion boards and unguided student interaction to explore the implications of course material, which is often the case in MOOCs.

Assessing Readiness

Although informal self-tests may not be ideal criteria for admission to a program, administering a readiness test for students who are embarking on an online educational experience may be appropriate. Maggie McVay, as a part of her dissertation, developed the touchstone readiness test for online learning. The test consists of a short series of questions that focus on general learning attributes such as the ability to work independently and acquire adequate interpersonal skills. As online learning has become more widespread, efforts to improve the diagnostic assessment of incoming students has multiplied. Assessment of incoming students can help with retention and overall student success (Dray, B., Lowenthal, P. R., Miszkiewicz, M. J., Ruiz-Primoa, M. A., & Marczynskid, K. 2011).

These new approaches argue that in addition to having students assess their personal attributes, understanding their engagement with technology is also significant. It is important to understand not only whether students have access both to the necessary computer hardware, software and network access, but also how comfortable they are with using technology generally. Understanding prospective students' general attitudes and beliefs about technology may be helpful in assessing readiness. Non-traditional students, in particular, may not be as adventurous in exploring new computer applications. Success in online learning is not just dependent upon the personality of the students, as they must be able to successfully utilize technology. Consequently, scales for assessment of personal characteristics, as well as measures of technology skills and capability may be employed to gauge likely success in an online program (Miszkiewicz, & Dray 2010). Overall, assessment tools have only limited value in predicting if a student will thrive in an online environment. Nonetheless, depending on the size of the class and the institutional support for online learners, the results of readiness assessments can be used to craft appropriate remedial and other services that can improve the likelihood of student success.

Orientation

Given the variations in admissions processes for online programs, a comprehensive orientation program is essential. In fact, the Middle States requires institutions to create a robust orientation program as a part of its accrediting evaluation process for online educational programs (Middle States 2011). The Middle States guidelines make it clear that students need to understand the nature of independent learning and the challenges of learning in a technology-based environment.

Historically, orientations even for distance learners have been conceptualized as events, either pre-recorded or as a live webinar. Some programs may require students to travel to the campus for an on-site orientation (Wilson 2008). The amount of material that needs to be covered in an orientation is too much for a single event, however, although an event could be used as the kick-off. And if an orientation is conducted on campus, the content must also be available online for reference in the future. An orientation program should have six major components (Fotia, Holtzman, & Dagavarian 2010). The orientation of the program should provide students with the following: a clear sense of the expectations; introduction to the technology that will be used in the program to ensure that they will be able to use the technology; an opportunity to "meet" the faculty in the orientation; an explanation of relevant policies and procedures including the honor code, policy on academic integrity and course netiquette; and, students should learn how to access the other student services provided to online students, including the tech support infrastructure, library services and academic support, among other services. The range of necessary services required will be discussed in Chapter 6.

One approach to structuring an orientation program is to set it up as a course in the learning management system. In this way, in addition to systematically moving through the orientation, students will also get a sense of progressing through a course. The orientation introduces students to the way a course module in the learning management system is set up, how the content is organized, and the technological requirements needed to accomplish the various tasks that will be assigned. With this in mind, the orientation should incorporate all the content types—video, text, slide shows, etc.—that will be utilized in the courses as well as have tasks that require the use of all the technology such as discussion boards, chat rooms, video conferencing, among other activities that students will experience in their online course. Orientation periods can run for different lengths of times, but should have a specific start and end date. The orientation, however, should be extensive enough that it will not be completed in one sitting, in most cases. Rather, the orientation is most useful to transition students into the regular program. Consequently, the orientation period should end either immediately prior to the beginning of the first class or during the first week of classes. Even if the orientation module opens several weeks prior to the start of classes, many students will not start until much closer to the course start date. One of the primary goals of the orientation is for students to understand and learn time management skills needed in an online program. Ideally, the professor in the first class or student support personnel will monitor individuals' progress through the orientation and intervene appropriately if a student lags behind.

The first module in the orientation introduces and explains the goals of the program and the expectations of the students both for the program overall and for the orientation itself. Since students generally have a defined period of time to complete the orientation, many online educational programs do not have a specific start date. Students start at a date and time of their own choosing or engage with the course when discussions are open or an assignment is due. They do not experience the nervous excitement of going to campus for the first time, finding their classroom, looking around and meeting their professor and interacting with other students. Instead they just have the unnerving experience of attempting to log onto the learning management system for the first time. The instructions about how to log on to the learning management system, along with any other administrative material, sent to the learner immediately prior to the first day of the orientation as well as periodically throughout the orientation, serve as a reminder to work through the orientation and to solicit questions if a student needs help. The first login to an online course can be a challenge for some students; email provides an alternative channel of communication.

The content of the first module serves three goals. First, it should excite them about the program and motivate them to plunge into the work. Not only is retention a major problem in online programs, even getting people to start the program is often a formidable task (Rivard 2013). If a student actually does login to the class, the first content should be as engaging and motivational as possible. It is not enough to simply post material and explain the program. The first encounter with the orientation should spark enthusiasm for the program and course, and remind students why they enrolled and the benefits that they will receive from the program.

The United States Distance Learning Association maintains: "All first-time distance education students should be given a clear statement of course requirements in advance. This should include: 1) all course requirements; 2) the weekly time commitment and specific computer skills required by the course; and 3) a presentation of the practical difficulties of working at a distance and what is needed to manage those challenges successfully" (United States Distance Learning Association, n.d.).

In 2010, Both Rowan University and The Richard Stockton College of New Jersey presented what at that time would be considered best practices for orientation to online learning. However, for online learning, with a rapidly changing technological environment and greater understanding of processes associated with the online learning experience, orientations have to be updated on a regular basis. In other words, best practices today will not likely be best practices in the future. The main content of the orientation will introduce students to the faculty and their other classmates, alert them to the school and course policies, introduce them to various student services, and, most important, train them in the use the technology involved in the program. The training in technology can be efficiently accomplished by using the tools to complete activities associated with the other goals. For example, students should have the opportunity to meet the faculty, perhaps in a virtual manner through a video, associated with the program. Once they review the content about faculty, they can be required to send an email either to a faculty member with whom they anticipate studying or to an appropriate support person. Along the same lines, to help students introduce themselves to each other, they can be instructed to post their learning aims on a Wiki and write and post a short biography in a discussion forum. In this way, they learn how to use the technology in a realistic setting that maximizes the chances that they will be successful when called upon to use various tools in a course. To maximize the effectiveness of the technology training, online tutorials, preferably video, should be available for each application utilized in a course. In addition to learning the design or flow of the course sites and the use of the technology tools, the most critical content areas in the orientation are familiarizing students with support services, netiquette and strategies about how to succeed in an online course.

Technology Support

Almost invariably in an online course or program, at some point students are going to encounter difficulty with the technology. The student support services that universities are required to provide online students will be more fully discussed Chapter 6. Technology support is most critical. Online students must have the same access to technology support services as residential students. That means if the school help desk is available until 10 p.m. Eastern time, help desk support must be available to 10 p.m. Pacific time, if the program enrolls students from California.

Providing technology support to online students poses many problems that must be addressed in the orientation. The first is for the students and the technology support services to understand the technology the students' own and plan to use. Commonly, the technological needs of the program, including what type of computer, which operating system and web browsers, are posted on the orientation Web site. Unfortunately, even so-called digital natives are not necessary computer or digital literates (Berg 2013). While younger students may be more willing than older students to push buttons to see what will happen when things go wrong, that does not mean they are more capable of solving a problem if the browser or operating system they are using is obsolete or unstable. Along the same lines, they may not be able to determine if there is a problem with their computer, their Internet connection, the university's servers or the learning management system. The best way to address those potential issues is to integrate an activity in the orientation that requires students to contact the help desk directly. Not only will students learn the process they can use if they need technical support, but also the tech support people will be able to ensure that the students have the right level of technology to succeed in the program. Faculty, program directors and technology administrators can alert support staff when to expect to be contacted by the online students.

Netiquette

The issue of netiquette, or the information code of conduct for online inter-action, has been around since people began insulting each other online during the early days of the Internet (Harris 2010). In general, netiquette refers to people using intemperate language and bullying behavior in their interactions online, often hiding behind the cloak of anonymity. But neti-quette for online education extends far beyond language and inappropriate responses to students and colleagues. During the orientation, expectations can be set regarding the way students will communicate in one to one and one-to-many situations, both in real time and asynchronously. For example, for one-to-one communication, students may be instructed to check their email daily and to reply to email within a 48-hour period. Different programs have a different tolerance concerning how formal an email should be. Do all the words need to be spelled correctly? Should there be a salutation? Par-ticipants need to be aware of and accepting of their colleagues' differences in their use of email.

As commonly used as email is (and for younger students it is actually being replaced by texting and other forms of direct communication), it cannot be assumed that students will know what is meant by proper communication eti-quette. Students need instructions and strategies to avoid engaging in email volleys on points of disagreement. To that end, publishing a policy at the outset will provide clear understanding of what mode of communication is best for different assignments. Similarly, complete sets of instructions and netiquette should be developed for group and collaborative interaction as well. When students collaborate in real time, a meeting time should be cooperatively estab-lished and students should log on early to check their technology. Meetings should start and end at the appointed times and participants should create an environment in which they can be fully engaged during the collaboration, and so on.

Communicating online is rife with the potential for misunderstanding. Those misunderstandings can be driven by a wide variety of factors. In tra-ditional educational settings, the instructor largely controls the interactions among students, at least in the classroom. The instructor is in a position to moderate and help repair relationships among students should they rupture or otherwise interfere with the work of the class; that same presence does not exist in online education. The code of conduct established at the outset of the course will cover as many aspects of communication—use of language, expectations for responses, rules for setting up appointments and group meetings. Online students, particularly non-traditional students, often believe that they should be able to settle conflicts on their own. But the online educational environment is unlike a face-to-face class, as students find themselves engaging in ongoing interaction with people they do not know, may never meet, and possibly do not like or respect.

Mechanisms may be put in place to ensure students abide by the netiquette code. For example, students can be required to email their consent to abide by the code to the appropriate person such as the program administrator. Requiring an acknowledgment of the code and consent from the student achieves three goals: it motivates students to read the entire code; it puts them on the record, agreeing to behave in a certain way; and, it opens the door for using that consent to demand changes in behavior if necessary.

Informal Student–Teacher Interaction

While netiquette codes set the overall parameters for interaction, general expectations for student–teacher interaction may also be established during the orientation. More importantly, however, as discussed in Chapter 3, from a faculty perspective, each instructor will benefit from establishing guidelines for each particular class, and then, as much as possible adhere to those guidelines. From a student perspective, effective and efficient communication with the faculty can play a definitive role in the overall educational experience.

Informal student–teacher interaction falls into three categories. The first is informal contact initiated by the student. In general, if a student has a problem or question, the individual will email the instructor. The guidelines should specify within what time period the student should receive a response. The expected response times can be framed in different ways. For example, an instructor may indicate that students should expect to hear a response to an email with 24 hours or perhaps 48 hours. If emails are sent over the weekend, expectations will need to be clarified. As students opt for online education in order to capitalize on its flexibility, they are often doing their assignments over the weekend. A second option for emailing students is to establish that the instructor will respond by a specific day of the week, Tuesday and Thursday, for example. In this way, faculty are not tied to their computers if other responsibilities make it impossible for them to respond to an email within 24 hours. Instead, responding to email can be a set part of the faculty schedule in the same way that teaching face to face is a fixed part of the schedule. The drawback to establishing response times fixed to the days of the week is that if a student has a question on a Saturday, and the response may not arrive until Tuesday afternoon, perhaps the student's study schedule and ability to complete assignments will be disrupted.

As students may not be entirely in control of when an instructor may respond to a query, the guidelines should make clear what happens if a student contacts the instructor with a problem or a question and does not receive a timely answer. Two factors come into play in this scenario. First, students may get anxious if it appears they will not be able to meet a deadline because their questions have not been answered in a timely manner. Second, their relationship to the instructor may be damaged. In addition to establishing the timeframe for informal one-to-one student–teacher interaction, instructors may develop a menu for what kinds of queries should be sent directly to them and what information and queries should be directed to other administrators, such as tech support, records or the financial aid office. In online education, the instructor may be viewed as the primary point of contact and might wind up serving as the traffic cop, so to speak, fielding all sorts of questions to which the answers are to be found elsewhere.

Over time, faculty will receive many "housekeeping" kinds of questions—requests for clarifications on instructions or deadlines. In a face-to-face class, these questions are often asked and answered at the beginning of a session. An effective method to answer these kinds of general questions is to set up a special discussion forum—a water-cooler forum of sorts—to which every student subscribes. When a student asks a question to which the answer will be of interest to the entire class, direct the student to post it on the discussion forum. More often than not, if one student is unclear on instructions, let's say, other students may be confused as well. By directing these kinds of questions to the discussion forum, the instructor only has to answer the question once, for everyone concerned.

Direct interaction initiated by the student is only one mode of interaction between the instructor and the student. As in face-to-face classrooms, instructors may set up "office hours" during which instructors and students can interact informally about classroom and non-classroom matters. As with traditional educational settings, not all students will take advantage of office hours. Nonetheless, it is a good practice to designate a time during which students feel free to perhaps video conference with or otherwise interact with the instructor. Depending on which time zones students are in, instructors may have to include some morning hours and some evening hours when they will be available.

The third mode of interaction is communication initiated by the instructor. In the traditional classroom setting, students more than likely come to the instructor for assistance. However, in online education, students may never reach out to the professor. They may never have any questions or wish to interact informally. The burden is on the instructor to build relationships with students. This kind of outreach plays an important role in keeping students engaged and on schedule. The first kind of proactive outreach that a faculty member may want to set up is a Frequently Asked Questions page. This page can be used to describe the common problems that arise in a classroom and further direct students to appropriate sources of information. Faculty may also want to set up a blog or create podcasts through which they can communicate on a regular basis. While potentially helpful, FAQs, blogs, and podcasts are passive forms of communication. Students have to remember to interact with them. Beyond passive means of communication, perhaps the easiest way to reach out to students is to send a regular email update, perhaps weekly, detailing where the student should be in the class schedule and what to expect over the next week or two, perhaps reminding them of assignment due dates. Depending on the subject matter, faculty can intermittently email supplementary readings or material. A third idea, depending on the size of the class, is to require students to "meet" with the professor either via telephone or video conferencing to discuss their progress in the class or to discuss other issues. The purpose of the telephone or video conference is to strengthen the student–teacher bond and reinforce that the instructor is paying attention.

The burden of ongoing, informal communication may not have to be carried entirely by the professor. In larger classes, discussion leaders or teaching assistants are also involved. In these cases, students need to be made aware of the proper person to address a particular issue or concern. Even with the availability of teaching assistants or discussion leaders, in non-MOOC settings, direct communication can substantially enhance the student experience. Effectively managing interactions with students is a critical issue for both the instructor and the student. If appropriate guidelines are not put in place, the instructor may feel tethered to the class at the same time that the student feels the instructor is being unresponsive. Without limitations, younger students who are used to texting and getting instantaneous responses may develop unrealistic expectations about when they will get a reply from the instructor.

Appropriate informal interaction between the instructor and the students as well as among students themselves through discussion forums and other means is an important factor in student satisfaction (Northrup 2002). Ongoing research suggests that in many settings including self-paced learning environments, informal interactions are as valuable as formal interactions in creating a high quality online learning experience (Rhode 2009). It is essential for faculty to play a proactive role in communicating with students, and if possible, have at least some opportunity for synchronous interaction with individual students. More important, however, is to establish a system through which the instructor is able respond to inquiries in a reasonable timeframe.

Policies and Procedures

As with other aspects of online education, communicating policies and procedures for online students requires more outreach than may generally be found in traditional education. The roadmap for creating a student handbook specifically for online students will be discussed in Chapter 6. A safe assumption is that online students are generally less connected to a campus than students taking residential courses and, as a result, have fewer obvious strategies to have their questions answered and issues resolved; online students cannot fall back on just going to the office and finding a person to ask. Policies and procedures have to be spelled out at both the program and individual class level. Many of the policies about which students must be aware concern the general operation of the university, including easy links to the academic calendar, the financial aid office, registration and records. Key dates on the academic calendar such as the beginning of the school year, the deadline for registering for classes and the last day to withdraw from classes without failing should be clearly visible as should the refund policy. Letting students know the policy about withdrawing is critical. If students do not withdraw from a class in a timely fashion, they may fail the class, which can put their financial aid in jeopardy. Online students are not immersed in the campus culture so there is no campus buzz about deadlines. And frequently, online students do not know their colleagues well and only interact with them within the context of the class and so they do not have a support network. While emails reminding students about critical deadlines are appropriate, the information needs to be easily accessible at the moment the student needs it. Other key policies and procedures that need to be readily available to online students include the registration process and how to receive or replace a student identification card, the procedure for appealing a grade, and the process for appealing dismissals. If the program has established its own grading standards that students have to meet to remain in good standing, those standards need to be readily accessible. Each link to the various policies and procedures might include a short explanation of what the office does, the key personnel and the best way to get service. On the flip side, the directors of online educational programs have to work with the various offices to make sure they are prepared for online students. A pivotal policy that must not only be published but should be publicized as well is the university honor code and policy on academic integrity. Technical solutions to protect against cheating and the need to establish an institutional commitment and appropriate environment to cut down on cheating will be explored in Chapter 6. And it is clear that technology in general has made it much easier for students to compromise their academic integrity. It is easy to cut and paste material from the Internet, for example, without properly crediting the source. Faculty report that even in traditional classrooms, as many as 50% of the students will plagiarize at least part of their papers (Carr 2014).

Despite the obstacles involved in eliminating cheating online, programs and instructors can take several steps to reduce the instances of cheating by students in online programs. One simple step is for instructors to clearly communicate how they define cheating and otherwise dishonest and unacceptable behavior. The first step in cutting down cheating for students is to clarify what constitutes cheating. Although this point may seem obvious, it is not always the case. Academic dishonesty can be grouped into five categories, the most obvious being plagiarism. But students can also simply falsify or fabricate information or turn in work done by other people, misrepresenting it as their own. And, students can act inappropriately, perhaps by offering help to a classmate (Gallant 2008). Examples of each of these forms of cheating should be made clear to the online student.

Online students need to be fully aware of the behaviors that violate the academic integrity policy, the sanctions for those violations need to be spelled out, and the processes for adjudicating accusations of academic dishonesty need to be clearly described. Other steps that may be taken are to present guidelines for acceptable collaboration, as well as alerting students when a plagiarism service, like Turnitin.com may be used to scan student work. Finally, the sanctions against a student for academic dishonesty need to be clearly spelled out (UT Telecampus, WCET, & Instructional Technology Council 2009). As with netiquette policies, students can be asked to sign the academic integrity policy.

In addition to communicating expectations, faculty can take other measures to cut down on cheating. One concrete step is to design assignments that make it difficult to cheat. Research papers can be required to include course material that may be only accessible through the LMS. Tests can be drawn from a large bank of questions and randomized on the LMS. Perhaps the most important step is for instructors to try to get know their students personally. Short writing assignments, for example, can be given at the beginning of an online course to get a sense of how an individual student writes, and students can be asked to document the steps they took to complete an assignment. None of these strategies will eliminate academic dishonesty and cheating—in fact, cheating is, unfortunately, too commonplace throughout higher education. But taking concrete steps can cut down on the amount of cheating. There is evidence to suggest that, coupled with a strong honor code, if students feel a connection to the instructor, the instances of cheating can be reduced (LoSchiavo, & Shatz 2011). Online students may not actually cheat at a higher rate than students taking classes on campus, but instructors must work to build a community of integrity by involving students in discussions about academic honesty (McNabb, & Olmstead 2009).

Building a Community

In many ways, reducing academic dishonesty relies most heavily on facilitating real bonds between the instructor and the student and among the students. The temptation to cheat is greatest when students feel that they are isolated and believe that nobody is watching or that nobody really cares. The same feelings of isolation that can lead to increased cheating may also hurt the overall academic experience for online students. That isolation can take many forms. Obviously, students are geographically dispersed, and in asynchronous programs, inevitably, students are online at different times. Under such circumstances students may feel socially isolated. In many cases, they will not know any of the other students in the program so they have no colleague or peer to turn to for advice or help (Croft, Dalton, & Grant 2011).

On the flip side, the same sense of camaraderie and identification that helps reduce cheating can also help improve the overall student experience. There is a large body of research reaching back to the beginning of the Internet that shows that people who interact online can build a strong sense of community or interconnectedness (Rheingold 1993). The challenge is determining what a community or cohort should be in online education and how to realize the benefits of a community (Conrad 2005). A community can best be understood as a group of people who have a sense of identification with each other and a sense that they share something in common. In campus-based education, that sense of identification comes from several sources, including the year they entered their program of study or the year they will graduate; and, their major, or the sense that they have had a common set of experiences. The key to developing a sense of a group identity is ongoing informal communication in addition to the formal instruction. When students get to know each other, they have the opportunity to bond.

To build a sense of community among online learners, elements of the online program should be designed to specifically address the root causes of those feelings of isolation. The faculty, program directors and course designers have to incorporate methods and activities that provide students with the environment and motivation to interact with each other without the surveillance of the faculty or program director. This can be facilitated in many ways. The first task in building a sense of community is for faculty to be aware of the ways they interact with students and engage with students in order to nurture a sense of community. Overall, the ways that instructors interact with learners can be grouped into six categories. They include providing information, participating and guiding discussions, offering support and encouragement, supplying feedback and modeling behavior. Other factors that have an impact on the ways instructors and students interact are the modes of communication used and if student participation is required. While providing timely feedback and creating a sense of the instructor's social presence is important to the overall perceived quality of a course, a recent study of graduate students found that the most important modes of interaction for fostering a sense of community were the instructor modeling what was desired, offering support and encouragement and effectively facilitating discussions. Instructor modeling provides strategies for students to initiate conversations and interactions, defines the scope of permissible interactions, and modeling can encourage or solicit engagement (Shackelford, & Maxwell 2012).

The most straightforward method for creating a sense of community is to create assignments in which students are paired off with each other or work in small groups. The pairs or small groups should be required to organize themselves as part of the assignment. In this way, students will have the chance to learn more about each other and begin to build a connection. This strategy works better if students can video conference. Face-to-face communication brings about a greater sense of intimacy, even if it is at a distance. A second vehicle for building a sense of identification is to invite students to participate in special events online and then establish special channels of communication for them to subsequently interact with each other. For example, students can be invited to watch a guest speaker whose talk is streamed over the Internet and then comment on the speaker using a Twitter hashtag or a real-time chat room. Not all students will be able to attend a synchronous event, but some will and even the simple act of inviting students to a special event helps build a sense of identification. A third approach to building a sense of community or a cohort is to set up a discussion forum for students to post content that falls outside the course material, like a coffee-shop forum. Earlier in this chapter the concept of a water-cooler forum was introduced as a means to generate discussion about the course. The advantage of the second ongoing coffee-shop forum is to create a space where students can bring up issues, ideas, events, or experiences that extend beyond the course. An interesting approach is to send students who have enrolled in the program an item with the school or program's logo on it. Students can be encouraged to take a "selfie" wearing or using the item and post it to the discussion board or through some other shared channel of communication, like Twitter. Making the activity into a contest could add to the incentives for students to participate.

In many cases, a large percentage of students in an online program will live relatively close to the campus. In those cases, an online program may want to plan some face-to-face events or perhaps schedule a weekend event. Even very short periods of face-to-face interaction can encourage the development of stronger bonds among students and help generate a stronger learning community. In low-residency, hybrid programs that are primarily online but where students visit campuses for classes that last for a week or two, time should be taken to plan social events and other activities designed to get students to know each other better. Some online programs take a cohort approach, in which a relatively small group of students start the program together, take the same classes, and then end the program together. The obvious advantage of a cohort–based approach is that through their shared experiences and ongoing interaction, it is easier to build a sense of community. But there are drawbacks as well, as students interact with only a set group of colleagues for the entire program. Moreover, the structure of a cohort reduces the flexibility that attracts people to online learning (Browning 2013).

The benefits of building a learning community in an online educational program are clear. A community helps cut down the isolation participants may feel. A community can help to motivate students. Indeed, when a sense of community has been established, students are more willing to engage more deeply with the course material, as well as reveal more of themselves and allow others to get to know them (Pfeifer-Luckett, & Skibba 2011). Paradoxically, in face-to-face education, the role of community varies greatly. In professional schools such as law and medicine, cohorts form communities in response to the intense workload. At the undergraduate level, on the other hand, students are often left to their own devices to create support communities. Approximately 75% of all students in higher education complete their studies without feeling connected enough to others to overcome the pressures in their lives (Johnson, Rochkind, Ott, & DuPont 2014). Among 18 to 24 year-olds who attend residential colleges full time, where the drop-out rate is far lower, one of the primary reasons for leaving is the inability to establish an appropriate community supportive of learning (stateuniversity.com n.d.).

Individual Class Orientation

The issues confronting students in online learning programs have to be addressed at a programmatic level. Every student, for example, needs to go through the orientation and all faculty members have to be trained to be alert and sensitive to the challenges that online students face. And while the program orientation should remain online and accessible throughout students' participation, this is not sufficient. Each online course needs to contain at least a subset of the most important information contained in the program orientation. For example, in each class, the faculty member clearly presents the policies that apply to that class, including, perhaps most importantly, the honor code and the rules defining academic integrity. Each class orientation will have information about what to do if the technology fails, along with a policy about the implication of technology failure and missed deadlines in general. In many cases, students starting out in an online program will not use the tools often enough to become comfortable with them right away. Some students need ongoing support and reminders of how to navigate through the technology. The assumption for each class should be that the students would have retained very little information from the program orientation. Compounding the challenge, online students can be expected to have very little knowledge about how the university as a whole functions.

Strategies for Success

When students enter an online educational program, they are entering a new learning environment, perhaps unlike anything they have experienced before. Even students who were very successful in traditional educational settings may find adjusting to the parameters and conditions of online education difficult and will need continued support to help them succeed. Without that support, even the most prepared and motivated students may find the experience overwhelming or unfulfilling. However, students can take several steps to thrive in an online environment (King, & Alperstein 2014). The first step online students must take is to establish a study schedule. While the primary attraction for online education for many students is its flexibility, that is also one of the primary pitfalls. In the case where there are no set classroom times, as in an asynchronous course structure, students left to their own devices may not complete their work in a timely manner, and ultimately fail the course or drop out of the program. A well-constructed, rigorous online class should require approximately the same amount of time as a class delivered in a traditional format, approximately 8 to 10 hours per week. Students should be encouraged to identify times in their schedules to devote exclusively to their course work.

The flow of the workload in an online class can be very different than in a traditional setting. Attending class is often a passive experience for many students. Too frequently students come to class unprepared but are able to recover in time for the tests or other grading activities. To thrive in an online program, ideally students will work at a steady rate throughout the semester. This suggestion does not mean that they have to devote an equal amount of time to the class each week, as that would remove one of the chief benefits of online education. However, students should identify each milestone in a course and block out in advance the time needed to successfully achieve the milestone. It has been emphasized that students need to be prepared to use the technology. This process has three phases. First, students must become comfortable with the learning management system prior to the beginning of the class to be certain that they can navigate through the site easily and that all the tools work correctly. Different professors may use different sets of tools and students must be prepared for that. Metaphorically, the learning management system can be thought of as the pencil and paper students brought with them when they entered primary school. Students have to be ready. And just as pencil points break, the technology in online classes will inevitably fail at some point in the class. While some students many have friends or family that can help them if a piece of technology is not working correctly, that is not a reliable or long-term solution. At the beginning of the semester, a process will have been established regarding the steps to take if a piece of technology does not work according to expectations. Most importantly, students should know when and how to contact the technology help desk and how fast they can expect to receive technical support.

The third phase is to understand the professor's policy concerning missed deadlines caused by technical malfunctions. If the rules are very strict and the professor will not accept late work, for example, students should be prepared to complete assignments a few days before the actual due date, taking into account the possibility of a technology failure. Along the same lines, students should be aware of how the instructor anticipates interacting with them regarding technical issues. Is the instructor, who is the person with whom the student has the most ongoing contact, willing to serve as the first line of support? Does the instructor want to be alerted to technical problems at all, or will a mechanism be in place whereby students can go directly to the technology help desk?

One strategy that can help students to thrive online is to proactively build connections with faculty, other students and the campus itself. Online students inevitably lead busy lives. On its own, online education does not open up a lot of opportunities to informally mingle with students, as might happen before or after a class, or with the faculty. It is worth emphasizing, the more connected students feel to their classmates, their instructors and the college or university through which the program is offered, the richer and fuller the educational experience will be. If students do not live too far away from the campus, they should try to visit and set up face-to-face appointments with faculty or perhaps attend an on-campus event. Mechanisms for student interaction, like video conferencing, should be in place to encourage collaboration. And faculty should proactively create times and mechanism that allow students to interact with them informally.

Learning from Failure

The pressure is building for academic institutions to improve the overall student experience for online programs. More and more students are opting for online programs and online programs attract a lot of non-traditional students who may have a whole set of additional obstacles standing in the way of their academic success. Taken together, these factors and others lead to retention and graduation rates among online universities that are significantly lower than for traditional universities. The U.S. Department of Education defines retention rate as the number of first-time students who enroll in a school who remain at the school the following year. In 2011, the University of Maryland University College, the University of Maryland's division geared to adult learners, which has a significant online component, had a retention rate among full-time students of 29% and among part-time students of 17%, and the overall graduation rate was 4% for students who had started their studies in 2006. For Western Governors University, the first-year retention rate for students starting their studies in 2011 was a respectable 89%, but the six-year graduation rate was only 27% for students who began school in 2006. For the University of Phoenix, the first-year retention rate is 33% and the six-year graduate rate is 19% (National Center for Educational Statistics n.d.). Even for well-established, relatively mature programs like these, the question remains as to why the retention and graduation rates, as defined by the failure to stay in school and complete a degree program, are so high. According to surveys conducted over the past decade by researchers at Monroe Community College, the top reason that students drop out is falling behind in their work. Another reason students offered to explain why they withdrew from a class included personal reasons that made it difficult to continue, like their inability to manage both their educational and family responsibilities, or they cited their inability to negotiate the technical and educational challenges of learning online. Their final explanation for dropping out was that they did not like the class (Fetzner 2013). Other surveys have returned similar results

(Tyler-Smith 2006). Virtually every element involved in online learning has the potential to result in failure. Students can have unsuitable technology or have difficulty using the technology associated with the program, including the learning management system. Students can enroll in courses for which they are not qualified, or they are simply unsuited for online learning. And, for a variety of reasons, student may not be able to manage the flexibility that online educational programs offer—the very reason that attracted them to online education initially.

Conclusion

To draw an analogy between spending for online programs and spending per student in regular programs illustrates the chasm that exists. In 2010, for example, the spending per regular student at the universities in the Southeastern Athletic Conference (SEC) was a little more than $13,400 a year. In the Big 12, spending per regular student was a little more that $13,700 and in the Big 10 it was just over $17,000. When it comes to expenditures per college athlete, the figures are significantly higher: $144,500, $124,000 and $115,500 respectively. The debate, however, is not whether college athletics makes a contribution to campus life. Beyond spending on sports, colleges have invested in other ways to enhance student life. Over the past ten years, the increase in spending on student services has far outstripped the increase in spending in either instruction or research in virtually every category of the institution except in public community colleges where spending on student services fell at half the rate it fell for instruction (Curtis, & Thornton 2014). Perhaps to their credit, in a market driven economy, colleges and universities have invested in new dormitories, fitness facilities and other amenities of college life.

On the other hand, online educational programs seem to strip away everything that is extraneous to the core student–teacher relationship. While significant, and perhaps often critical to the student success in online learning, from the student perspective, a myriad of factors stand in the way of having as rich an experience as traditional college students. In fact, the directors of online educational programs have to work hard to overcome all the disadvantages generated by online education's greatest benefit. Online education is often seen as a low-cost stepchild of the university; however, online students need as much or more support than students who study on campus. This chapter has outlined the kinds of support and the high level of communication that is required to sustain an online course and in the end develop an online program whose retention and graduation rates are at least as high as those for traditional on-campus programs. In short, online students simply don't know what they are getting themselves into, and faculty and staff have to be educated, as well, in order to engineer an environment that is supportive and gives students the best chance of success.

References

ALCTS Association for Library Collections and Technical Services (n.d.). Are you ready for online learning? Retrieved from http://www.ala.org/alcts/confevents/upcoming/web-course/webctready

Aslanian, C., & Clinefelter, D. (2012). *Online college students 2012: Comprehensive data on demands and preferences.* Retrieved from http://www.learninghouse.com/files/documents/resources/Online%20College%20Students%202012.pdf

Aslanian, C., & Clinefelter, D. (2013). *Online college students 2013: Comprehensive data on demands and preferences.* A joint project of The Learning House, Inc. and Aslanian Market Research. Retrieved from http://www.learninghouse.com/ocs2013-report/

Berg, S. (2013, March 22). Digital literacy for digital natives and their professors. Retrieved from https://www.hastac.org/blogs/steven-l-berg/2013/03/22/digital-literacy-dignital-natives-and-their-professors

Bolkan, J. (2013, June 24). *Report: Students taking online courses jumps 96% over 5 years.* Retrieved from http://campustechnology.com/articles/2013/06/24/report-students-taking-online-courses-jumps-96-percent-over-5-years.aspx

Browning, B. (2013, June 11). Q&A: What is a cohort? Retrieved from http://www.onlineschools.com/ask/what-is-a-cohort

Carr, C. (2014). College cheating? Equal time television show (video file). San Jose State University. Retrieved from https://www.youtube.com/watch?v=0ZbBjBNtuKk

Conrad, D. (2005). Building and maintaining community in cohort-based online learning. *Journal of Distance Education*, Spring, *20*(1), 1–20. Retrieved from http://files.eric.ed.gov/fulltext/EJ807822.pdf

Croft, N., Dalton, A., & Grant, M. (2011). Overcoming isolation in distance learning: Building a learning community through time and space. *CEBE Working Paper No. 18*, February. Retrieved from http://www.heacademy.ac.uk/assets/cebe/documents/resources/workingpapers/WorkingPaper_18.pdf

Curtis, J., & Thornton, S. (2014). Losing focus: The annual report on the economic status of the profession 2013–2014. *Academe*, March–April. Retrieved from http://www.aaup.org/file/zreport.pdf

Dray, B., Lowenthal, P. R., Miszkiewicz, M. J., Ruiz-Primoa, M. A., & Marczynskid, K. (2011). Developing an instrument to assess student readiness for online learning: A validation study. *Distance Education*, *32*(1), May, 29–47.

Fetzner, M. (2013). What do unsuccessful online students want us to know? *Journal of Asynchronous Learning Networks*, *17*(1), January. Retrieved from http://sloanconsortium.org/node/386931

Fishman, R., (2013, May 21). Technology and the next generation university: Issue brief. *New America Foundation.* http://higheredwatch.newamerica.net/publications/policy/technology_and_the_next_generation_university

Fotia, D., Holtzman, D., & Dagavarian, D. (2010, June 10). Developing student orientation modules of online education programs. Presented at the National Institute on the Assessment of Adult Learning, Atlantic City.

Gallant, B. (2008). Moral panic: The contemporary context of academic integrity. In *Academic integrity in the twenty-first century: A teaching and learning imperative.* Jossey-Basse: *ASHE Higher Education Report*, *33*(5), 1–12.

Hall, M. (2011). A predictive validity study of the revised Mcvay Readiness for Online Learning Questionnaire. *Online Journal of Distance Learning Administration*, *14*(3), Fall. Retrieved from http://www.westga.edu/~distance/ojdla/fall143/hall143.html

Harris, S. (2010, April 30). Top 10 Internet flame wars. Retrieved from http://www.toptenz.net/top-10-internet-flame-wars.php

Herbert, M. (2006). Staying the course: A Study in online student satisfaction and retention. *Online Journal of Distance Learning Administration*, *9*(4), Winter. Retrieved from http://www.westga.edu/~distance/ojdla/winter94/herbert94.htm

Ho Yu, C,, Digangi, S., Jannasch-Pennell, A. K., & Kaprolet C.(2008). Profiling students who take online courses using data mining methods. *Online Journal of Distance Learning Administration*, *11*(2) Summer. Retrieved from http://www.westga.edu/~distance/ojdla/summer112/yu112.html

Johnson, J., Rochkind J., Ott, A., & DuPont, S. (2014). With their whole lives ahead of them. *Public Agenda.* Retrieved from http://www.publicagenda.org/files/theirwholelivesaheadofthem.pdf

Johnson, T. (2013). Did i really go to Harvard if i got my degree taking online classes? *The Atlantic*, September. Retrieved from http://www.theatlantic.com/education/archive/2013/09/did-i-really-go-to-harvard-if-i-got-my-degree-taking-online-classes/279644/

King, E., & Alperstein, N. (2014). *How to thrive in an online graduate program*. Whitpaper. Retrieved from http://www.loyola.edu/Emergingmedia

Knight Commission on Intercollegiate Athletics (2010). Restoring the balance: Dollars, values and the future of college sports. Retrieved from http://www.knightcommission.org/component/content/article/22-press-room/583-june-17-2010-knight-commission-calls-for-college-sports-reform-recommends-public-transparency-of-finances-and-new-financial-incentives

Kolowich, S. (2014, January 16). Exactly how many students take online courses? *The Chronicle of Higher Education*. Retrieved from http://chronicle.com/blogs/wiredcampus/exactly-how-many-students-take-online-courses/49455

LoSchiavo, F., & Shatz, M. A. (2011). The impact of an honor code on cheating in online courses. *MERLOT Journal of Online Learning and Teaching*, 7(2) June. Retrieved from http://jolt.merlot.org/vol7no2/loschiavo_0611.htm

McKeown, K. D. (2012, March 13). *Can online learning reproduce the full college experience?* The Heritage Foundation Discussion Paper. Retrieved from http://www.heritage.org/research/reports/2012/03/can-online-learning-reproduce-the-full-college-experience

McNabb, L., & Olmstead, A. (2009). Communities of integrity in online courses: Faculty member beliefs and strategies. *MERLOT Journal of Online Learning and Teaching*, 5:2, June. Retrieved from http://jolt.merlot.org/vol5no2/mcnabb_0609.pdf

McVay, M. (2001). *How to be a successful distance education student: Learning on the Internet*. New York: Prentice Hall.

Middle States Commission on Higher Education (2011). Distance education programs: Interregional guidelines for the evaluation of distance education (online learning). Retrieved from http://www.msche.org/publications/Guidelines-for-the-Evaluation-of-Distance-Education-Programs.pdf

Miszkiewicz, M., & Dray, B. J. (2010, November 4). Surveying for online readiness: What does ready mean? 16th Annual Sloan Consortium International Conference on Online Learning. Retrieved from http://sloanconsortium.org/2010aln/presentation/surveying-online-readiness-what-does-ready-mean

The National Center for Educational Statistics (n.d.). College navigator. Retrieved from http://nces.ed.gov/collegenavigator/?q=University+of+Maryland+University+College&s=all&id=163204#retgrad

Northrup, P. (2002). Online learners? Preferences for interaction. *The Quarterly Review of Distance Learning*, 3(2), Summer. 219–26.

Perez-Pena, R. (2014, April 8). Best, brightest and rejected: Elite colleges turn away up to 95%. *The New York Times*. Retrieved from http://www.nytimes.com/2014/04/09/us/led-by-stanfords-5-top-colleges-acceptance-rates-hit-new-lows.html?ref=todayspaper&_r=0

Pfeifer-Luckett, R., & Skibba, K. (2011, November 11). How to build thriving online learning communities. Sloan-C International Conference on Online Learning. Retrieved from http://sloanconsortium.org/conferences/2011/aln/how-build-thriving-online-learning-communities

Rheingold, H. (1993). *Virtual communities: Homesteading on the electronic frontier*, Cambridge: MIT Press Cambridge.

Rhode, J. F. (2009). Interaction equivalency in self-paced online learning environments: An exploration of learner preferences. *International Review of Research in Open and Distance Learning*, February, http://www.irrodl.org/index.php/irrodl/article/view/603/1178

Rivard, R. (2013, March 8). Measuring the MOOC dropout rate. *Inside Higher Ed*. Retrieved from http://www.insidehighered.com/news/2013/03/08/researchers-explore-who-taking-moocs-and-why-so-many-drop-out#ixzz2z2x67d9P

Shackelford, J., & Maxwell, M. (2012). Contribution of learner? Instructor interaction to sense of community in graduate online education. *MERLOT Journal of Online Learning and Teaching*, 8(4), December. Retrieved from http://jolt.merlot.org/vol8no4/shackelford_1212.pdf

Sheehy, K. (2012, March 15). 10 business schools with the lowest acceptance rates. *U.S. News and World Report*. Retrieved from http://www.usnews.com/education/best-graduate-schools/the-short-list-grad-school/articles/2012/03/15/10-business-schools-with-the-lowest-acceptance-rates

Sheehy, K. (2012, October 24). States, districts require online ed for high school graduation: Requiring online classes may not benefit all students. *U.S. News and World Report*. Retrieved from http://www.usnews.com/education/blogs/high-school-notes/2012/10/24/states-districts-require-online-ed-for-high-school-graduation

Shulock, N. (2010). Beyond the rhetoric: Improving college readiness through coherent state policy. National Center for Public Policy in Higher Education, June. Retrieved from http://www.highereducation.org/reports/college_readiness/CollegeReadiness

stateuniversity.com (n.d.). 7 reasons why students drop out of college. Retrieved from http://www.stateuniversity.com/blog/permalink/7-Reasons-Why-Students-Drop-Out-Of-College.html#ixzz2zKNY8o1J

Tyler-Smith, K. (2006). Early attrition among first time elearners: A review of factors that contribute to drop-out, withdrawal and non-completion rates of adult learners undertaking elearning programmes," MERLOT Journal of Online Learning and Teaching, 2(2), June. Retrieved from http://jolt.merlot.org/documents/Vol2_No2_TylerSmith_000.pdf

United States Distance Learning Association (n.d.). Guidelines for online orientation. Retrieved from http://www.usdla.org/html/journal/NOV01_Issue/article03.html

UT Telecampus, WCET, & Instructional Technology Council (2009). Best practice strategies to promote academic integrity in online education version 2.0. Retrieved from http://www.wascsenior.org/files/Best_Practices_for_Academic_Integrity_in_Online_Education.pdf

Western Governors University (n.d.). Admissions requirements. Retrieved from http://www.wgu.edu/admissions/requirements.pdf

Wilson, M. (2008). An investigation into the perceptions of first-time online undergraduate learners on orientation events. MERLOT Journal of Online Learning and Teaching, 4(1), March. Retrieved from http://jolt.merlot.org/vol4no1/wilson0308.pdf

6

The Institutional Needs of
Online Programs

In the spring of 2014, the Maryland Higher Education Commission (MHEC) began to send letters to the presidents of colleges and universities around the country. The letter informed the presidents that as of June 2012, any institution of higher education that offered online education to a resident of Maryland had to register with MHEC, and their letter identified a student living in Maryland enrolled in one of their online programs. If that were so, the letter continued, the school would have three options. It could affirm that it enrolled the online student and pay a registration fee of $1000 and post a bond equal to five times the annual tuition, or it could express an interest in enrolling students from Maryland that meet the financial requirements. Or the institution could indicate that it would not accept students into its programs from Maryland (Straumsheim 2014).

The MHEC letter came in the middle of an ongoing national discussion about what role the Federal government should play, if any, in regulating institutions offering online education across state lines. While the proposed rules would make it easier for states to engage in reciprocity agreements to authorize online education—if an institution was authorized to offer online education in a state that was part of a reciprocity agreement, it would be automatically authorized in all the states that were party to the agreement—states that did not participate in those agreements may have to not only establish more precise authorizations, but also review the applications of hundreds of new schools, which many states may not have the resources to handle (Stratford 2014). Under the proposed rules, colleges would have to provide proof of authorization to be eligible for Federal financial aid. And states would not be allowed to exempt online education from their regulatory purview, as many do now (Field 2014). The net result is that many colleges and universities have to invest more resources into gaining state authorizations, and many states have to invest more resources into developing approval processes. At the same time, the demand for online education continues to grow.

The debate demonstrates the elevated status that online education has on the regulatory agenda. The irony of the MHEC letter, however, is that some of the college and university presidents who received the letter may not even be aware that their institution offers online classes to students in Maryland. In fact, they might not even be aware that their institution offers online classes at all. Not infrequently, the idea for teaching online has come from an individual faculty member or department and was approved without understanding the full implications of a move online.

The multiple levels of authorizations required for online programs were generally described in Chapter 2. State and accrediting agencies have, in most instances, set general standards that institutions—particularly in-state institutions—must meet in order to receive authorizations. These standards touch on every part of the operation of a college or university, ranging from the reconciliation of online learning and the institution's mission, to the availability of library services. But the institutional demands of online education stretch well beyond those spelled out in the regulatory documents. Launching and sustaining an online program may require changes in the operation of everything from the registration process to the records office to graduation ceremonies. Online programs may require personnel to be added to support the specific needs of online students. Online programs are generally marketed differently than traditional programs. And perhaps most profoundly, the introduction of online programs may reshape the character and identity of the institution. Online educational programs are not just about faculty and students. And they are not just about educational outcomes. In many ways, the addition of online educational programs can have a profound impact on the very nature of the institution of higher learning.

Standards Overview

While regulatory commissions have developed standards for evaluating online education, perhaps the most significant standards are those promoted by accrediting agencies. Those standards are utilized for evaluation during the accrediting process, and the single most important criteria in selecting an online program is ensuring that it is offered by an accredited institution (Sheehy 2012). Conversely, no respected college or university wants its reputation damaged or its accreditation threatened because of the way it mismanaged online learning. The Middle States Commission on Higher Education (2011) established nine "hallmarks" or standards of quality for online education. The first three hallmarks examine the role of online education within the general context of the institution as a whole, in particular whether the institution has reconciled and integrated online education with its overall mission and purpose. Therefore, online education has to be integrated into an institution's regular strategic planning processes, which would lead to the establishment of a roadmap for sustaining, developing and, if appropriate, expanding online programs.

The second set of hallmarks address the quality of the curricula and courses delivered to the students. The Commission demands that online curricula be coherent and academically rigorous, at least as rigorous as comparable traditional programs. Institutions need to develop procedures to assess whether the program goals are being achieved. And it is important for the institution to demonstrate that faculty teaching online have the support and training they need to be effective. The third set of hallmarks are concerned with student support and ensuring the academic integrity of the programs. Generally speaking, students taking courses online or who are enrolled in an online program should have the same access to the same student services as traditional students. Moreover, mechanisms need to be developed to ensure that students who take online classes are who they say they are. In the same vein, policies and programs will be established to cut down on cheating and to promote academic integrity.

Along with adherence to the general guidelines, colleges and universities will want to demonstrate to the accrediting agencies that they are meeting the hallmark standards. For example, to demonstrate that online education is consistent with the mission of the institution, the role of online education could be included in the institution's mission statement. Of course, for colleges and universities just beginning to offer programs online, it is very unlikely that this form of delivery will be included in the mission statement. And in most cases, to change a college's mission statement is a long and complex process. Nevertheless, by indicating that the mission statement could be a piece of evidence used to evaluate online programs, accrediting agencies have signaled that online programs must be addressed at the institutional level.

The evidence suggested by the Middle States Commission to demonstrate that an institution has met the standards is equally broad. They call on the faculty to have a role in the development and implementation of online learning. Approval and evaluation of online learning must adhere to the same procedures used elsewhere for course approval and evaluation. Evidence should demonstrate that the curricula are coherent and that program objectives can be easily described in appropriate documents and so on. Overall, the accrediting agencies want to make sure that the college or university has made an appropriate commitment to online learning at an institutional level (Office of College and University Approval and Evaluation n.d.).

Institutional Commitment

The need to build a vision for online programs, to incorporate that vision into the ongoing governance of the college or university and to shepherd a proposal through various approval processes was discussed in Chapter 2. But commitment to online learning has to be ongoing, which means that administrative processes have to be established that ensure the online education can be managed within the same parameters as on-campus programs.

Building a robust university-wide online educational strategy as well as specific programs is a cross-institutional, interdisciplinary, disruptive endeavor. Even a single program in a single department places demands across the university. The first, and perhaps most significant step, in setting the framework for building an institutional commitment to online education is to identify strong institutional leadership for the effort. Many institutions delegate the responsibility and leadership for online education to a director, perhaps of instructional or academic technology, or maybe the institution appoints a director of online and blended learning, often working with a small support staff within the information technology group (Polk State College 2012). Such an administrative structure can be useful to systematically implement an online program. A centralized office can effectively serve as a liaison to various stakeholders in the institution that are impacted by online education, and a centralized administration can provide support services to faculty to develop a program. However, a director of online learning is not appropriately positioned within the overall organization to drive the vision for online education. While directors of instructional technology and their colleagues have often been charged with facilitating online education, over time, programs have been administratively housed in several different ways. The most logical place for an online program is within the context of an academic department, and that is the most common institutional structure. But online programs are also frequently found in administrative units that focus primarily on continuing education. And to a growing degree, distance education efforts are being nurtured in specific units created specifically for online education (Paolucci, & Gambescia 2007). Each of those organizational approaches is sufficient for the operation of an individual online program; however, they usually are not sufficient to provide an institutional perspective. Academic departments are generally cloistered. Continuing education and distance education units, while perhaps valuable for producing revenue, are frequently seen as outside the main academic thrust of most colleges and universities. For online education to be integrated into the ongoing educational operation of an institution, it needs high-level administrative sponsorship. The chief education officer of the academic units offering an online program will have to publicly express support and commitment to the project or projects. If more than one academic unit has launched an online educational program, the academic officer who supervises all the units offering programs has to demonstrably support the initiatives, not only developing an administrative structure, but also laying out a vision for online education, placing it squarely within the mission of the college or university.

Perhaps the most direct method to cultivate ongoing public commitment to online education that potentially would meet the standards set by the accrediting agencies is to create a strategic plan specifically for online education. Developing a strategic plan for online educational programs at the institutional level is not unlike the strategic planning process in which many colleges and institutions already engage. A common methodology used has ten steps, starting with building a team and assigning tasks and ending with a strategic plan for periodic review. Moving from an ad hoc approach to a more systematic approach, the committee developing the strategic plan will, among other things, survey the current state of online education and ascertain the institution's strengths and weaknesses, articulate a vision, consistent with the college or university's mission, assess the resources available and resource needs, establish goals and objectives, and create a timeline for implementing the goals. Finally, an assessment plan, not only for online courses, but also for the program or programs, as well, should be put in place followed by the periodic review of the entire plan (Pisel 2008).

In 2014, the Ohio State University released the strategic plan of its Office of Distance Education and eLearning (Ohio State University 2014). An associate vice president heads the office, and its strategic vision is to "enhance education technology-empowered learning experiences." Its mission statement calls for it to "provide students on and off campus with an enriched educational experience for a lifetime of learning through technology-ready classrooms, centralized learning systems, innovations in technological pedagogy, and distance education opportunities." That said, the plan's first goal is to generate $25 million in revenue. The plan details the investment the university will need to make to achieve the goal. And it sets a goal of creating 200 open online courses. It is in that last goal that strategic planning differs dramatically from most campus-based planning processes. To develop 200 courses over the course of four years including ten undergraduate and five graduate programs requires the Office of Distance Education and eLearning recruit numerous faculty to develop programs and courses and teach online. In many cases, faculty that embrace online opportunities will relinquish tasks that will, going forward, have to be completed by others. The alternative to drawing on regular faculty, of course, is to hire part-time and affiliate faculty, but part-time faculty are a slender reed on which to base major new educational initiatives that are supposed to operate at a world class level. To its credit, The Ohio State University plan calls for $500,000 in faculty development funds and support for faculty to publish appropriate academic scholarship. It envisions producing 35 digital publications and opening a digital online bookstore. Interestingly, The Ohio State University already supports eight online programs ranging from a Master of Science in Welding Engineering and a Registered Nurse program, to a Bachelor of Science in nursing program. The university moved to a centralized planning process and implementation model, because initially there was inconsistent quality in the programs and inefficient use of resources. Moreover, without centralized oversight, the university could not be sure that all the programs complied with the appropriate regulations, putting the institution as risk. And if programs were developed haphazardly, the institution as a whole could not integrate online learning efficiently throughout the institution.

A centralized, strategic planning effort has many benefits; however, there is a downside when individuals responsible for moving the program forward need to motivate all the stakeholders to embrace the vision. The faculty involved in the program need to be willing to invest time and effort—and endure some risk as well—to make the program work. It is necessary for every supporting administrative office to be on-board; The Ohio State University strategic plan calls for a marketing plan, a project focused on electronic student records, and student services enhancements. As a strategic plan for online education involves so many moving parts, representatives from all the stakeholders across the university will be involved. Those representatives have a two-part task: making sure the plan does not call for practices beyond their capacity; and, preparing various constituencies for the demands of online education. At Virginia Tech, for example, the strategic plan was put together by a steering committee that included 20 members. With a charge from the deputy provost for undergraduate education, the committee included administrators, academic leaders, faculty and staff, and staff members of the Institute of Distance and Distributed Learning. Their strategic plan bridged the university's overall strategic plan, as well as connecting to the plans of individual units involved in distance learning (Virginia Tech 2012). Over time, to develop a vibrant, flexible online program, universities and colleges will engage in a strategic planning process that leads to the integration of online education with the university's overall mission and vision. But the plan is only one part of the challenge. Institutionally, colleges and universities also have to address a plethora of operational issues. Some are new issues posed by online students, such as the authentication of students. Some issues involve determining how to provide services that are routinely offered to students who come to campus to students who never set foot on campus. Some are ongoing issues that present themselves differently for online programs, including retention and assessment.

Student Authentication

Of the nine standards laid out by the accrediting agencies, the U.S. government mandates only one. The Higher Education Opportunity Act (HEOP) of 2008 requires that all institutions offering online courses verify that the person who registers for the course is actually the person who takes the course. In some ways, this mandate addresses the long-standing question of how to cut down on cheating in online classes (Sloan Consortium 2010). But for online education, student authentication starts at program registration. Are the students enrolling who they say they are? Different institutions have different approaches to verify students when they register for programs. The most common is to simply accept a registration with the appropriate information. Other institutions require new students to provide photo identification issued by a governmental body such as a driver's license or passport. The most stringent approach is to require students to submit a notarized statement attesting to their identity. Generally, if a college or university is going to subject a student to additional charges to verify their identity at registration, the school must clearly notify the students of those charges (Southern Association of Colleges and Schools 2012). While the idea that somebody may fraudulently present himself or herself presents a risk, making the enrollment and registration process too cumbersome also presents problems. Ease of registration is seen as one of the most important advantages of online education (Noel-Levitz, Inc. 2011). A complex and burdensome enrollment and registration process, no matter how well meaning it is, may be an inhibiting factor for some students wishing to enroll in an online course or program. Student authentication goes beyond registration and strikes to the very heart of online education. If nobody— faculty, administrators, or staff—at the institution ever meets the students how do they know if the students are who they say they are? Furthermore, how can colleges and universities be sure that the individual who has registered for the class is actually the person doing the work?

With HEOP and regulations that followed, many college and university administrators worried they would be required to put costly technology into place to verify online students. In fact, some institutions have invested in sophisticated technologies or partnered with companies capable of using advanced techniques to confirm somebody's identity (Bailie, & Jortberg 2009). For example, companies have introduced biometric and video recording solutions that can capture a typing signature or voiceprint. Of course, storing that level of personal identification raises significant privacy issues. Another approach involves recording students taking tests via Webcams, and as long as the video recordings are not saved, they do not pose privacy issues. In one very sophisticated and even elegant solution, the National American University, which started offering online education in 1998, partnered with the Axciom Corporation, one of the largest aggregators of third-party consumer data in the world, to use third-party information to verify the identities of online students. In the pilot, the student released some information that was checked against consumer databases. Based on the results, the student's identity was verified (2009).

While these sophisticated approaches help address the challenge of student authentication, they also require an investment in HEOP which mandates that programs use a secure login and pass code, proctor exams and have technology in place to verify identity. Safeguards were initially left to the college or university to cut down on academic fraud and cheating, and the adoption of minimum standards has been slow and uneven. In 2013, one survey indicated that around 80% of private, non-profit institutions did not use student authentication technology or proctor exams. For larger schools that use test centers for proctoring exams, approximately three-quarters require the students to pay for the costs of proctoring, which may be seen as a hidden cost for those programs.

UMUC was one of the schools that formerly required that undergraduate final exams be proctored, but like some other institutions, they no longer require it. Thomas Edison State College, however, has a proctored exam program for online courses that allows students to take the exam at home, for example. However, students would need a Webcam and microphone for monitoring purposes. All programs meet the HEOP requirement that students have a secure log in and password to the learning management system, and 90% use that system for quizzes and exams (UPCEA 2013).

The challenges of student identification and authentication promise to grow as the prevalence of online education grows and becomes more seamlessly integrated into higher education. Both high-tech and low-tech solutions such as requiring students to attend physical centers where exams could be proctored in person will grow. Over the next several years, it is anticipated that in many institutions of higher learning only minimal standards will be in place. In the interim, at an institutional level, colleges and universities can put into place as many policies and procedures as possible to cut down on academic fraud—when one person poses as another—and the other kinds of cheating. In general, to help cut down on cheating, institutions can develop vigorous and visible standards, and they can demonstrate a willingness to punish academic dishonesty when it is discovered. In one interesting approach, Kansas State University developed an online course about academic honesty. The course has five modules. The first focuses on integrity and student development. The second directly addresses the issue of academic integrity and the Kansas State honor code. The subject of the third module is plagiarism, and how to give credit to academic sources. The fourth module is about ethical decision-making, and the last delves into notions of moral development. The course is taught in weekly units over a ten-week period (Roberts, & Hai-Jew 2009). By requiring students to take the courses, Kansas State has sent a university-wide message about the importance of academic integrity. However, it is not clear if the course has had an impact on the level of academic honesty at Kansas State. Nevertheless, the course does undoubtedly make a contribution to the overall campus climate regarding cheating and ensures that the students know the rules and the expectations.

Student Services

In 2013, a joint legislative review committee sent a report to the Virginia legislature and the governor detailing the trends in spending at the state's 15 public universities. The study examines higher education from a variety of angles, but one finding stood out. Most of the growth in the cost for higher education in Virginia did not come from increased costs for instruction. In fact, the cost for instruction remained relatively flat for the period reviewed, accounting only for about one-third of the costs. The bulk of the expenditures were for ancillary services such as student services, including dining and the dormitories (Joint Legislative Audit and Review Commission 2013). The universities in Virginia were not an anomaly regarding the investment in student services. Over the past two years, student services and the growth in the number of administrators have been the two major factors in the jump in costs in higher education. The rationale behind increasing student services is straightforward. For students to succeed, they often need support in many areas outside of the classroom (Carlson 2014). And there is evidence to support the idea that robust student services can play a role in student retention and graduation rates, particularly at universities that serve a large number of students who are disadvantaged educationally or economically (Ehrenberg 2010). According to one report, an increase in spending on student services by $500 per student increased retention rates by 0.7%, twice the rate of increasing instruction or academic support services by a similar amount (Eisen 2009). Unfortunately, extending services to off-campus students generally and to online learners specifically has not been a part of the mainstream campus agenda. The issue is two-fold: first, it is not always clear what services should be available to students who do not come to campus; and second, whether an institution can flexibly, efficiently and appropriately provide those services (Shea, & Armitage 2002). As Shea and Armitage point out, the term "student services" encompasses many different functions ranging from financial aid and the bookstore to the career center (2002). Not infrequently, student services have been added at different campuses as a response to specific demands. And different services are housed and managed by different administrative offices in the university. The haphazard development and distribution of responsibilities for various student services can lead either to organizational silos of services or a generally chaotic administrative structure. To reduce the complexity implicit in understanding how student services are structured in specific institutions, Shea and Armitage clustered services that should be available to online learners into five categories or suites (2002). They include an administrative core, academic services, personal services, student life, and a general communications suite. Admission, registration and financial aid, for example, fall into the administrative core. Academic advising is part of the academic services suite. Career and personal counseling are in the personal services suite and so on. In total, Shea and Armitage identify more than 30 student services that should be available to online students (2002).

There are different approaches to providing appropriate services for online students. One approach, to address academic support services in institutions with large numbers of online students, is to develop specialized teams and case managers trained to address the needs of online students (Britto, & Rush 2013). For example, Lone Star College in Houston, Texas, is the fastest growing community college system in the country. In the fall of 2012, it had nearly 90,000 enrollments and approximately one-third of them were online students.

To respond to the needs of those online students, Lone Star launched what it called Lone Star College-Online (LSC-Online), a specialized department to provide support to online students and faculty teaching online. Initially responsible for course development and faculty/technology support, in 2011 a third unit was added—an Online Student Support Services group. This group launched three programs. They launched an early alert assistance system that was integrated into the learning management system to alert instructors when students had not logged into the system for a specified period. The second program was Online Advising for students who took no classes on campus at all and consequently had no access to the regular advising infrastructure. Online students could activate an instant chat button and ask a question that would be routed for a response to an available adviser. The third element in the Online Student Support Services group was a Case Management Advising unit that proactively reached out to at-risk students. The Online Student Support Services group also absorbed student services being offered to online students through other resources, including Online Readiness Assessment, Online Student Orientation, and Online Tutoring. The unit had a straightforward, two part mission. Its goals were to increase the retention and graduation rates and to ensure that online students had the same access to services as those students on campus. The unit also created an online newsletter to facilitate better communication with online learners. Student use of the system grew sharply in the first year and within a short period of time the LSC-Online was offering more services to online students for advising than residential students. The LSC-Online student support effort has not been in operation long enough to measure its impact on retention and student success but at the very least it brings added individualized attention to online learners. But the effort clearly has its limits. The program focuses on academic achievement and support. But student services across the board may need to be revamped to address the individualized needs of online students.

Library Services

Appropriately extending library services to online students is one of the most significant but challenging elements in creating a menu of services that online students need and deserve (Buchanan 2011). In fact, the Association of College and Research Libraries (ACRL) mandates that every student, faculty member, administrator and staff member is entitled to the full range of library services regardless of where they are located geographically (Standards for Distance Learning Library Services 2008). As many students already access the library remotely (if at all), and the use of actual library materials such as books or paper-based course reserves appears to be dropping, ensuring the library is prepared to meet the needs of online students may be relegated to an afterthought. Paradoxically, the reverse is true. As students increasingly have alternatives to physically visiting the library building, more and more library users should be thought of as distance learners, even if they reside on campus.

The first task to be addressed is training students how to effectively use the library. While it is commonplace for university libraries to provide extensive online access to their holdings, most students—residential or otherwise—usually need some sort of training. Students don't intuitively know what is in the library and which resources can help them. Many don't understand the role of the librarians in supporting their studies. And the idea of "going to the campus library" may never cross an online student's mind. On the other hand, as more students take classes online, libraries may have to examine their policies and procedures to ensure that they accommodate online students. For example, online students need credentials to be able to access material online, particularly if the university has a separate process to activate a library account. The library staff will likely need training to deal with students enrolled in online courses and programs, so they can get the same help and support as on-campus students. At a minimum, online chat services can be provided in time periods in which it would be convenient for online students to use. Given the growth of texting, some libraries also encourage online students to text questions to them. Finally, many libraries participate in consortia with other institutions, to which online students may have geographic access. Online students need to be apprised of such arrangements with other libraries. As online programs grow compelling libraries to review their policies and procedures, two issues can prove to be particularly vexing. The first is providing online students with physical artifacts, such as actual books. The rule of thumb is that online students need to be allowed to check books out of the library and receive the actual book. Libraries have taken different steps to address this problem. In some cases, libraries define a geographical area within which students are expected to come onto campus to pick material up. Universities with many locations may define those pick-up service areas for each of their campuses. For example, let's say an online student lives within 50 miles of the campus or any remote facility, the student would be expected to pick up the material at one of those locations. While not unreasonable, requiring physical pick-up under any circumstances can be awkward and inconvenient. Online learners may not know where the library is or be able to travel to the campus easily. Parking can also be an issue. And in any case, libraries have to provide books to students who live outside of these geographical service areas anyway. So most commonly, if an online student wants to check a book out of the library, the library will simply send the book through a delivery service without charge, generally within a two-to-three day window. Some universities will also cover the cost of returning the items as well. In that case, they use a less expensive return service, which may take two to three weeks. Putting a delivery system in place requires libraries to establish appropriate policies and procedures and those policies must be clearly communicated to the borrowers and the staff, and there must be sufficient and appropriately trained personnel to execute the procedures. Obviously, most online students will not be able to check out a book at the library; therefore, they must be given instructions on how to obtain a book or other printed material, and the staff must be trained to respond appropriately to those requests. Even small items, like the borrowing time for materials, may need to be modified to accommodate online students.

The second challenge libraries face is communicating the services they offer to online students (Nicholas, & Tomeo 2005). Many libraries have established specific Internet portals that cluster together much of the information and services that online students need; however, the pathways to those portals are often not obvious. Indeed, the terminology can be confusing with some colleges referring to distance education, others to online learning, yet others using eLearning and so on. The link to the specialized portal is often buried on the library home page under headings such as Academics, Academic Support for Library Resources. Since the resources available to online students are not easy to find and access, in many cases, students are not aware of those services.

At a minimum, libraries have to take several steps to begin to address the specialized needs of online educational programs. First, they must review their policies, procedures and staffing assignments to ensure that online students have the same access to library resources as other students. Second, they should gather the services available to online students in a single portal. Finally, libraries must aggressively communicate the availability of the services. As a first step, the link to the portal should be clearly communicated on the library's home page. Second, a link to the library's distance learning Internet portal should be integrated into the course pages in the LMS. Third, a link to the library's distance learning portal should be made visible on the course site for each online class. Finally, an orientation to the library and library services should be a part of the mandatory orientation for students, both when they first join the online program and then at the beginning of each class. There are several different ways in which the orientation can be implemented, including live online sessions with the appropriate librarian, videos describing the services and providing visual directions regarding how to utilize the library portal, or perhaps simply a series of clearly written explanations regarding how and when to use various library services. In any case, as with other parts of the orientation sequence, the online program will better serve students by giving them a concrete task to complete to demonstrate that they have completed the library module.

University libraries can move beyond simply being a repository of books and other materials for online learners. The library can be an ongoing touchstone for students, a service of the university that students may need to use class after class, and consequently can serve as a ongoing focal point for online students or an additional place of connection for students (Grabowsky 2013). In recognition of that opportunity, for example, some librarians have created a special position devoted to online education (Gandhi 2003). The distance education

(DE) librarians serve as a liaison and resource for the faculty teaching online classes, the programs or departments in which those courses are situated, and the learners. DE librarians can proactively reach out to every constituency ensuring that learners know how to appropriately use the library resources and that the materials the faculty need to be online are available and easy to find. They can manage questions of copyright and fair use and even assist faculty in devising appropriate assignments that rely on the library resources. DE librarians can also solicit feedback from their constituencies about interface design, the suitability of collections and other usage issues, and DE librarians can work with the other departments in the library and around campus to continually improve library services for online students.

Creating the position of DE librarian may be considered a significant change within the library's administrative structure. A major initiative some academic libraries have undertaken is to establish their role in teaching information literacy to online students. Through the lens of the library, the term distance literacy encompasses several elements including network literacy, computer literacy, media literacy, visual literacy and the more traditional expectations of literacy (Mnkeni-Saurombe 2012). One approach for libraries to assume leadership in the instruction of information literacy to online students is to embed academic librarians into online courses. An embedded librarian logs on to specific online courses through the LMS and is available to provide instruction and research skills training (Hoffman 2011). While this approach has yielded positive results, it is labor-intensive and difficult to scale up from pilot program to university-wide implementation. The Internet has had a profound and ongoing impact on library operations (IMLS 2008). The challenge of designing and implementing suitable services for online students is one more step in the process of adjusting to the digitally connected world. With regard to library services, the solutions devised to address the needs of online students may be appropriate for residential students as well.

Technology Services

The development of online educational programs places a greater demand on academic computing and technology support services than merely putting in place processes so students can use the technologies through which the programs operate; they have to be available to solve technology problems as they occur. The most critical responsibility for the technology group is to guarantee that the LMS and other tools are constantly online and operational. One of the primary advantages of online education is its flexibility, and that advantage disappears if students cannot access the LMS at their convenience. The ability to access the LMS is the very basis of a technology-based online education program. If students are unable log onto the LMS, they often have difficulty determining the problem—with their computer, their Internet connection, or the LMS. This leads to frustration and, as importantly, lost learning time.

To achieve acceptable levels of support, campus technology services may enter into service level agreements (SLAs) with the online program in which the expected levels of services are defined. Service level agreements, however, can range far beyond commitments for support personnel to be available at various times during the day. SLAs should clearly describe the capabilities of the LMS as well as the limitations. The SLA should describe the operation of the systems and reasonable user expectations. And lines of communication for the user community and the technology services group to interact will need to be established (Emory n.d.). Among the specific points a service level agreement can include are incident response times, incident escalation procedures, support commitments and reporting intervals. The SLA is the basic contract between IT services and those generally responsible for managing the online programs.

But the information technology team does not just provide a support function. While many faculty routinely use the LMS and other education technology in their classrooms, the learning environments in online educational programs are fundamentally and qualitatively different than the technology-enhanced classroom. In online education, the learning environment is completely defined by the technology. It is the role of the technology services group or the academic computing group to ensure that the learning management system and other technology tools are appropriate, up to date, useful to the faculty and easy for students to use. To fulfill this mission, the technology services team must continually monitor new developments in educational technology. Unlike the traditional classroom, learning management systems are constantly evolving; the technology support team must constantly evaluate when a system should be upgraded or even replaced.

Changing or upgrading an LMS is a complicated task and decisions regarding the LMS should not be made in a vacuum. A group that includes faculty teaching courses that are entirely online, faculty active in the implementation of the technology-enhanced classroom, faculty who are not yet involved in the application of technology in teaching and learning, and students, should be involved in the decision making process. But convening a small group of stakeholders is not enough. Academic computing teams should regularly survey each of the user communities—students and teachers—to understand what features of the LMS and other technology tools are working effectively and which are not. Comfort with the technology and ease of use are critical determinants of student satisfaction and success for online programs, and it is the responsibility of the technology support team that the technology infrastructure provides adequate support for both the faculty and students. Ultimately, the technology team working in conjunction with the program directors and other stakeholders should specify which applications will be supported within the learning management systems and which will not. In general, faculty should only use supported applications. The team—IT, faculty and program director—should meet on a regular basis to see what is working well and which technologies are not working as promised. A year-end meeting will serve as an opportunity to assess technologies and to determine which, if any, tools should be dropped in the coming semester and what tools might be added. As adding new tools may incur costs, such considerations should be made within the university's normal budget cycle. Having a technology-based learning environment can allow technology services to reach beyond their traditional boundaries.

Most learning management systems gather a significant amount of usage data. The technology support group can partner to determine how to use that data for program assessment and perhaps to help with student retention. As the technology services group monitors the development of the platform and applications for online learning, it must also institute a systematic purchasing program that is clearly communicated to the stakeholders, including the faculty. Among the key issues is that applications should be selected with specific learning outcomes in mind. They should be tested. In most situations, selected faculty or other users should be able to pilot the new software first (Curriculum Associates 2014).

Online program development places significant new demands on the Information Technology unit as well as the technology infrastructure itself. In some cases, colleges and universities will not be able to meet those demands but still want to develop online programs. To respond to that demand, third-party providers have emerged that offer a complete technology platform for online courses and programs. For example, companies like Udacity, which started as providers of MOOCs, have shifted their business model to offer platform services to colleges and universities that want to offer online courses. Other companies provide a more extensive range of services. Known as bundled services providers, companies like Deltek, which was bought in 2012 by educational publisher John Wiley and Sons for $220 million, SchoolNet and Embanet, which were both bought by Pearson for a combined total of nearly $900 million in 2011 and 2012, provide a full range of services for online education from course development and support, to marketing, student recruiting and admission, student support and retention, and data management and assessment. These companies generally take a percentage of the tuition generated by the courses over an extended period of time (futureofhighered.org n.d.).

Opting for a bundled service provider (BSP) could prove to be a viable option for many colleges and universities just launching online programs or rapidly expanding their offerings. Because BSPs are focused on creating the appropriate ecosystem for successful online learning, they can invest more readily in the needed technology infrastructure and the human resources required. And since they have a strong interest in the success of the program, they can assist schools in marketing as well. But working with a BSP has tradeoffs. In addition to the potentially high fees, BSPs generally require long-term contracts, which can in some ways cut down on an institution's flexibility over time. Moreover, since BSP fees are generally calculated as a percentage of tuition, the BSP may be less interested in supporting smaller, more targeted programs that will generate less revenue. Opting for a third party either for the technology platform or for a bundle of services places different kinds of demands on colleges and universities. The contract with the service provider has to be managed and that can require the attention of many different offices in the university. A BSP, for example, has to interact with every department that provides the same service—admissions, technology services, marketing and so on. The BSP may want to deal with a single point of contact at the university and the university official managing the BSP contract will have to consult widely to make sure the BSP is meeting all the needs and expectations. Since the primary service the BSP provides is the technology platform, it may seem that the technology services group or the CIO, perhaps, should be the main point of contact, but that may not be the case in many situations.

Accessibility

Building and supporting the appropriate technology ecosystem for an online educational program requires planning and investment. One of the critical areas to address is accommodating students with disabilities. Federal law requires that colleges and universities provide students with disabilities equal access and equal opportunity to all their programs, including online programs. Students must have the same benefits as other students; however, colleges and universities should not offer separate programs and activities to accommodate people with disabilities, except under specific circumstances. As technology has become more complex throughout the university, the issue of accommodating individuals with disabilities has become more complex and is not limited to online education. Many university functions and services are now provided online, and colleges and universities have to make those services accessible to everyone. Every division of a university has to be alert to disabilities, which can no longer be suitably addressed by a single office (Betts 2013).

The use of technology to communicate across many different functions within the university represents one of the major advantages of online education. However, guaranteeing access to people with disabilities represents a pressing issue. More than 10% of all post-secondary school students have a disability—either physical or mental, one associated with a communication function such as vision or hearing, or a specific learning disability (U.S. Government Accountability Office 2009). To receive accommodations, the student must report and document the disability with an appropriate person or office to request accommodations. The institution is then obligated to assess the impact of the disability on student performance and determine corrective actions. There are many different approaches to addressing disabilities issues. There is a range of technical solutions that address a broad range of disabilities. For example, screen readers can be used to convert text to speech, for vision-impaired students. Along the same lines, speech recognition software can convert speech to text for the hearing impaired. Mobile technologies are routinely incorporating more flexible control mechanisms such as gesture-based interfaces (Betts et al. 2013).

Unfortunately, many of the key technologies for online education were not developed with accessibility in mind. For example, many learning management systems were designed with the idea that users would be able to see the screen, the mouse would be the main navigational device, and that users would be able to glance over the entire screen and understand how to find what they need. None of those assumptions necessarily applies to disabled students. In fact, each activity in an LMS can pose significant difficulties for students with disabilities. For example, students may have trouble following the scroll of comments in a chat room or if papers are uploaded and graded online with comments in different-colored text, an adaptive technology may not be able to segregate the comments from the other text. Online forms also can present problems for screen readers. Along the same lines, certain kinds of online content are more accessible than others. For example, PDFs do not actually contain any text and are impossible for screen readers to decipher. Documents marked up in HTML are easier for adaptive devices to convert to speech than Microsoft Word documents. And making Adobe Flash content accessible is extremely challenging (CANnect 2014).

Accessibility is only part of the equation, however. Usability is equally important. Accessibility means that content is within reach of users. Usability refers to content that can actually be utilized with equal ease by everybody (Horton 2005). Students with disabilities should be able to access content on an equal footing with other students, and they should not be at a disadvantage in navigating a course Web site, or be disadvantaged in any other way. The most prudent approach to developing online educational content and platforms that are both accessible and useable is to adhere to the seven principles of universal design for Web pages and determine how they can be applied to address the needs for disabled students. For example, the first principle of universal design is equitable use—that students should have access to the same attractive and intuitive interface. In the context of online programs, that may mean that Web sites can be navigated by keyboard as well as mouse or with the assistance of a screen reader. The second principle of universal design is flexibility in use, which means, among other things, that students should be able to use a wide range of access devices that address different capabilities (CANnect 2014). As with other aspects of addressing the needs of people with disabilities in an increasingly technologically driven environment, the need to apply the principles of universal design to Web development is not limited to online education. In fact, adhering to the principles of universal design benefits all students (Horton 1997). However, the stakes are higher with online education because common solutions such as hiring a student to read or take notes, for an online disabled student is more difficult, if not impossible, to implement. Nor can disabilities issues be addressed within the development process for an individual course. Compliance with the Americans for Disabilities Act poses a major liability for online education and the responses required to address that liability must be institutional (Parry 2010).

Retention

Perhaps the primary institutional adjustment to nurture online education is to improve retention rates. The dramatic MOOC drop-out rates, which typically reach 85 to 90%, have captured national attention and in some ways have called into question the limits of online education. Like many other aspects of MOOCs, the drop-out rates need to be scrutinized and understood—one insight, for example, is that because it is very easy to enroll in a MOOC, many people sign up without really having a deep commitment to taking the course. High MOOC drop-out rates, however, are not generally applicable to online education in general (Haber 2013). While not as alarming as with MOOCs, the drop-out rate for online education does run higher than the drop-out rate for traditional education, perhaps as much as 15 to 20% more (Parry 2010). Improving retention rates for online students is not an easy task. In fact, a study by professors at Kennesaw State University showed that some of the more common approaches to improving retention, such as professors emailing students regularly during the semester, were not sufficient to reduce the drop-out rate (Brunset 2010).

Of course, as discussed earlier, students drop out from online courses for many reasons and not all of those reasons can be addressed. As many students take online courses because their life circumstances do not allow them to attend traditional courses; their life circumstances may intrude on their studies in a way that prevents their completion. As they may access advising and other student services less, online students may take courses for which they are not prepared, which can lead to them dropping out. Or online students, like MOOC students, may have less of a commitment to completing their education than those in traditional settings.

Despite the personal reasons that may lead a person to quit prior to the completion of a course or a program, institutions can take several steps that potentially can help improve retention. One promising approach is to provide ongoing, proactive student mentoring and monitoring. This strategy involves going well beyond simply having the teacher reach out periodically to students, which increases the teaching burden significantly. Rather, such an approach involves building a support staff that engages regularly with students who are identified as at risk of dropping out. For example, the University System of Georgia established a 14-person support team that calls students to guide them to the academic support services they can access to help them succeed. The initiative has helped the University of West Georgia raise its retention rate for online students from 68% in 2007 to 92% in 2012; putting it ahead of the 91% retention rate the university has for traditional students (Zatynski 2013).

Interestingly, the structure of online educational programs can make it easier to identify at risk students. Learning management systems track when students actually log onto the system and students who do not log on for extended periods of time can be flagged and contacted. In a traditional class, a student may inadvertently miss a class or two because of circumstances. But given the flexibility of online education, students' failure to engage with the course material is a troublesome signal. Implementing an early warning and system of intervention is not without costs. Either the faculty member has to be trained to access the LMS usage statistics and then report at-risk students to a support team, or the support team has to monitor student engagement and query the professor about the appropriate intervention. Expecting the professor to intervene extends faculty responsibilities beyond traditional boundaries and therefore raises the burden for faculty teaching online.

A second method for increasing retention rates has come from research into MOOCs. One predictor as to whether a person will complete a MOOC is the degree to which the student is socially integrated with other students (Yang, Tanmay, Adamson, & Penstein Rose n.d.). Students in MOOCs build social relationships through their interactions on discussion boards. The research suggests that if discussion boards are structured in a way that fosters the development of bonds among students, retention rates increase. However, the best predictor for retention is student success (Wilson, & Allen n.d.). In the same way that students with higher grade point averages in high school generally perform better in college, students who have already done well in college level courses are more likely to succeed in online classes. Creating an environment for success in online education, however, is not automatic. In traditional education, the overall ecology and atmosphere of a college education can help students to persist in their studies. Many students actually enjoy coming to campus. They take pride that they are a student at a specific university. Older and non-traditional students often look forward to that set period in which they can focus on their studies and not their day-to-day responsibilities. Traditional students have often built their social lives around being in school and may participate in a wide range of extra-curricular activities that helps keep them in school. None of those non-academic motivations to remain in school exists in online education and strategies need to be devised to substitute for them.

Assessment

Improving retention rates is a fundamental challenge facing online education, but assessment is an essential element of providing a high quality online education that is meaningful to students. Assessment for online education has to be carried out on three levels—the program level, the technology level and the institutional level. Ongoing program assessment has emerged as an issue throughout both K-12 and higher education. A wide variety of stakeholders want educational institutions to be able to demonstrate that students actually achieve something specific. On the programmatic level, assessment generally looks at the program's learning aims and is geared to defining and applying measures that can demonstrate how well those learning aims are met. But program assessment can and perhaps should address a broader set of questions (Miller, & Leskes 2005). A program must be assessed both as a whole and as a sum of the parts. Are the individual courses and the course sequences and sub-categories appropriate and clearly connected to the program learning aims and outcomes? How do the program's aims and outcomes fit into the overall curriculum and student learning experience? The data for assessment can come from both direct and indirect measures. Students, for example, can be surveyed during and after completion of the program, and selected students can be asked to participate in exit interviews. Direct measures can include having students create a portfolio of work during the program, perhaps an ePortfolio, and have third party reviewers examine the work for evidence that the program goals have been achieved. Capstone courses and major projects and theses can also serve as direct evidence for assessment purposes.

The need for ongoing monitoring of the technological infrastructure was discussed earlier in this chapter. But the assessment and evaluation of technology should also be linked to the program assessment. Do the technology platform and associated tools support the learning goals? For example, if a portfolio of work is going to be used as direct evidence in program assessment, is appropriate ePortfolio technology in place? Have the faculty been alerted to the ePortfolio's function and how to incorporate assignments that may be used for assessment into their courses? Do students know how to upload those assignments appropriately into the ePortfolio? The assessment process should reflect the use of technology in online educational programs, as technology is closely linked to program learning aims and outcomes.

Finally, as discussed in Chapters 1 and 2, online educational programs represent a major shift and new direction for most colleges and universities. The role of online education should be delineated in the institution's strategic plan. Moreover, colleges and universities, as discussed earlier, can develop strategic plans specifically for online programs. Those plans should be assessed and reviewed on a regular basis to measure if goals have been achieved of if new goals should be determined. The purpose of this type of assessment is to create institutional norms for online programs across the college or university. In addition to the traditional levels of assessment, online education produces new forms of data that could allow new assessment questions to be asked and answered (Prineas, & Cini 2011). Learning management systems capture a huge amount of data on every student. There is a record of when students log onto the system and the length of each session. Every word posted to a discussion board or blog is captured. The LMS details which files students access and when. If tests are given online, the learning management system has a record of the grades, one of the simplest forms of assessment. Time spent on assignments in the LMS can provide a measure of student engagement. Using advanced data analytics and data mining techniques, this data can be used to better understand student learning experiences. Early efforts geared to identify students at risk of dropping out were developed at Purdue University. Their system consists of monitoring 20 data points and a student receives a green, yellow or red signal, indicating levels of engagement in a course. The novel aspect of the initiative is that the signal is not generated by performance on graded assignments alone but on engagement with course material and involvement in course activities as well. The ability to capture statistics on the behavior and performance of each student opens many other possibilities for assessment. The time it takes for students to complete self-paced assignments can provide evidence of mastery of a specific skill or body of content. Learning management systems provide feedback not available in the traditional classroom. If that data is aggregated, it can also provide program level feedback. The application of large-scale data mining and analytic techniques to the data amassed by learning management systems, or learning analytics, is still in its early stages. And as LMSs are increasingly used in the traditional classroom, the data can be useful for assessment across higher education. The potential benefit and impact for online program development is clear.

Intellectual Property

As online education matures, new issues will emerge that will have to be addressed on an institutional level. Intellectual property rights promises to be one of the more complex ones. An example of what may emerge comes from the experience of Sebastian Thrun, who offered his first MOOC in artificial intelligence—one of the first courses that thrust MOOCs into the public eye and online education onto the public agenda. Several observers wonder, if Thrun developed the course while he was a professor at Stanford University, whether Stanford owned the intellectual property rights to the video lectures developed for the course. The answer was that Thrun had already left Stanford by the time the course was offered, and the course was not hosted on Stanford servers. But that raised another question. Though the course was not branded as a Stanford course, it was marketed as being nearly identical to the one offered at Stanford (Salmon 2012).

The issue of who owns what material in online courses is just coming into focus. When Cathy Davidson, a professor at Duke University and a leader in online education, moved to the City University of New York, Duke allowed her to take the name of her MOOC, "History and Future of (Mostly) Higher

Education," with her. Duke made that determination in light of guidelines that allowed professors to keep the rights to courses that Duke funds (Shah 2014). Indeed the issue regarding who owns the content of online courses has been percolating at least since 2000, when 14 leaders in higher education met to discuss the issue at the Biltmore Hotel in Miami, Florida. The group sought to understand if the content developed for online courses would have commercial appeal, and therefore a need for copyright protection, and if so, who should own the rights to the material. The outcome of their deliberations was inconclusive, asserting that universities need to develop policies regarding intellectual property rights, and that those policies need to be communicated early in the course development process. Unfortunately, many colleges and universities are not prepared to easily address that issue (Twigg 2000).

In most settings, professors are seen as the owners of the content of their courses, but that content may consist of little more than their lecture notes and slides. Online courses, however, may require a much more significant investment from the university, including video production. In light of that investment, should the university also retain some rights to the content? The situation becomes more complicated in online programs that are not structured as one-off courses like a MOOC, but are part of an ongoing program. If another instructor replaces the one who developed the course, should the second professor be able to use lectures or other material that has already been recorded? Does the content, including the lectures, reside with the university and the course, or with the faculty member who created them? What rights do professors have to the use of their own images? Can podcasts or lectures be largely retained but still modified by subsequent instructors? These are not merely theoretical questions. In 2011, Jeff MacSwan and Kellie Rolstad, former professors at Arizona State University, learned that another professor without attribution or authorization was teaching an online course they had developed. MacSwan and Rolstad, who by that time had moved to the University of Maryland, sued for $3 million, claiming ASU had violated its own intellectual policy guides that define online course content as scholarly work (Basu 2012).

Developing intellectual property guidelines for online course content is part of a larger ongoing dialogue between faculty and institutions about intellectual property (Nelson 2012). The growth of online education requires a wide-ranging discussion to assess if the current intellectual property rights policy is adequate and sufficient to address the salient issues involved in online course development. Some of the critical issues involve fair use of materials, use of the university's name, ownership, student rights and licenses. With such a broad array of issues, the development or revision of intellectual property rules requires collaboration of faculty, academic administrators, the legal team and others. The results of their deliberations must be clearly communicated to and approved by the relevant stakeholders (Cate, Drooz, Hohenbert, & Schulz 2007).

Marketing

As with other areas, online program development presents specific issues in marketing as well. On one level, online programs can call for a change in marketing tactics. Students who may be responsive to studying online generally can be reached through online marketing tactics and social media. As prospective students search for appropriate programs, how and where a program shows up in search engine results can play an important role in generating leads. Moreover, the Web sites for online programs have to be informational, easy to navigate and interactive. Since many individuals access the Internet through their smart phones, Web sites for online programs should be optimized for mobile and not too text intensive or have a lot of high resolution images. But the tactics for marketing an online program are easy to address and can be a part of the ongoing discussion about marketing generally. But the stakes for a university when it launches an online program are much higher than simply attracting students. Online education shifts an institution's potential market reach and consequently can have a profound impact on its image.

Universities like Arizona State and Southern New Hampshire State have invested heavily in national advertising campaigns. They may now be on the agenda—top of mind awareness in advertising parlance—for students who may never have considered enrolling in one of those schools before. By aggressively promoting their online programs, Arizona State, Southern New Hampshire State, and many other colleges and universities have changed their public profile. The challenge is to maintain or improve the brand equity they have built over the years. In many cases, long established non-profit colleges and universities have not been able to effectively differentiate their online offerings from those offered by online-only universities, for-profit universities and non-accredited universities. They often use the same terminology and make the same claims on their Web sites (Adams, & Eveland n.d.).

If not marketed correctly, the move online could hold considerable risk for institutions. A high-profile experiment in online education was initiated by the Georgia Institute of Technology partnered with Udacity and AT&T to offer a completely online master's program in engineering for only $6000, compared to the $26,000 plus the school normally charges (Empson 2013). The idea, of course, is to attract many more students to its program. The Georgia Tech engineering program is currently ranked very high, but what happens to its reputation if the distinction between its traditional program and the online engineering program is blurred? For colleges and universities that have historically attracted students from regional or local markets, the move online will be their first foray into promoting their name nationally. The marketing campaign is the vehicle these schools have at their disposal to define what their name will mean to completely new audiences and potential new students.

Conclusion

A commitment to developing high quality online education programs requires a deep commitment from many different stakeholders across the institution. Indeed, most approaches to assessing the quality of an online educational program have the institutional dimension as a key factor for success (Shelton 2011). In its landmark study "Quality on the Line: Benchmarks for Success in Internet-based Distance Learning," the Institute for Higher Education Policy laid out 24 benchmarks for measuring online educational programs (Merisotis, & Phipps 2000). Those benchmarks could be grouped into several major themes. The institutional benchmarks were listed first and included using appropriate technology, the development of quality standards, and security and authentication measures.

Since that report was issued, online educational programs have proliferated and the demands on institutions have grown proportionally. In response, colleges and universities have to work strategically and tactically. On the strategic level, institutions must understand where online education fits into the overall educational mission. They need to cultivate sensitivity to the demands placed on the institution by online programs and provide support for the adjustments that will be needed to meet the needs of online students. A deep commitment to online learning may require an investment in time and money from virtually every part of the institution.

On a tactical level, every office that has contact with students has to review their operations, policies and procedures to ensure they provide the same level of service to online students as they do to traditional students. In the case of key academic components such as the library and support mechanisms like technology services, online education requires serious self-evaluation. High quality online education relies on an appropriate technology platform and support services and the library can serve as an important, ongoing focal point for online students. In many cases, such as with the library and the use of assessment data from learning management systems, the adjustments made for online education can be used to benefit face-to-face learning as well. At its best, online learning for most institutions will be incorporated seamlessly into the institution's overall educational effort.

Institutional change in higher education is often difficult. Colleges and universities are not organized in a way that allows them to move too quickly. Developing high quality online programs requires institutions of higher learning to move forward at several levels ranging from the strategic vision for the school to the intellectual property policies, and the enrollment processes and beyond. But everything does not have to be done at once. In many cases, individual faculty members have been able to conduct very successful online classes on their own and individual departments have launched successful programs without much support from other parts of the university. While individual initiative is a way to move into online programs at the beginning, building a sustainable program and a sustainable online infrastructure requires a deep institutional commitment.

References

Adams, J., & Eveland V. (n.d.). Marketing online degree programs: How do traditional-residential programs compete? Retrieved from http://pilotmedia.com/adams/xPDF/market_online.pdf

Arnold, K. (2010). Signals: Applying academic analytics. *Educause Quarterly, 33*(1), November 1. Retrieved from http://www.educause.edu/EDUCAUSE+Quarterly/EDUCAUSEQuarterly MagazineVolum/ SignalsApplyingAcademicAnalyti/199385

Bailie, J. L., & Jortberg, M. A. (2009). Online learner authentication: Verifying the identity of online users. *MERLOT Journal of Online Learning and Teaching, 5*(2), June. Retrieved from http://jolt.merlot.org/vol5no2/bailie_0609.htm

Basu, K. (2012). Loss of control. *Inside Higher Ed*, March 14. Retrieved from http://www.insidehighered.com/news/2012/03/14/former-asu-professors-threatens-litigation-over-online-course-ownership#ixzz30O3tD6UF

Betts, K. (2013). Legal perspective: Q&A with Daniel F. Goldstein. *Journal of Asynchronous Learning Network, 17*(3), October. Retrieved from http://sloanconsortium.org/jaln/v17n3/legal-perspective-qa-daniel-f-goldstein

Betts, K., Welsh, B., Pruitt, C., Hermann, K., Deietrich, G., Watson, T. L., Trevino, J. G., Brooks, M., Cohen, A. H., & Coombs, N. (2013). Understanding disabilities & online student success. *Journal of Asynchronous Learning Networks, 17*(3) October. Retrieved from http://sloanconsortium.org/jaln/v17n3/understanding-disabilities-online-student-success

Britto, M., & Rush, S. (2013). Services for online students. *Journal of Asynchronous Learning Networks, 17*(1). Retrieved from http://sloanconsortium.org/jaln/v17n1/developing_and_implementing_comprehensive_student_support_services_online

Brunset, B. (2010, October 20). Curtailing dropouts at online universities. *U.S. News and World Report*. Retrieved from http://www.usnews.com/education/onlineeducation/articles/2010/10/20/curtailing-dropouts-at-online-universities

Buchanan, E. A. (2011). Institutional support for distance education. Retrieved from http://learningdesign.psu.edu/deos/deosnews10_8.pdf

CANnect (2014). How-to guide for creating accessible online learning content: Web accessibility for online learning. Retrieved from http://projectone.cannect.org/

Carlson, S. (2014, February 5). Administrator hiring drove 28% boom in higher-ed work force, report says. *Chronicle of Higher Education*. Retrieved from https://chronicle.com/article/Administrator-Hiring-Drove-28-/144519/

Cate, B., Drooz, D., Hohenbert, P., & Schulz, K. (2007). Creating intellectual property policies and current issues in administering online courses. The National Association of College and University Attorneys. Retrieved from http://www.insidehighered.com/sites/default/server_files/files/nacuaPDF.pdf

Curriculum Associates (2014). Guide to purchasing EDTECH the right way: 4 steps to making a successful EDTECH purchase. Retrieved from http://www.prnewswire.com/news-releases/new-guide-to-edtech-procurement-released-240333701.html

Ehrenbert, R. (2010, August 23). Student services matter. *The New York Times*, http://www.nytimes.com/roomfordebate/2010/08/22/why-are-college-students-studying-less/student-service-expenditures-matter

Eisen, B. (2009, July 29). Cut student services? Think again. *Inside Higher Ed*. http://www.insidehighered.com/news/2009/07/29/gradrate#ixzz2zrImrlY9.

Emory University (n.d.) Technology services service level agreement. Retrieved from http://it.emory.edu/documentation/Learning%20Management%20System%20SLA.pdf

Empson, R. (2013, May 15). Georgia Tech teams up with Udacity, AT&T to offer $6K Master's degree in computer science, entirely online. *Tech Crunc*. http://techcrunch.com/2013/05/15/top-10-engineering-college-teams-up-with-udacity-att-to-offer-6k-online-masters-degree-in-computer-science/

Feeney, M. (2004). Centralizing information about library services and resources: Delivering the library to users at any distance. *Internet Reference Services Quarterly* 9, 129–46.

Field, K. (2014, March 27). Negotiators tussle over proposed rule to compel state scrutiny of online ed. *The Chronicle of Higher Education*. futureofhighered.org (n.d.) The "promises" of online higher education: Profits campaign for *The Future of Higher Education*. Retrieved from http://futureofhighered.org/promises-online-higher-education-profits/#_edn11

Gandhi, S. (2003). Academic librarians and distance education: Challenges and opportunities. *Reference & User Services Quarterly, 43*(2) Winter,138–54 http://web.simmons.edu/~benoit/lis403/readGandhi.pdf

Grabowsky, A. (2013). Information and interaction needs of distance students: Are academic libraries meeting the challenge? *Georgia Library Quarterly 50*(2), http://digitalcommons.kennesaw.edu/cgi/viewcontent.cgi?article=1662&context=glq

Haber, J. (2013, November 25). MOOC attrition rates—running the numbers. *Huffington Post College.* http://www.huffingtonpost.com/jonathan-haber/mooc-attrition-rates-runn_b_4325299.html

Hoffman, S. (2011). Embedded academic librarian experiences in online courses: Roles, faculty collaboration, and opinion. *Library Management, 32*(6/7), 444–56. Retrieved from http://www.emeraldinsight.com.ezp.lndlibrary.org/journals.htm?issn=0143-5124&volume=32&issue=6&articleid=1939464&show=html#sthash.qy6xgiRE.dpuf

Horton, S. (1997). The 7 Principles: A universal design approach to Web usability. Center for Excellence in Universal Design. Retrieved from http://www.universaldesign.ie/exploreampdiscover/the7principles.

Horton, S. (2005). Access by design: A guide to universal usability for Web designers. Berkeley, CA: New Riders Press.

IMLS (2008) The IMLS national study on the use of libraries, museums and the Internet. Retrieved from http://interconnectionsreport.org/

Joint Legislative Audit and Review Commission (2013). Trends in higher education funding, enrollment and student costs report to the Governor and General Assembly, State of Virginia. Retrieved from http://jlarc.virginia.gov/reports/Rpt441.pdf

Merisotis, J., & Phipps, R. (2000). Quality on the line: Benchmarks for success in Internet-based distance learning. Institute for Higher Education Policy. Retrieved from http://www.ihep.org/Publications/publications-detail.cfm?id=69

Middle States Commission on Higher Education (2011). Distance education programs: Interregional guidelines for the evaluation of distance education (online learning). Retrieved from http://www.msche.org/publications/Guidelines-for-the-Evaluation-of-Distance-Education-Programs.pdf

Miller, R., & Leskes, A. (2005). Levels of assessment: From the student to the institution. Association of American Colleges and Universities. Retrieved from https://www.aacu.org/pdf/LevelsOfAssessment.pdf

Mnkeni-Saurombe, N. (2012). Information literacy: A cornerstone of open distance learning. A University of South Africa perspective. Retrieved from http://iflasatellitetampere2012.files.wordpress.com/2012/08/session3b_mnkeni-saurombe.pdf

Nelson, C. (2012, June 21). Whose intellectual property? *Inside Higher Ed.* Retrieved from http://www.insidehighered.com/views/2012/06/21/essay-faculty-members-and-intellectual-property-rights#ixzz30O5kZIo6

Nicholas, M., & Melba, T. (2005). Can you hear me now? Communicating library services to distance education students and faculty. *Online Journal of Distance Learning Administration, 8*(2), Summer. *Retrieved from* http://www.westga.edu/~distance/ojdla/summer82/nicholas82.htm

Noel-Levitz, Inc. (2011) *National online learners priorities report.* Retrieved from https://www.noellevitz.com/upload/Papers_and_Research/2011/PSOL_report%202011.pdf

Office of College and University Approval and Evaluation (n.d.) Review process for approval of programs in the distance education format. Retrieved from http://www.highered.nysed.gov/ocue/aipr/guidance/gpr17.html#b

Ohio State University (2014) Strategic plan 2014–2018, The Office of Distance Education and eLearning. Retrieved from https://odee.osu.edu/sites/default/files/odee-strategicplan.pdf

Paolucci, R., & Gambescia, S. (2007). Current administrative structures used for online degree program offerings in higher education. *Online Journal of Distance Learning Administration, 10*(3), Fall. http://www.westga.edu/~distance/ojdla/fall103/gambescia103.htm

Parry, M. (2010, September 22). Preventing online dropouts: Does anything work? *The Chronicle of Higher Education.* Retrieved from http://chronicle.com/blogPost/blogPost-content/27108/

Parry, M. (2010, November 12). ADA compliance is a "major vulnerability" for online programs. *Chronicle of Higher Ed.* Retrieved from http://chronicle.com/blogs/wiredcampus/ada-compliance-a-major-vulnerability-for-online-programs/28136

Pisel, K., (2008). A strategic planning process model for distance education. *Online Journal of Distance Learning Administration, 11*(2), Summer. Retrieved from http://www.westga.edu/~distance/ojdla/summer112/pisel112.html

Polk State College (2012). Distance learning strategic plan. Retrieved from http://www.polk.edu/wp-content/uploads/Distance-Learning-Strategic-Plan.pdf

Prineas, M., & Cini, M. (2011). Assessing learning in online education: The role of technology in improving student outcomes. National Institute for Learning Outcomes Assessment. Retrieved from http://www.learningoutcomeassessment.org/documents/onlineed.pdf

Roberts, C. J., & Hai-Jew, S. (2009). Issues of academic integrity: An online course for students addressing academic dishonesty. *MERLOT Journal of Online Learning and Teaching*, 5(2) June. Retrieved from http://jolt.merlot.org/vol5no2/roberts_0609.pdf

Salmon, F. (2012, January 31). Udacity's model. *Reuters U.S. Edition* Retrieved from http://blogs.reuters.com/felix-salmon/2012/01/31/udacitys-model/

Shah, A. (2014, April 17). In light of MOOCs, intellectual property policy remains flexible. *The Chronicle of Higher Education*. Retrieved from http://www.dukechronicle.com/articles/2014/04/17/light-moocs-intellectual-property-policy-remains-flexible

Shea, P., & Armitage, S. (2002). Guidelines for creating student services online. WCET LAAP Project "Beyond the administrative core: Creating Web-based student services for online learners. Retrieved from http://wcet.wiche.edu/wcet/docs/beyond/overview.pdf

Sheehy, K. (2012, November 9). Online degree programs: How to tell the good from the bad. U.S. News and World Report. http://www.usnews.com/education/online-education/articles/2012/11/09/online-degree-programs-how-to-tell-the-good-from-the-bad

Shelton, K. (2011). A review of paradigms for evaluating the quality of online education programs. *Online Journal of Distance Learning Administration*, 4(1), Spring. Retrieved from http://www.westga.edu/~distance/ojdla/spring141/shelton141.html

Sloan Consortium (2010). Student authentication, academic integrity, and the Higher Education Opportunity Act of 2008. Retrieved from http://sloanconsortium.org/node/160521

Southern Association of Colleges and Schools (2012). Distance and correspondence education. Retrieved from http://sacscoc.org/pdf/Distance%20and%20correspondence%20policy%20final.pdf Standards for Distance Learning Library Services (2008) Association of College and Research Libraries. Retrieved from http://www.ala.org/acrl/standards/guidelinesdistancelearning#exsum

Stratford, M. (2014, March 26). Fight on state authorization. *Inside Higher Ed*. Retrieved from http://www.insidehighered.com/news/2014/03/26/state-regulators-express-concern-over-education-departments-new-draft-state#ixzz2zSlfdkgr

Straumsheim, C. (2014, April 16). Stand up and be counted. *Inside Higher Ed*. Retrieved from, http://www.insidehighered.com/news/2014/04/16/armed-federal-data-maryland-goes-after-out-state-distance-education-providers#ixzz2zShEIGih

Twigg, C. (2000). Who owns online courses and course materials? Intellectual property policies for a new learning environment. The National Center for Academic Transformation. Retrieved from http://www.thencat.org/Monographs/Whoowns.html

United States Government Accountability Office (2009). *Higher education & disability: Education needs a coordinated approach to improve its assistance to schools in supporting students.* Report to the Chairman, Committee on Education and Labor, House of Representatives (October 2009). Retrieved from http://www.gao.gov/new.items/d1033.pdf

University Professional and Continuing Education Association (UPCEA) (2013). *Center for Research and Consulting, student authentication and online proctoring report* . Retrieved from http://bvirtualinc.com/wp-content/uploads/2013/09/UPCEA_Proctoring_Authentication_Report_Final.pdf

Virginia Tech (2012) University's six-year distance learning strategic plan unveiled. *Virginia Tech News*. Retrieved from https://www.vtnews.vt.edu/articles/2012/10/101612-dlss-dlsp.html

Wilson, D., & Allen, D. (n.d.). Success rates of online versus traditional college students. *Research in Higher Education Journal*. Retrieved from http://www.aabri.com/manuscripts/11761.pdf

Yang, D., Sinha, T., Adamson, D., & Penstein Rose, C. (n.d.). "Turn on, Tune in, Drop out": Anticipating student dropouts in Massive Open Online Courses.Retrieved from http://lytics.stanford.edu/datadriveneducation/papers/yangetal.pdf

Zatynski, M. (2013, January 16). Calling for success: Online retention rates get boost from personal outreach. Education Sector at American Institutes for Reach. Retrieved from http://www.educationsector.org/publications/calling-success-online-retention-rates-get-boost-personal-outreach

7

The Generational Model of Online Program Development

As they have grown over the last 125 years, colleges and universities are complex organizations. In many ways, institutions of higher learning are organizationally much more complicated than many business enterprises including massive public companies. For example, due to the nature of their development, some key components of universities are hierarchical and others non-hierarchical (Duarte, & Martins 2013). The key tension between the hierarchical and non-hierarchical elements in higher education is at its very core. Faculty see themselves as autonomous professionals, while administrators may work within more formalized structures. Traditionally faculty see themselves as the sole guardians of the academic project—teaching, learning and research—of the university and resist other elements of the university intruding on that space. While the faculty may see academics as their sole domain, the current structure of higher education is made up of a wide range of stakeholders with competing interests. Federal and state governments have one set of concerns. Boards of trustees and other university governing boards may have a different understanding of the needs of the institutions for which they are responsible. Various stakeholders within the university may also have their own agenda, particularly the administrative leadership.

As Clayton Christensen argued, the growth of the use of technology in general and online educational programs in particular is profoundly disruptive for higher education (Hovland 2014). Through online learning, colleges can compete to attract both traditional and non-traditional students in ways that were not possible before the emergence of widespread, high-speed access to the Internet coupled with the complex technological platform needed to deliver online education. As Nazir, Pujeri, & Rizvi (2013) point out, the university is "no longer bounded by geographical place" (p. 609). And the new potential reach for individual institutions can have an impact on every aspect of the university, not just teaching and learning. While for much of its development, online education has focused primarily, though not exclusively, on teaching and learning, as online programs are developed, they reside within the complex ecosystem of the university. Colleges and universities have multiple, multi-layered functions that are made up of many sub-systems. Those functions often reside in organizational silos with a minimal degree of inter-organizational communication. Enrollment management, for example, may have very little contact with the library. Library staff does not generally worry about the financial aid office. And though the different functional units may be organized within a bureaucratic structure, faculty still view themselves as the centerpiece of the traditional university. Faculty governance is collegial and not directive. While willing to zealously defend what it sees as its domain, many faculty members want little if anything to do with the other parts of the university. Successful online programs demand change and support from every part of the university from public safety (particularly with the rise of cybercrime) to the bookstore. Online programs must meet the expectations of state legislatures, accrediting bodies, boards of trustees, and the students that are to be served. Well-designed courses will fail if the technology platform is inadequate and faculty are inadequately trained. And students will reject the course or program if it is too difficult to enroll. The lack of student support and library services can make it more likely for students to drop out and so on. Unfortunately, most universities are not organized to make complex changes of the magnitude required to offer programs online. So while the failure of online programs is often attributed to technology issues, it often comes from weaknesses in organizational processes (Curtis, & Alden 2007).

A cursory survey of program managers for online programs indicates that in many cases, online program development has been ad hoc, driven by unique factors. Some schools developed online programs primarily as a business opportunity to supplement falling tuition revenues by increasing their geographic market, or in the case of for-profit universities, offering programs online is the basis of their business model. Others developed online programs with the idea of cutting costs. The need to cut costs has been particularly acute, as state aid to higher education has been challenged to provide more benefit at a lower cost. Other institutions offer online programs to reach out to nontraditional students such as those who left college with only a few courses left to complete their degree, or to reach out to those who are looking for specific career-enhancement. In fact, professional and continuing education are the most vibrant areas of online program development among traditional non-profit colleges and universities. Finally, the emergence of MOOCs has led some institutions to launch high profile online efforts to ensure they remain in the public mind in the same category as top echelon schools such as Stanford and Harvard. These ad hoc efforts, in some instances, have produced significant results and have placed online education firmly on the agenda; however, the next generation of online program development requires a new approach. Online programs must be a part of the strategic vision of colleges and universities, and online programs must be incorporated into the ongoing operations of every aspect of the university, because the impact of online education is pervasive.

Many of the questions online program development raises are just starting to be considered. For example, will increasing the number of online-only students and graduates have an influence on advancement and alumni fundraising?

Because of the organizational silos and the fact that faculty frequently see themselves as independent from the other parts of the university, the university has no unified administrative mechanism regarding online programming to promote and manage the changes needed across the university. Even if faculty embrace online education, if technology services, for example, is not sufficiently ramped-up to handle online programs, those programs will suffer. Consequently, online education is constantly evolving, as is the technology on which it so heavily relies and the support services that are required to create and maintain a successful online program. Ad hoc efforts may succeed in the short term. But for a college or university to weather the disruption online education presents, it needs to develop a more systematic approach—an approach both to judge and measure the level of development of the online educational effort and to develop a common informational platform through which the various stakeholders can communicate. Through this common informational platform, appropriate stakeholders can gauge the investment they need to make to provide adequate support for their online educational efforts.

Maturity Models

One approach to an informational platform for different stakeholders engaged in disparate activities in the support of online programs is referred to as a maturity model. The first maturity models were developed in the 1980s at Carnegie Mellon University with funding by the U.S. military. The models were developed at a time when computer technology was rapidly growing. As the computer industry was young, there were experienced and non-experienced developers engaged in those developing technologies, and a method or model of assessment was needed to avoid the inconsistencies brought on by many groups working independently but toward a common goal. The first maturity model determined if contractors had the ability to complete government projects. Some U.S. government departments, for example, "require software development contractors achieve and operate at a level 3 standard" (Select Business Solutions n.d.). This particular model was referred to as a capability model, intended to describe processes based on a structured collection of practices. In due time, other types of organizations, beyond computer software contractors, adapted the capability maturity model (CMM). Typically such models utilize five levels to determine the maturity of an organization at any given point in the development of a project or program. The structured levels, which are described below, suggest that level one is an immature phase of development and level five represents the mature level, where consistency has been achieved through the systematic processes developed over time. Maturity models have now been applied to a wide variety of organizations and in a number of countries around the world.

Levels of a Capability Maturity Model

- **Level 1: Initial** Common to all of the models is the idea that organizational process begins on an ad hoc basis. At this level, someone within the organization champions a specific change. Because there may be organizational resistance to the change, the actions of those individuals advocating the new directions or activities are commonly labeled "heroics." The success of implementing the change may be described as a "test of wills," because advocating for change often breeds organizational struggle and strife. Such changes are fostered by an individual or small group of individuals, and organizations may not be committed to these processes and may be quick to abandon them, before they have had the opportunity to develop.
- **Level 2: Repeatable** This level refers to the establishment of a process orientation utilized in the development of the project. This level has been utilized, for example in the development of computer software, where costs and production schedule need to be followed on a repeatable basis. Each software development project is approached in the same way and goes through the same process. In complex organizations, however, while some processes may be repeatable, and consequently at the second level in a maturity model, other functions or processes may not.
- **Level 3: Defined** Once standards are developed and perhaps codified, organizations will have established a process that can be applied with consistency. This is a reasonable level to achieve, as it suggests that organizations have achieved a consistent level of continuity in the development of projects. Most important, at this third level, the processes can be utilized for other units within an organization. For the institution of higher learning that has established one online program, the standards and organizational systems initially established in Level 2 can be applied in the development of other online programs. Standards at this level are a threshold, but not a plateau; as such standards will become the basis for improvement as they are applied across the organization.
- **Level 4: Managed** As the development of projects within various types of organizations may not be exactly the same, it may be necessary to adjust and adapt in order to accommodate differences in projects. At level four, as quantitative standards are developed, a baseline provides ways to measure progress with particular concern for understanding and managing deviations from the standard processes. The goal of

this level of maturity is to establish quantitative measures across all the functions associated with online programs, with the end-goal of establishing some quantitative predictability.

- **Level 5: Optimizing** This level emphasizes the need to revisit the project with the goal of continuous improvement. In other words, once a project has been initiated, standards will be established, the organization has mechanisms in place to apply those standards across the board, with an eye toward modifying those standards and practices as needed. This level represents a process-oriented approach that requires revisiting projects across the organization, as opposed to within a project, in order to monitor variations and optimize the objectives of the organization.

The value of a maturity model is to determine the level the organization enters into the process. It is a way for administrators within organizations to better understand how they are executing their projects and processes. The goal is not necessarily an assessment to determine deficiencies in the organization. Not infrequently, ad hoc processes are sufficient to achieve a specific goal. In many cases, ad hoc processes are not good enough. Moreover, partner agencies such as the government or accrediting agencies may have standards that define how a certain process or procedure should be carried out. A maturity model can be used to help define those standards and help organizations achieve them. But the long-term value of maturity models is that they provide a road map for a systematic and strategic approach to project development. When companies and organizations understand where they are in the development of a project or program, they can devise strategies to help get to where they want to be.

The Generational Model

Assessing the online program development and associated process improvement model requires a systematic approach in order to help institutions of higher learning optimize their efforts to establish a set of best practices. The goal is to develop a set of routines that are not just reliable and repeatable across the institution among all the stakeholders in online programs. The processes examined are evolutionary, and should be viewed in terms of a road map. In fact, many programs have been established using what will be called first generation processes, ad hoc efforts spearheaded by a small group of faculty or administrators. While these programs can succeed, inevitably they will not function at an optimal level. Nor will it be easy to follow those processes for subsequent programs.

Duarte and Martins state that maturity models are "repositories of practices that have proven effective through extensive application in industrial and government organizations" (2013). Processes described in the model can be measured, and as a result, such processes can be improved through succeeding generations with the goal of achieving sustainability. Once a baseline has been established, comparative results can be measured across the institution, based on a four-step process: 1) research and mechanisms establishing the program, 2) implementation of the program, 3) evaluation and assessment of results leading to 4) improvement.

Paulk presented a five-level model that was intended to overcome the failures of past attempts at developing process-oriented models (1999). The capability maturity model (CMM) was designed to increase the effectiveness of processes associated with software design. The model is based on the following five levels: Initial, repeatable, defined, managed and optimized (Paulk 1999). The initial level refers to the ad hoc process that may be borne out of chaos. The second level establishes management processes, like cost tracking and scheduling, that bring discipline to a project. The third level provides standardization to the processes that may be documented and useful across the organization. Fourth, quality control measures are established to allow for measurement of progress. And, the fifth level of the CMM model allows for continuous improvement through the establishment of a feedback loop that leads to new ideas and implementation of new technologies.

Adapting Maturity Models to Online Educational Programs

The Generational Model of Online Program Development™ that we have developed applies the general concepts of a maturity model to online program development. In some respects, online education currently has parallels to the early days of the computer software industry. Online education is proliferating in the same way that the need for software exploded. Many different organizations are plunging into the arena for different reasons and implementing different approaches. The pioneers in the field are exploring and promoting the use of best practices but except in a few areas, those practices are not widely accepted or implemented. In many areas such as enrollment management or bookstores, no widespread best practices have emerged. While maturity models have been in use by business organizations for some time, there have been only a few attempts to adapt such models to online educational programs (Duarte, & Martins 2013; Marshall 2012; Nazir, Pujeri, & Rizvi 2013). Some of the models have focused primarily on one particular aspect of the education enterprise, namely, online course development and delivery, or one central unit for analysis such as student outcomes or technology infrastructure. The framework developed by Marshall has a wider scope and attempts to help universities understand and assess their capacity to develop online educational programs.

The Generational Model of Online Program Development™ builds on that work but has a different orientation. It is based on four underlying principles.

First, many institutions have entered and will launch online educational programs at the initiative of only one of the stakeholders involved, often the administration or the board of trustees. When a program is launched from one vantage point, there can be no expectation that other departments in the university will be aware of or be prepared to take on additional responsibilities. Therefore, the Generational Model is intended to serve to facilitate communication among the different departments involved in online education development. The Generational Model is not a blueprint of a progressive process. To move from a first generation process to a fourth generation process, individual administrators and departments do not have to first go through the second generation or the third generation. Nor is it technically a capability model. Some schools may technically have the capability to implement fourth generation processes but other obstacles may stand in the way. The assumption is that most colleges and universities will not have fourth generation processes when they launch programs and may never actually implement fourth generation processes in many areas. In some cases, first generation processes may be completely sufficient. The model is not aspirational in the sense that all departments involved in online education should strive to achieve fourth generational processes. It is a method for all the stakeholders to orient themselves and to be aware of how their partners in other parts of the university are operating. The Generational Model is scalable. That means the process can be used to examine very granular processes or look at processes from a broader institutional level. For example, in terms of governance, the Generational Model can be used to look at how a specific program is launched as well as how programs are managed at the department, school or university level. Each level or stage is not necessarily dependent on the other. At the university level, governance may be very well developed while individual programs are being created on an ad hoc basis.

Drawing on the key strengths of the CMM model, including its avoidance of a prescribed methodology and a singular organizational model, the Generational Model for Online Program Development™ provides a roadmap for developing institutional resources in the establishment of online programs across the university. The model provides indicators similar to the CMM model as it relies on a generational structure; such generations provide an understanding of the status of institutional development when it comes to online programs. While they provide insight into an end point that represents an optimized level for each process to aid long-term institutional planning for online education, the assumption is that an institution of higher learning will not have established optimal practices and processes before engaging in online program development; at any moment different processes will be at different generational levels. The model can help institutions determine the level at which they are presently operating, and the model provides guidance regarding areas of focus in order to achieve a process of continual improvement.

The Four Generations

The Generational Model of Online Program Development™ proposed four generations or stages. The stages are expressed as generations, so as to avoid the idea that one set of processes or stage of process development is necessarily better than another; rather they are offered as a means to identify the institution's capabilities or actual procedures at any given stage of online program development within a wide variety of institutional settings and practices. Those settings, like size of the university, and practices, like administrative hierarchies, are going to vary greatly based on a number of institutional factors.

- **Generation 1 (Ad hoc)** is concerned with the initial stages of creating an online program. It begins with a small cadre of people who see an opportunity to do something different, which drives this generation. They may have become enamored with the potential of educational technology or perhaps see an opportunity to generate revenue. Ad hoc development is often very creative. The people driving the development are consciously trying to push the envelope and often are unaware of or unconcerned with the rules and regulations that may impede their progress. Ad hoc processes, however, are often untested and can lead to unintentional consequences. This generation is most at risk for failure or the inability to consistently deliver high quality education based on limited resources. Moreover, this generation often rests on the passions of the first generation of people involved in the project and requires too much commitment for others to take up the mantle. In general, they do not serve as a stable foundation for incorporating online programs into institutional flow of university life.
- **Generation 2 (Repeatable)** At this stage a process, or several processes associated with an online program, has been routinized. Whenever that process comes into play, it is executed in the same way. One of the most central features of online program development that often moves quickly into the second generation is course development. If a faculty member wants to create an online course, the person must go through a predefined set of steps designed to meet certain standards. Technology support often quickly becomes a second-generation process.
- **Generation 3 (Managed)** In this third generation, the processes have not only become standardized, but also they are subject to routine planning through established management structures and related practices. They are reviewed and regularly assessed according to established standards, guidelines, and policies. In most cases, appropriate administrative hierarchical structures have been put in place that will oversee the development, implementation and assessment of processes.

- **Generation 4 (Integrated)** At this stage, administrative structures for online education are embedded in the hierarchy of the institution, therefore, attention can turn to measuring and assuring the quality of the online program. More granular processes are integrated into the assessment of the larger processes in which they are implicated. For example, individual course assessments can be integrated into overall program assessment and overall program assessment can be used in ongoing program development, which, in turn, shapes course development. Moreover, online processes can be measured against the processes used traditionally by the university enabling the development of university-wide best practices.

Once the program or programs are established, the institution enters into a cycle of improvement. In other words, the Generational Model is not a static operation. It is intended as a dynamic process that is intended to continually look for ways to improve the quality of online programs. As capabilities within the institution grow, it is expected that a culture of continuous improvement will be established and maintained. In addition to the four generations described above, the model elaborates on the processes and associated practices. The practices associated with online program development are presented as general ones that can be modified given the particular institution of higher learning where the model is applied, based on its technological sophistication, instructor training and program development, as well as the organizational culture of the institution. By contextualizing the generational processes and the associated practices, institutions of higher learning will be better able to develop strategies leading to successful online program development, and in that minimize the possibility of failure.

Issues for Assessment

The organizational structure of colleges and universities differs greatly from the typical business enterprise. Colleges and universities are generally divided into four or five major divisions including academic affairs, student life, administration, enrollment management and recruitment, and so on. Each of those divisions is headed by a single chief administrator, often a vice president (or the provost in academic affairs). And while the faculty view themselves as autonomous, institutions as a whole still have many hierarchical elements. What they lack is a clear governance structure to bridge those camps. One of the reasons that online educational programs are often launched on an ad hoc basis is that each unit of the university has very little accountability to other units. So if an English Department, let's say, wants to offer online classes, it may begin to do so without notifying the library (or even the office that would be in charge of getting regulatory approvals). While administrators within the university operate within more centralized functions and may adhere to more formal practices, faculty may see those practices both as bureaucratic and infringing on their academic authority and freedom.

Consequently, the Generational Model assumes each organizational unit of the university will assess itself independently. Only fourth generation institutions have integrated governance processes.

The list of functions and the number of processes that are involved in creating a sustainable, robust online educational program is long and can always be adjusted, depending on the level of granularity at which the analysis is to take place. The length is indicative of the complexity of institutions of higher education and the complexity of initiating change within the context of the university. The following are a sample of the eight functions and processes that must be addressed and developed in online learning. The functions and processes are: administration, governance, faculty development and support, course and program development, pedagogy, student services, institutional commitment, and assessment. These functions roughly follow the best practices laid out by the Commission on Colleges, Southern Association of Colleges and Schools, and the nine hallmarks for quality in online learning in the Interregional Guidelines for the Evaluation of Distance Learning published by the Middle States Commission on Higher Education (Commission on Colleges Southern Association of Colleges and Schools 2000; MSCHE 2011). Each of these functions and processes has been discussed at length in the earlier chapters. In the section below, one example from each will be discussed to clarify how the different generations of development appear in practice.

Administration: Program Administration

All programs in a university need to be administered in some way. In a first generation or ad hoc process, the administrator may be one of the core group involved in launching the program. The administrative function may be an added responsibility with no time or compensation pegged specifically for the additional administrative duties. The person fulfills the administrative functions because of a commitment to the program and does not have an official standing that would allow the administrator to call on other resources in the university for support or development. If the administrator were to step down, there would be no obvious replacement. In a second generation or repeatable process, the administrator would be formally recognized as the program director and receive some compensation, perhaps in the form of a course release or monetary compensation. The role would be recognized across the university and the person would be empowered to interact with other parts of the university that need to provide services to the program. In this way, should the administrator step down, a replacement could be found and have the authority needed to operate. In a third generation or managed process, there would be a formal job description for the administrator. The duties and rights would be carefully defined and the expectations carefully presented. There may be a training period or systematic way to prepare and introduce a new person to the position. And the department chair with which the program was associated or an alternative direct supervisor would periodically review the administrator. In a fourth generation or integrated process, an administrator would have formal interaction with all the other online program administrators to share best practices and other ideas. New administrators would have formal training and be introduced to the other stakeholders across the university to learn about and better understand the level of development of those services. Regular meetings between program administrators and other stakeholders will routinely explore what services need to be improved and identify new opportunities to serve online students. Assessment practices would be standardized. The program administrator would interact both with an immediate supervisor and also a manager with expertise in online programs.

Governance: Decision-making

Governance refers to the way in which decisions regarding a specific program are made. Governance reflects and shapes the way programs are constructed including their requirements: how they are staffed; how changes to the program are made; and, who is admitted to the program, among other issues. In first generation processes, the program founders, the faculty teaching in the program, or in some cases, perhaps just the program administrator, makes and enforces governance decisions. In the second generation, governance is a department responsibility. In many cases, a department committee that includes both faculty members teaching in the program and those who are not teaching in the program will make critical decisions about the shape and direction of the program. This committee may be answerable both to the program director and the department chair. It is also responsible for regularly reviewing the program's operations. In the third generation, governance will be lodged in the ongoing governing procedures of the department and the university. Changes in curriculum or requirements would be subjected to the same scrutiny to which other changes in other parts of the curriculum are subjected. Rules and processes needed to manage the program—what is the process for changing specific requirements, for example—are spelled out and codified. In the fourth generation, an administrator charged with supervising online education would ensure that processes and procedures were consistent across all online programs. Administrators and others responsible for program supervision and governance would meet regularly to share best practices and improve processes and procedures where necessary. Online programs would be recognized in the university governance processes as well, and online programs would be formally represented and addressed in the official governing structure of the institution. For example, the university or faculty senate would have a subcommittee charged with oversight for online programs in the same way they have committees performing oversight regarding curricula.

Faculty Development: Faculty Training

Faculty development is one of the most critical areas of online program development. In traditional higher education, many faculty have no training as teachers. The depth of their coursework and research and their experience as practitioners or as students in the classroom is what they bring. With online education, most faculty do not even have experience teaching online. In the first generation, faculty are not trained at all and learn on the job. This is not necessarily bad. First generation faculty are often those most committed to online education, and they are willing to spend hours and hours mastering the technology and learning it with their students—students and teacher as co-learners. The problem with the first generation approach is that ongoing, sustainable programs cannot rely on faculty suddenly devoting 50 to 60 hours to each class they teach. The danger is that instructors will not be able to sustain 50 to 60 hours contact hours with students. As a result they are likely not to spend enough time to create an appropriate bond with students and the classes will devolve into self-learning exercises for the students. The student learning outcomes in self-learning environments are not necessarily bad, but generally when students enroll in a college course, they expect some reasonable amount of student–teacher interaction. In the second generation, faculty members receive some training. This can come in the form of a workshop prior to teaching a course, a self-paced online learning experience, or some sort of mentoring arrangement with more experienced faculty. Second generation programs are often sufficient to satisfy the standards set by accrediting agencies and can be effective in introducing faculty to the basics of online teaching. The third generation of faculty development is an ongoing process. It links faculty development, having instructors proactively seek out new techniques and approaches to online learning, from early adopters, to reporting successful approaches back to the faculty. There is a mechanism to regularly introduce faculty to new technology tools and instruction and how to use them effectively for various learning activities. This is premised on the idea that teaching techniques for online education must constantly develop since online education itself is still in a period of great changes. The fourth generation of faculty development links faculty development with student evaluations, course assessments and technology support services. Mechanisms are put into place that allow those managing the program as well as individual faculty to collect data to see what technologies and techniques are working and which ones aren't. All faculty are expected to periodically participate in training, with more experienced faculty regularly meeting with less experienced faculty. Moreover, data collected from the learning management system can be incorporated into the process to assess what is working well, and perhaps what is not.

Course and Program Development: Course Development

Course development is one of the most mature areas in online education. Instructors have been creating online courses for more than 20 years now and the experience has been codified into a set of best practices that are broadly accepted. Nevertheless, since many aspects of online program development are still in the first generation and performed on an ad hoc basis, best practices in course development are not appropriately communicated or implemented.

In the first generation of course development, faculty create courses according to their own intuition and insight. This is the method that is often utilized in traditional on-campus courses and, in fact, course materials are seen as the intellectual property of individual faculty members, indicating that courses are original and in some ways uniquely linked to an individual faculty member. While online courses may also be original and unique to each faculty member, the development process cannot be. On just one level, state regulators and accrediting agencies have set more complicated standards for online courses requiring that students receive a sufficient amount of instruction. Furthermore, learning activities have to be more carefully matched to the available technology. In the second generation of course development, programs have set procedures and a format to which faculty adhere. An instructional designer may be available to assist the faculty member. Each course has a defined set of learning aims and learning outcomes and the learning activities are linked to those goals and outcomes. In the course development process, a blueprint for the course is established. The Quality Matters procedure or a similar procedure like the Cal State rubric, represent the third generation of course development. Courses are subjected to outside peer review to verify that they meet quality standards. There is an expectation that courses require the input from individuals with expertise in online learning and the input will be incorporated into the course. Course development is seen as an iterative process and not solely the domain of the individual instructor. In the fourth generation, courses are periodically reviewed and revised. Course development is linked to continuous improvement processes. In addition, program-wide or institution-wide mechanisms are in place for best practices and new ideas to be broadly shared. The knowledge base created through the course development process is captured and available to teachers devising new online courses.

Pedagogy: Student–Teacher Interaction

Teaching online requires a different set of skills and techniques than teaching in a classroom. It is much harder to be witty and interactive via videotaped lectures than it is online. Creating a social presence so students feel that the instructor is paying attention to them and their participation in the class is one of the essential components of a successful online class experience.

When examining student–teacher interaction, in the first generation, the interaction may be limited to only one or two modes of communication— perhaps email and discussion boards. The instructor may participate in discussion boards only intermittently or not at all, and students may not have the feeling that the instructor is paying attention to their efforts. In the second generation, the instructor clearly lays out what students should anticipate in terms of communication. Guidelines should include how the instructor will participate in ongoing discussions, the response time for email, opportunities to interact with students on a one-to-one basis and in what ways the teacher will be available for informal interaction with the students, either to resolve questions that may come up concerning the management of the course or just to build a more personal relationship. In the third generation, the instructor uses many different modes of communication. In addition to discussion boards, other asynchronous interactive channels of communication such as blogs, Wikis and audio or video annotation tools are utilized in the course. The instructor establishes virtual office hours during which students can expect a more immediate response to their inquiries or the instructor will be an active participant in the course's "water-cooler" discussion board. Depending on the size of the class, professors may also make themselves available via telephone or video conferencing. In the fourth generation, expectations for student–teacher interaction are standardized for both instructors and students across the program and for certain communication activities such as virtual office hours, across the university. The instructor monitors student–teacher interaction, and insights into how to better facilitate student–teacher interaction and create a stronger student–teacher learning relationship are shared.

Student Services: Technology Support

Online programs cannot thrive without outstanding technical support. Technology support refers to the selection of technologies to be utilized in online courses, and to the availability of staff to solve technological problems as they arise during the semester. If the technology does not work correctly, and learning is impeded, in the worst-case scenario, students drop out of the program.

In the first generation, technology support for online students mirrors the support given traditional students. They may receive information about how to access technical support online and via the telephone and the hours of operation. Requests for support from online students are handled in the same way as requests from residential or on-campus students. Indeed, often there may be the assumption that online students should be equipped to manage their own technology but that is too often a faulty assumption. In the second generation, technology support services are designed in a way that recognizes the special needs of online students. The available support services are carefully communicated to online students both in their orientation sessions and in each class. A system to triage technical problems that online students may face is developed and communicated so online students know exactly where to turn when problems arise. In the third generation, technology support teams try to anticipate the issues that online students may encounter and devise strategies to minimize or ameliorate them. Instructional videos are created specifically for online students on the use of each technology tool. Once again these videos are made available both in the orientation and in each course. The technology tools used are regularly assessed to identify which ones cause the most problems and strategies are devised to reduce or eliminate those programs. In the fourth generation, technology support is an integral part of course development and faculty training. Support teams are available to faculty to explore new technologies and report to faculty which tools are the most effective and which generate the greatest number of problems. The data generated though the assessments is broadly disseminated and is reviewed by appropriate stakeholders to improve the underlying learning technology platform in ways that could improve teaching and learning.

Institutional Commitment: Planning

Institutional commitment is one of the hardest aspects of online program development to measure. In the broadest sense, institutional commitment means that the college or university is willing to provide enough resources to implement an effective online learning program. But institutional commitment is not just a question of resources. Online educational programs have to be seen as significant enough that every office will make them a priority and implement the changes needed to address the special requirements of online learners.

Planning is a key component of institutional commitment. In the first generation, there is very little overall planning for online education. Courses and programs are launched because individual faculty members or departments get interested in online learning, or a separate unit is created for continuing education, or for some other reason, like generating additional revenue. In the second generation, online education is incorporated into the planning process at the departmental or school level. Online program development is seen as an integral part of the overall educational project that requires an ongoing commitment of resources. Moreover, initiatives to improve the overall delivery of the online educational program can be crafted. In the third generation, an institution-wide strategic plan for online education is established. At this stage, goals for online education generally are set along with milestones to achieve those goals. The overall vision for online education is established and stakeholders have a clear idea of how they can participate in the process. The resources needed for the plan to succeed are identified and strategies are crafted to gather those resources. In the fourth generation, online program development is part of the overall strategic plan for the college or the university. The goals of online education are blended and harmonized with overall institutional goals. Online education has a recognized role and is part of the fabric and identity of the university.

Assessment: Teacher Evaluations

Assessment has emerged as a critical issue throughout education starting with pre-school. Governments, regulators, administrators and teachers want to measure what students are actually learning and how effective teachers are. One of the tools utilized in that process is teacher evaluation.

For online educational programs, in the first generation, teacher evaluations are individual, generally linked only to the faculty member. The teacher evaluation tool is developed on an ad-hoc basis and may consist solely of an online survey. Participation in the survey may be voluntary and little concern is paid to the response rate. An important factor is that the data produced by the survey cannot be compared to the data produced by standard teacher evaluation surveys. In the second generation, data produced by the course evaluations is aggregated and seen as a shared resource. Through the aggregation of data, average performance can be identified so instructors know how their performance compares to their colleagues. Performance goals and standards can be set and utilized to shape faculty training programs. In the third generation, additional types of data beyond the course evaluation can be collected. Many accrediting agencies want to review direct evidence of student learning, and strategies utilized to collect that evidence can also be incorporated into the course evaluation process. Individual course evaluation data is explored and discussed by the instructor and the direct supervisor and aggregated data is discussed on a program-wide level. Procedures to improve the response rates to the course evaluation surveys are put into place. In the fourth generation, course evaluation data is aggregated from across the university. Efforts to compare course evaluation data generated in online educational programs to the data generated in traditional classroom settings are put in place. The qualitative differences between teaching online and teaching in the classroom are recognized and accounted for in all the places that course evaluations are utilized, including annual evaluation, and tenure and promotion decisions.

The functions above are just a small subset of the myriad functions involved in implementing a successful online educational program. For example, administration also includes recruitment and retention, the acceptance process, registration, financial aid and so on. Student Services includes advising, academic support, psychological support, the library, and the bookstore among others. In addition to course evaluations, there are program, technology, and administrative assessment, as well as institutional effectiveness measures. And each of these areas can be further subdivided into yet more specific functions. For example, Technology support can be broken down into incident reporting, incident resolution and follow-up communication, and these functions can be assessed on the generational continuum from an ad hoc process to an integrated process within the ongoing functioning of the program and the university.

Sample Generational Model Worksheets

The challenge in applying the Generational Model is the range of services involved in the successful implementation and management of an online educational program. As online education is currently most commonly structured, nobody can fully understand the activities and concerns of each stakeholder, how their services are currently implemented and how those services may need to be revised to meet the specific needs of online learners. The Generational Model, however, provides a guide for those most responsible for managing online educational programs on a day-to-day basis. At the institutional level, the model may be utilized to consult with different stakeholders by working through the development worksheets that can help orient those stakeholders. The worksheets provide stakeholders with a means to better understand the generation in which they are operating, identify which generation of services they could potentially provide, and consider the resources they need to achieve associated goals.

Worksheets consist of three elements. First, there are the broad themes associated with online education such as administration or pedagogy. Second are the granular practices, functions or elements that support those themes. For example, determining learning outcomes is a granular part of course development. Third is the generational status of each granular practice, function or element. In the case of learning outcomes, in the first generation, individual faculty members decide on their own learning outcomes. In the second generation, course-learning outcomes are developed within the context of program outcomes. In the third generation, course outcomes are regularly reassessed and reviewed. And in the fourth generation, course outcomes are measured against institutional learning goals.

The Generational Model to Assess Institutional Commitment

On the following page is a sample worksheet that looks at the issue of institutional commitment. Many of the practices, functions and elements are drawn from the Southern Colleges and Universities best practices statement.

Theme	Process/Function/Element	1st Generation (Ad Hoc)	2nd Generation (Repeatable)	3rd Generation (Managed)	4th Generation (Integrated)
Institutional Commitment	Vision	No articulated vision statement.	Vision is expressed at the program or departmental level and focuses primarily on program content and outcomes.	Vision has been developed in conjunction with college or university-wide input.	Vision is clearly articulated with the parameter of the university-wide mission statement and accounts for any changes in students served, geographic reach, etc.
	Planning	Planning is done at the course or program level.	Program planning is incorporated into departmental planning processes.	Strategic plan for online educational programs has been developed.	Online education is incorporated into the university's strategic plan.
	Budget	Program is run within the ongoing budget framework with no allowances for online programming.	Budgeting for online educational programs is a negotiated process and addresses specific tasks such as investments in course development.	Online educational programs have independent budgets that account for all the needs of the program.	Budgeting for online educational programs is part of the standard budget development process and reflects a commitment to meeting the needs of online students in activities across the university.
	Technology Infrastructure	Program is expected to run on existing technology infrastructure.	Program consults with appropriate stakeholders to determine and request technology needs.	Technology infrastructure is subject to ongoing review and investment.	University manages technology infrastructure to insure that privacy, reliability, safety and security needs are met.

Internal Organization	Program has only internal organization.	Program is lodged with the ongoing work of the department or unit.	University has established an appropriate university wide administrative infrastructure to meet the needs of online programs.	Online programs are integrated into the organization across the university. Every office that must provide services to online programs has the necessary staff trained to do so.
Legal and regulatory capacity	Courses and programs are launched with little regard or awareness of legal or regulatory requirements.	Program personnel are tasked with monitoring and responding to legal and regulatory matters.	The university office tasked with monitoring legal and regulatory affairs is responsible for proactively supervising the legal and regulatory requirements of online programs including copyright issues and intellectual property issues.	Legal and regulatory affairs are routinely reviewed for compliance. University forecasts implications of new online program initiatives.
Marketing	Primarily word of mouth marketing aimed at people who already have a commitment to the university.	The program or department is the driving force behind the marketing strategy.	Marketing program is managed as a part of the overall university marketing effort.	The marketing program reflects the unique demands and opportunities posed by online learning in conjunction with the overall marketing strategy.
Institutional review	No institutional review.	Programs are reviewed at the department level.	Programs are periodically reviewed on the same schedule that other academic programs are reviewed.	Online education is a component of major institutional reviews including reaccreditation processes.
Transfer policies	No articulated policy.	Department determines if transfer credit will be accepted.	Standard university processes for transfer credit are used.	Transfer policies are clearly articulated and consistently applied.

The functions and elements in the chart are not intended to be comprehensive, even to assess just institutional commitment. Moreover, many of the functions can be broken down into smaller sub-components, for example, legal and regulatory matters, including obtaining state authorizations, accrediting agency approval, copyright issues, intellectual property guidelines, student privacy issues, records retention, among others. Each of those sub-components potentially could be assessed within the generational framework. Not all functions connected with the development of an online program will move into the fourth generation. In many cases, with many functions, first or second generation approaches will be sufficient and successful. In fact, in some cases, stakeholders may resist moving into the third or fourth generation, as they may find that generation too bureaucratic and not nimble enough, depending on specifically how those frameworks are constructed and managed. Even in those cases, however, the Generation Model provides the groundwork and a common basis for discussion and negotiation. For the Generational Model to be the most effective, different stakeholders should reflect on the functions they need to execute to support the success of online educational components and break those functions into their constituent components. They should then reflect on how those functions are performed currently and what is the most effective way to perform them in the future.

Conclusion

In the spring of 2014, Richard Lyos, the dean of the Haas School of Business at the University of California, Berkeley predicted within a decade or less half of the 420 accredited masters of Business Administration programs in the United States could be out of business (Clark 2014). Some of the top business schools in America were beginning to offer high quality programs online and those programs were attracting a lot of students. For example, the Kelley School of Business at Indiana University, whose program is ranked in the Top 20 nationally, has more than 1000 students enrolled—twice the number enrolled in its regular two-year program. Moreover, the online program costs one-third less than the traditional program. And that is not the only threat. Online education is particularly attractive to students in part-time and executive MBA programs, which often are more lucrative for universities as the students have less need for financial aid. Some of the highest ranked business schools including the University of Pennsylvania's Wharton School and Stanford's Graduate School of Business have offered MOOCs that have attracted thousands of students. At the same time, the overall pool of students interested in obtaining MBAs is shrinking.

Dire predictions regarding the growth of online education at the expense of traditional on-campus programs is forcing programs, college or universities to shut down if they are able to adapt to the new environment. But that does not have to be the case. Online education opens up opportunities for colleges and universities to move in new directions by broadening their educational offerings and by making new contributions to their students and their communities. As discussed in Chapter 1, higher education is at a major pivot point. Many believe that higher education has become too costly, and its benefits are not as clear as they once were. Too many students are saddled with too much debt. The time and money students invest in higher education is not rewarded with well-paying career-oriented jobs. Ironically, at the same time that public support is diminishing, policy makers from the Federal and state governments and accrediting agencies are demanding more accountability.

Though it has a reputation for being slow to change, higher education has had several other critical moments of change in the last 150 years or so. In the 1860s, land grant universities were formed to teach the practical skills needed in an industrializing society. At the beginning of the 20th Century, universities assumed the responsibility both for research and for the exclusive training of professionals in medicine and law. And in the 1960s and 1970s, access to higher education was thrown wide open to women and other previously excluded groups. In each case, colleges and universities had to respond in some way. And those who found the right formula to work with their mission or redefined their mission to match the new circumstances flourished.

Although online education has been growing steadily over the past 20 years or more, only now has it reached the point that it will have an impact across the entire universe of higher education. Until recently, while many students may have taken an online class here or there, most online programs were targeted and often outside the main educational thrust of many institutions. They were geared to non-traditional students, continuing education or higher focused professional education. For many reasons, that is changing. Online education is entering the mainstream.

Developing a high quality online educational program is not a simple or trivial project. It requires change from every part of the university. It requires vision, resources and commitment. It requires institutions to examine themselves and decide what will be their character for the next epoch of higher education.

The Generational Model for Online Program Development™ is a tool both for self-assessment and a blueprint for action. With it, colleges and universities can understand if they have examined themselves in a way that will allow them to succeed in offering online educational programs. It gives an institution a way to measure the readiness of each part of the university to play its role in the development of online programs. And it provides insight into what can be considered best practices now and a methodology for examining and developing best practices in the future. In short, the model offers a framework within which successful online educational programs can be developed and maintained.

And what are the components of a successful online educational program? That formula had not changed. Successful programs attract students with a sound educational background, and they create a structure in which students can succeed academically. It helps them to build authentic student–teacher, student–student and student–technology learning relationships and trains them to be independent learners for life. But most importantly, a successful online program enables students to achieve their educational goals and learn what they have set out to accomplish.

References

Clark, P. (2014, May 5). Online B-schools threaten the traditional classroom. *Bloomberg Business-week*, p. 51.

Commission on Colleges Southern Association of Colleges and Schools (2000). Best practices for electronically offered degree and certificate programs. Retrieved from http://www.sacscoc.org/pdf/081705/commadap.pdf

Curtis, B., & Alden, J. (2007). Maturity model du jour: A recipe for side dishes. Retrieved from http://www.bptrends.com/publicationfiles/10-07-COL-maturitymodeldujour-CurtisAldenfinal.pdf

Duarte, D., & Martins, P. (2013). A maturity model for higher education institutions. *Journal of Spatial and Organizational Dynamics, 1*(1), 25–45.

Hammond, T. (2002). Herding cats in university hierarchies: The impact of formal structure on decision-making in American research universities. Retrieved from http://www.ilr.cornell.edu/cheri/conferences/upload/2002/chericonf2002_04.pdf

Hovland, M. (2014). The distruption of higher education. Retrieved from http://facultyecommons.org/disruption-higher-education/

Marshall, S. (2012). E-learning and higher education: Understanding and supporting organizational change. *Journal of Open, Flexible and Distance Learning, 16*(1). Retrieved from http://journals.akoaotearoa.ac.nz/index.php/JOFDL/article/view/96z

Marshall, S., & Mitchell, G. (2002). An e-learning maturity model? In A. Williamson, K. Gunn, A. Young, and T. Clear (eds), *Proceedings of the 19th Annual Conference of the Australian Society for Computers in Learning in Tertiary Education.* Retrieved from http://www.unitec.ac.nz/ascilite/proceedings/papers/173.pdf

Middle States Commission on Higher Education (2011) Distance education programs: Interregional guidelines for the evaluation of distance education (online learning). Retrieved from http://www.msche.org/publications/Guidelines-for-the-Evaluation-of-Distance-Education-Programs.pdf

Nazir, M. I. J., Pujeri R. V., & Rizvi A. H. (2013). Maturity level definitions for the evaluative framework to measure the maturity of skill based training program with multimedia support in an e-learning environment [SBTP-MSELE]: A learner's perspective. *International Journal of Computer and Information Technology, 2*(4), 609–16.

Paulk, M. (1999). Using the software CMM with good judgment. *Institute for Software Research*, Paper 12. http://repository.cmu.edu/isr/12

Quality Matters (n.d.) Higher education program. Retrieved from https://www.qualitymatters.org/higher-education-program

Select Business Solutions (n.d.). What is the capability maturity model? Retrieved from http://www.selectbs.com/process-maturity/what-is-the-capability-maturity-model

Index